PENGUIN BOOK

THE AMBITION DE(

Hana Schank is the Strategy Director for Public Interest Technology at New America, and a frequent contributor to the *New York Times*, the *Atlantic*, and the *Washington Post*. This is her second book.

Elizabeth Wallace worked for print magazines including *Vogue*, *Nylon*, *Seventeen*, *Us Weekly*, and *Lucky*, and is now a freelance editor and writer. She contributes regularly to *Domino* and *Architectural Digest*.

* * *

Praise for *The Ambition Decisions*

"The goal of *The Ambition Decisions* is to 'fill in [the] missing knowledge' for women trying to navigate work and life options, in part because the choices for women 'often look radically different from the way those very same decisions played out only a generation earlier.' . . . If anyone is feeling adrift in midlife, this may be the most useful advice." —*Wall Street Journal*

"Those looking for some solidarity reading or ideas about how other professional women mesh work, family, and the decisions related to them can find it here." —*Washington Post*

"There's not much historical precedent for the continual societal change around women and work. So journalists Schank and Wallace interviewed their former classmates to find out how a generation of women are grappling with questions of ambition, work, and balance." —*Elle*

"Get inspired . . . Curious about where their college friends ended up, Hana Schank and Elizabeth Wallace, authors of *The Ambition Decisions*, called and asked. What they found: Ambitions fluctuate, so don't throw in the towel if you haven't realized all your dreams by forty." —*Redbook*

"Insightful and clarifying in a way that traditional career-focused books for women rarely are." —*Salon*

"A big-picture read that explores the decisions women make over the arcs of their careers. Read it to know what to expect, or to feel heard."

—HelloGiggles

"*The Ambition Decisions* is willing to confront the possibility that perhaps the shape and sum of female ambition offers a better road map for all human beings, men as well as women. The lively and engaging stories that emerge from the authors' interviews add up to a larger point. Why should we all not be able to choose lives that allow for ambition of different kinds at different times?"   —Anne-Marie Slaughter, *New York Times* bestselling author of *Unfinished Business*

"Every woman who feels paralyzed by her life decisions should read this honest, insightful, and surprising book that explores the challenges of 'working while female'—and provides helpful advice on how to craft the life you want."

—Jancee Dunn, author of *How Not to Hate Your Husband After Kids*

"Schank and Wallace take readers on a heartfelt journey to discover whether and how it's possible for women to meaningfully combine work and life without losing our sanity, our health, or our souls. *The Ambition Decisions* reassures us we're not alone in our struggle, offers practical guideposts to forge our own paths, and reminds us that defining and redefining success and ambition on our own terms as we grow and change will light the way forward."

—Brigid Schulte, *New York Times* bestselling author of *Overwhelmed*

"Hana and Elizabeth illuminate a truth I wish more ambitious women trying to juggle it all understood: You're not alone and you're not going crazy. You just live in a world that hasn't evolved."

—Tiffany Dufu, author of *Drop the Ball*

"A fascinating look at how ambition is not easily contained or defined. Schank and Wallace examine broad questions, such as the relationship between passion and work, alongside practical questions. . . . Readers of all generations will learn from the authors' road map through life's transitions."

—*Booklist*

THE AMBITION DECISIONS

What Women Know About Work,
Family, and the Path
to Building a Life

HANA SCHANK AND ELIZABETH WALLACE

PENGUIN BOOKS

PENGUIN BOOKS
An imprint of Penguin Random House LLC
penguinrandomhouse.com

First published in the United States of America by Viking Penguin,
an imprint of Penguin Random House LLC, 2018
Published in Penguin Books 2019

ISBN 9780525558859 (paperback)

THE LIBRARY OF CONGRESS HAS CATALOGED THE
HARDCOVER EDITION AS FOLLOWS:

Names: Schank, Hana, author. | Wallace, Elizabeth (Freelance writer), author.
Title: The ambition decisions : what women know about work, family, and the
path to building a life / Hana Schank and Elizabeth Wallace.
Description: New York : Viking, [2018] | Includes bibliographical references.
Identifiers: LCCN 2018013959 (print) | LCCN 2018013218 (ebook) |
ISBN 9780525558811 (hardcover) | ISBN 9780525558828 (ebook)
Subjects: LCSH: Middle-aged women—United States—Psychology. |
Women—Decision making. | Ambition. | Career development. | Families.
Classification: LCC HQ1059.5.U5 S24 2018 (ebook) | LCC HQ1059.5.U5 (print) |
DDC 305.244/20973—dc23
LC record available at https://lccn.loc.gov/2018013959

Printed in the United States of America
10 9 8 7 6 5 4 3 2 1

Set in Times LT Pro
Designed by Amy Hill

For our children:
Clyde and Eli
&
Milo and Mira

You'll never fly as the crow flies
Get used to a country mile
When you're learning to face
The path at your pace
Every choice is worth your while

—"Watershed," Indigo Girls

CONTENTS

PROLOGUE

In 2012, the two of us were, individually, circling a crisis of faith. We hadn't mentioned this internal chaos to anyone, especially not to each other. We had both subscribed to the belief that if we went to a good college, graduated, worked hard, and made our way up through the professional world, things would fall into place and we'd achieve the dreams of our feminist foremothers. Along the way, we hoped, we would find people to love who would love us back. We would become mothers, we imagined. We would feel satisfied in our careers and happy in our home lives and it would all work out, the end.

In 2012, we had hit our early forties, and thanks to social media, there were suddenly a lot of reunion dinners with college friends passing through New York. The two of us saw each other infrequently then, and the dinners could involve as many as five or six women, which meant that each person got her turn to offer up a monologue about her life—bullet points on how's the job, how's the spouse, how's the family, say something self-deprecating, reveal some new triumph, share a funny, anodyne story, pass the mic to the next woman. There was no chance during these dinners to say how we really felt about anything. How even though from the outside our lives looked pretty good, when we slid into a cab alone after these dinners, we often returned to feeling frayed, rudderless, fumbling toward who-knew-what with only unanswered questions and nothing specific to guide us.

Hana had recently turned down a job with a technology consultancy that would have meant a prominent step up in her career, and more money, but also a dramatic change in lifestyle. For the past fifteen years she'd been first a freelancer and then a small-business owner. She worked from home, which meant she could be around for her two young children. She had what was, in theory, an ideal setup—she got to have a job and also be a physically present mother. But her career had stalled. She was taking on the same kinds of projects at forty that she'd been doing ten years earlier, and no longer finding them interesting. But how to move forward? Working in her field meant that most jobs came with hours that started at *always* and stretched to *forever*. Was it too much to ask to be challenged by work, earn a decent living, and also see one's children?

Liz, too, was living the dream, only to find it wanting. As a print-magazine editor, her industry was collapsing, her fast-track career derailed, and she was filling in the gaps by spending more time at home with her kids—which she both enjoyed and felt ambivalent about. What about that job? Without a heavy-hitting career, was she worth less? And financially, how were she and her partner going to survive without two incomes? Her professional sphere had felt glamorous and fun and important, if only to a tiny number of people, and like living at the whirling pulse of New York City. But even before the magazine industry began to disintegrate, she wondered if she really wanted to be clocking in to an office job in Midtown every day with an infant and a toddler at home, reaching new milestones without her. She'd moved into a freelance editing and writing career with little extra childcare, so now her days were a mad dash to finish 1,798 tasks in one abbreviated "workday."

Our group dinners didn't feel like the time or place to talk about any of that. There were too many people, and who wanted to hear that maybe we didn't have it all figured out, that we were both questioning whether the tenets we'd built our lives on, the very construct of what we'd been told a good life should look like, were all wrong? So we stayed quiet, until one evening we didn't.

We were eating at a small, dark Korean restaurant in the East Village.

The group was smaller than usual that evening, just the two of us and a third college friend. This friend had always been impressive. After college she'd gone to a prestigious graduate school and become a tenured professor at a large university. She traveled around the world giving talks. She was known in her field. She was also single. At one point in the evening Hana commented to our friend that, of the people in their sorority with whom they'd graduated, she was probably the most successful.

"That's funny," the friend replied. "Because I'd say that *you* are."

Hana was married and had a family and also ran a company, she pointed out. Then the three of us wondered: Do you have to have a family to be successful? What, exactly, is success? Is it climbing to the top of your career? Is it climbing to the top of your career while also being married and having children? Is it climbing to a midway point in your career and then saying screw it, this isn't actually what I wanted to do, and pivoting to something else that truly makes you happy?

We didn't know, but that dinner lasted three hours as we sat and tried to figure out the answers. That night, something cracked open for us, a small chink in the belief that there was only one way to do things, that if we just followed the road in front of us, it would lead to happiness and success. That evening, there was time and space to say the things we'd never gotten to in our other reunion dinners. We talked about how unexpectedly hard it all felt, how we didn't know what our lives were supposed to look like anymore, and wondered aloud if any of the women we'd graduated with had figured things out better than the three of us. That dinner was the start of a multiyear journey to find answers. The questions we were asking shifted over time as the goals of our project shifted, but the endpoint remained the same. We wanted to resolve our crisis of faith. We wanted to understand what other women knew so we could apply that knowledge to our own lives. Researching this book showed us that there isn't one true path to fulfillment. Writing it fed our ambition and helped us find our footing on our own paths, wherever they may lead.

THE AMBITION DECISIONS

INTRODUCTION

We were always ambitious.

We arrived at Northwestern University, outside of Chicago, in 1989, from opposite coasts, meeting in a part of the country that was foreign to both of us. Hana had grown up in a Connecticut college town, where she'd been a mediocre student at a highly competitive prep school. Her plan, when she got to Northwestern, was to spend a year improving her grades so she could transfer to a college back east famed for its writing program. She wanted to be a writer but was forbidden by her computer science professor father to major in English. And so she majored in biology. She'd always been interested in science and figured this was a reasonable route to a paying job. And maybe she could be a science writer, or a geneticist who wrote on the side.

Hana eventually abandoned the idea of transferring schools, content to take lots of writing classes and work for the school newspaper, switching majors from biology to political science. (Receiving a D in chemistry will do that to a person.) At the end of her junior year, she took a class on political campaigns, and was captivated. This was 1992, during the heated race between Bill Clinton and President George H. W. Bush. As part of her campaigns class, Hana began volunteering in the press room of the Clinton campaign's Chicago headquarters. As she watched the internal mechanics of the campaign and came to understand how important words and modes of communication could be to the fate of the nation, she knew she'd found a thing she could be passionate about. Shortly after graduation,

Hana was accepted into a program that trained recent college grads to run political campaigns, then staffed them on local races. That summer she packed up her car and drove to Northern Virginia to work on a House of Delegates race.

Liz came to Northwestern from Southern California, raised by a single mother who had emigrated from Vietnam in the mid-1960s, with frequent visits to her father and stepmother in Texas. She'd done well at her competitive public high school, where she'd been the editor in chief of the school newspaper and hung out with the other honors students, most of whom aspired to attend impressive colleges. She had wanted to be a journalist since age ten, was excited by the process of gathering news and turning it into a physical product, and she knew she wanted a dramatic life change from suburban San Diego. Liz had never heard of Northwestern until a close friend's mother, a Northwestern alumna, mentioned that the school housed Medill, the best journalism school in the country. Liz applied for early admission to Medill and was accepted. She visited the campus on a wintry weekend and saw snow falling, the academic buildings clustered around a frigid Lake Michigan, a world and a life that looked so different from her own that she knew she must have it. But once college began, Liz found Medill to be a hypercompetitive, not particularly nurturing nor enjoyable environment. She wasn't motivated by the culture of elbowing every other student out of the way to launch yourself to the top. The social aspects of college, on the other hand, enticed her. In a school that was fairly segmented by major, Liz knew and hung out with everyone. She had friends who were sorority sisters, theater and music majors, freaks and geeks from all walks of life (the last group of which she counted herself a member). She also invested a lot of time exploring her own identity, and her junior year, Liz came out as a lesbian. Even with the intensity of Medill, her enthusiasm for journalism never waned. Her senior year she completed an internship at the Ann Arbor News, in Michigan, and loved the environment of the newsroom and the progressive feel of the town. After graduation, Liz took an editorial assistantship at

Chicago's well-regarded gay and lesbian newspaper, *Windy City Times*, ready to launch her career.

The two of us lived in the same dorm freshman year. We had very different personality types—one more introverted, academic, cynical; the other earnest, giddy, perennially optimistic—but we discovered we had a lot in common. We came from quietly feminist homes where the working assumption was that we'd grow to be independent, successful career women; we were driven by a desire for new experiences; and we had found our way to a prestigious university in the Midwest where we didn't always feel we fit in. We arrived at college with no intention of joining a sorority. But Northwestern is heavily Greek, and rush is the primary social activity over the first week of school. So we somewhat unwittingly signed on. We were only acquaintances then, but we pledged the same house because we were drawn to the same sort of women: loud, smart, funny, sassy, outspoken.

It wasn't until our junior year that we became true friends. We spent many afternoons between and after classes and meals grappling with the philosophical questions of the day. In our college-aged minds, our conversations were wise, insightful, and often hilarious. One day we decided it would be a brilliant idea to get a tape recorder and preserve one of our marathon talking sessions. It was as self-indulgent as it sounds, and yet it provides a glimpse into how much joy and insight we gained from talking together and why, twenty-five years later, we're still continuing the conversation.

When we graduated from college, we were eager to position ourselves for success, to find careers that would make people take notice, and most of all, we craved interesting lives that would transform us into interesting people. Like most college students, we weren't sure how to get from graduation to . . . there. Separately, we meandered through the early part of our twenties. Hana quickly got burnt out on campaigning. The living conditions were inconsistent—on one campaign, she slept on someone's sun porch for three months; on another, she shared a house with the campaign staff, the candidate, and the candidate's monkey—and after meeting a bunch of real-life politicians, she discovered she disliked the sort of people who chose to run for office. She ended up taking a writing job at a large consulting firm, and eventually became a change management consultant, boarding a plane each Monday morning to fly to different client sites across the country, then returning home, laptop in hand, late on Friday evenings. Liz was promoted to news/features writer at *Windy City Times*. She followed her college girlfriend to Washington, DC, and took a pharma-trade reporter job covering FDA news.

And then, in 1997, unbeknownst to each other, we both moved to New York. Hana landed a job working for the soon-to-launch CBS News website; Liz broke up with the college girlfriend and promptly relocated to a coveted position at *Vogue* magazine. We moved into apartments downtown, and had the same thought: *Now my life is starting.*

We got back in touch with each other eventually, though we can no longer remember how. (Nor can we remember how, pre-Internet and social media, people even found each other after they fell out of touch. Did we run into each other on the street? Know someone who knew someone who reconnected us?) And over the next decade and a half, we became the kind of friends who had dinner once a year or so, usually following a long email exchange requesting date changes and venue changes and apologies for delayed responses. Our lives got busy. We were sucked into the swirl of our thirties, with marriages and pregnancies and children, the daily thrum of careers and commuting, clients and magazine-issue closings, both of us building our lives according to the aspirations we'd articulated in college.

But in our early forties, things changed. We were both still in New York; we'd both moved to Brooklyn, chased out of Manhattan—along with much of the rest of New York—by high real estate prices. Liz's wife discovered she had stage III breast cancer weeks before Liz gave birth to their second child. For a period of time, Liz was caregiver not only to her newborn and two-year-old, but to her wife as well, while still holding down a job as deputy editor at *Lucky*, a fashion magazine. That job, at that time in the publishing industry, was the brass ring for Liz—a senior-level position at a beloved glossy publication, a formidable salary, lots of perks and societal cachet. But after enduring her wife's yearlong cancer treatment, mastectomy, and oophorectomy, and coming home after work to three vulnerable people with pressing daily needs, Liz's heart just wasn't in editing shoe captions any longer. And the print publishing industry was in rapid decline. She soon found herself out of a job. Liz found regular freelance editing work after that, but appealing full-time jobs were becoming even fewer and farther between, and other glossy-magazine editors whose careers had diminished with their industry were scrambling for those same positions like pigs at a trough. Freelance work itself was increasingly difficult to monetize, as every digital outlet wanted groundbreaking content, most for paltry compensation. Like many former print editors, Liz's career had transformed from something glamorous and enviable to a constant hustle for often low-paying work and a quarterly reinvention of her skill set, stuck as she was in a race to keep up with everyone who had suddenly become "content creators."

Hana had been running a tech consultancy for more than a decade, but the thrill she'd once gotten from signing new clients and designing and launching new technologies had begun to fade. In her early thirties, the payoff for the work she was doing—which wasn't exactly what she'd intended to do out of college, but was interesting and engaging enough—was flexibility and time to spend with her young children. She worked from home, which meant that when someone had strep, she could be there to administer the Tylenol in between conference calls. She picked her kids up from school most days and spent a lot of afternoons with them. But objectively, by forty her career felt stuck. She found herself stalking LinkedIn, looking up people she'd worked with earlier in her career, glowering at their VP titles, imagining that their lives were full of fancy meetings in glassed-in conference rooms where they decided the fate of the world, while she was cramming a full workday in before three p.m.

and then spending her afternoons picking Cheerios off the floor. And also, what about the writing? She'd always intended for the tech piece to be only half her career, but running a company and a family left her with little space in her days to write.

We embarked on our careers with such certainty, building our résumés and checking off milestones as though our lives were giant invisible to-do lists. Work for fancy companies: check. Get promoted: check. Find someone you love, start to spend your life with them: check. Children: check. But now, in our early forties, for the first time in a long while, we were unsure where to go next.

So Hana emailed Liz: "I might be having a midlife crisis, or working on an idea for a documentary."

Twenty minutes later, Liz responded: "Tell me about your midlife crisis in a nutgraf. And I want to work on this idea with you."

That email led to other emails, which led to drinks and dinners and the realization that we didn't know anything about making a documentary, but that we did know about writing and research. Perhaps we should start researching what the hell was going on with us. We were at what felt like an unexpected transition point, with no idea what we might be transitioning from or to. It was like living through those uneasy post-graduation days again, except with kids and mortgages. Was it just us, we wondered, or were there others? We decided we would interview a few of our friends from college to find out. They were scattered across the country, which meant we'd be able to talk to people outside our New York City bubble. And they were ambitious. In-your-face ambitious. Northwestern grads were all over TV (Julia Louis-Dreyfus, class of '82; Kathryn Hahn, class of '95; Stephen Colbert, class of '86), dotted the political and business landscapes (Chicago mayor Rahm Emanuel, class of '85; IBM CEO Ginni Rometty, class of '79), and were some of the heaviest hitters in journalism, grabbing Pulitzer Prizes and heading bureaus of prominent news organizations.

And we immediately knew who we wanted to talk to from Northwestern. Our sorority sisters were the picture of ambition. They prioritized academics over aesthetics, wearing hastily styled ponytails and baggy sweatshirts, competing for slots on the dean's list. They were now spread out across the globe, living a panorama of different lives, and most important, they were women. That was essential, because we were sure that this thing that was happening to us, this gnawing uncertainty, this feeling that we were possibly doing it all wrong, had something to do with being female.

We sat down to Skype with a few of the women we'd been closest to in college and asked questions. We listened to where our friends took the conversations. Those first few interviews were focused primarily on work-life balance and having it all, tropes that had dominated the news around that time due to the recent publication of Sheryl Sandberg's *Lean In*, Anne-Marie Slaughter's essay a few years earlier about how women still can't have it all, and a *New York Times* cover story about highly educated women opting out of their careers to stay at home.

We asked our friends what their dreams had been back in college and how (or if) those dreams had materialized. We were searching, in those first interviews, for the root of *why everything felt so hard all the time*. Our friends wanted to talk. As we asked about the people they'd been at eighteen and the people they'd become, several of them brushed tears from the corners of their eyes. Most of them were living full, happy lives, but at the same time, their days felt unexpectedly harried. They were tired. Things hadn't turned out exactly as they'd planned. To everyone's and no one's shock, life had revealed itself to be more complex and less straightforward than we had anticipated back in college.

Those first interviews were exhilarating. We would close Skype and take a minute to catch our breath, then, fingers flying over our keyboards, text each other things like **WELCOME TO BEING A WOMAN** and **WHAT IS THE MEANING OF LIFE???** It was as though we had both been marooned on an uninhabited, desolate planet and had stumbled upon a small band of humans who were friendly, who took us in and gave us shelter and told us that they, too, had wandered around hopelessly, alone, but now we were all in this together. As our interview list grew, though, we also began to realize that the question we'd been asking ourselves—what are the systemic problems making it so hard for women to realize our dreams and succeed in the ways we'd envisioned as young girls and then college students?—would only reveal part of the answer.

After interviewing a series of friends who were wrestling with the same midlife, mid-career challenges we were facing, we ran through a bunch of interviews with women who were pretty happy with how things had worked out for them. Some of these women were high up in the business world, others had chosen careers that enabled them to spend time pursuing outside interests, and a few were stay-at-home mothers. They were occasionally beleaguered, or stressed, or sometimes screamed at their kids to finish their homework. They had unrealized dreams. But generally, they were pleased with where they had arrived.

We wrote up our initial findings for *The Atlantic* in a series called "The Ambition Interviews." Midway through writing the series, Hana was at dinner with a group of friends, one of whom had an infant at home. She'd left her job as a high-end textile designer to be at home with her daughter, but wasn't sure what to do next. She liked being home, but probably didn't want to stay at home forever. But she also didn't think she wanted to go back to work quite yet. How long was it okay to stay home? she wondered. Should she be looking to freelance or was it okay to focus all her attention on her daughter for the time being? And what about the economics of it all? Her husband earned enough that she could stay home for now, but their lives would be a lot more comfortable with two incomes, especially when it came to saving for college. On the other hand, her old job didn't pay much more than the cost of childcare. Should she try to find a higher-paying job? Something she was passionate about? She felt like she had a million options and no options, all at the same time. She didn't know which choice was the right one, or even how to begin making a decision. She lacked the data to help her understand her choices, the ramifications of her decisions, and how to assemble everything into the kind of life she wanted. After that dinner the two of us chatted, Hana sharing the details of her friend's dilemma. Together we realized that, based on our interviews, we probably had the data this woman needed.

So we went back and looked again at what we'd learned from our interviews. While our initial goal had been to understand something about our own lives, we were beginning to see patterns forming. After more than a year of conducting interviews with women on the decisions they'd made and how those decisions had played out, we now had answers. We could see predictable ways in which people's lives unfolded. (At one point, we joked about creating an online quiz called "Answer these ten questions to find out if you'll become a stay-at-home mom or an exec at a Fortune 500 company!") More than that, we had a valuable body of knowledge for women in transition, for the crisis points we all encounter at crossroad moments in our lives: starting or changing careers, getting married, having kids, hitting midlife. Four years after our first email exchange, with more than eighty hours of interviews stockpiled onto our hard drives, and innumerable synthesis sessions, text messages, and Slack conversations later, we have condensed that body of knowledge into the pages you now hold in your hands.

For generations, men have had other men's lives to observe to guide them through the process of putting the pieces together, models for different directions lives can take. But women don't. What women's lives look like has changed so quickly from generation to generation that the choices we have and the way those choices play out for women today often look radically different from the way those very same decisions played out only a generation earlier. We don't have a template to follow, a way to peek into the future to catch a glimpse of what leaving this job or marrying that person or even just choosing to be the person who unloads the dishwasher every evening might mean for us decades from now. As a result, we are often making what turn out to be important decisions blind, groping for a way forward, winging it, and hoping it all works out. This book is an attempt to fill in that missing knowledge, and to help women navigate these decisions. We are sharing our own stories, and the stories of our college friends, so that other women can learn from them and make their own choices. We all want to be able to shake a Magic 8 Ball and find out what our futures hold. We can't give you a Magic 8 Ball, but we can tell you what we know about how those same transition points turned out for other women, illuminate the patterns—the rewards and consequences— we've identified, and help you think about how to integrate that information into your own life.

We interviewed forty-three women, all of whom were in the same sorority at Northwestern between 1989 and 1993. Most of these interviews were conducted over Skype. Many of them were interrupted by children, dogs, UPS, visiting in-laws, one by birds, and another by an eight-year-old's impromptu dance performance. Some women spoke to us at work, with their office doors closed. One woman huddled in a closet, the only quiet space she could find. A few people preferred to answer questions over email. Two women connected with us on Facebook, giving us glimpses of their lives, but never managed to find time to sit down with us for an interview. (We did not include them in our final interview tally.) Some people we interviewed multiple times, in some cases for over an hour each time. Of the women we graduated with, we were able to locate all but one.

Our college friends are geographically diverse, spanning five countries and twenty-one states. Many of the women were originally from the Midwest, though others' states of origin included a number of southern and western states, a handful of eastern locales, and Hawaii. And despite the connotations associated with sororities, our friends' socioeconomic backgrounds were also diverse, with several women having earned scholarships to pay their tuition and sorority dues, many graduating with a heavy load of student loans to pay off, and some whose families had been able to foot the tuition bill in full. One woman was the first member of her family to attend college. Another was a second-generation Northwestern student— her mother was a member of the class of 1967. Some women had parents who were doctors or lawyers or professors. Others came from working-class backgrounds or farming communities. Five of the women were first-generation Americans, with parents who had come to the United States from Taiwan, the Philippines, Vietnam, and Korea. And while the word *sorority* conjures up the most heterosexual of communities (what is a sorority, after all, without fraternity date parties and formals?), two of the women (not including Liz) are in same-sex marriages or partnerships.

We understand that our interview set doesn't represent every woman, every race, or every possible experience. We know that there are women who don't have the advantages our friends had—the awareness to apply to a private school like Northwestern, the grades and test scores and extra-curriculars to earn acceptance into a top college, the resources and support to negotiate student loans and high tuition. We also know there are women who don't go to college, or whose dreams don't include running a multinational corporation or being a renowned screenwriter or any of the other dreams in this book. This book doesn't speak for all women everywhere. But for the women out there who identify themselves as ambitious, who seek help and guidance in structuring their lives, who crave a community of other women's stories from which to learn, who are looking to understand their own lives in the context of others, read on. This book is for you.

CHAPTER 1

CAREER

As we began to interview our college friends from two decades ago, connecting with them over Skype in their homes in the United States, Eastern and Central Europe, and South America, we were prepared to hear diverse narratives of women killing it across a broad spectrum of careers. Armed with their résumés, some vague details from their smiling Facebook feeds, and spotty but indelible twenty-year-old memories, we began each interview the same way, asking, "When you got to Northwestern, what was your plan? How did that turn out?"

And we were not disappointed. We talked to a legal director at a women's rights nonprofit who is raising two children but also carves out time each week for running trail marathons, a television writer turned advertising copywriter turned stay-at-home mom tooling away at her long-dreamt-of novel, a rabbi, several financial executives, an artist with a niche Etsy following, and an on-air reporter in a major media market. We spoke with a former friend who is a first-generation Vietnamese American, and learned that she has been wheelchair-bound since 2000 due to multiple sclerosis. She works sixty-plus hours a week as a rehabilitation physician at an academic hospital, and jokes with her patients that "walking is over-rated." We interviewed a teacher who uses her free summers to work for a nearby national park counting birds, and her evenings and weekends to shred it with her all-female hard-rock band. Many of these successful, dynamic women warned us that "my life isn't that interesting," as if they feared their stories wouldn't live up to those of their former college class-mates (this warning both irked us, prompting us to instantly message each other, "Stop diminishing yourself—you were a badass in college!" and had us identifying with our friends' inherent need to self-deprecate). We as-sured them that we had yet to find anyone's life a bore. These women all struck us as interesting, particularly in the context of our memories of them from our college days. Some life stories followed a trajectory we could have predicted back in college (had we bothered to give any thought to what our forty-year-old selves would be like); others took a sharp left turn into something radically different and often fascinating.

As varied as our conversations were, over time we began to see ele-ments of people's paths repeating; one woman would say something that sounded eerily similar to something we'd heard from another woman, even though those friends lived 3,000 miles away from each other and had gone without any contact for more than twenty years. Everyone asked, as we had asked each other when we started this process, "What happened to so and so?" And as we slowly, over a year's time, gathered the answers to those questions, we collected stories that were immensely relatable. Each one had us nodding our heads and thinking, *That sounds like my life.* Or *I've struggled with exactly that problem, too.* Or *My spouse and I have that conversation constantly.* The fact that the life details of this group of so-called ordinary women felt so resonant is precisely what drove us to want to share their stories. Woven together, they began to paint a tableau of what life has been like for this group of women, who came of age in early-'90s America, at a time full of hope and potential but also of economic instability and political change. These stories began to show us where we all collectively succeeded (creating generally "happy" lives) and what tripped us all up (moving up at work exactly when and how we wanted, balancing personal life and work ambition), and revealed some surprising commonalities along the way. When one person with a rock-star career shares that she's married to a stay-at-home dad, it's unique. When five people share that same partnership configuration, it's something else entirely. So we began to analyze each of our friends' paths, noting the similarities and the disparities. One overcaffeinated morning, we grabbed a scrap of paper and began sketching out our friends' trajectories. That's when we started to note significant crossover in their life choices and resulting arcs.

After graduation, most of the forty-three women we interviewed went on to either land a first job or pursue a graduate degree. Due to the dismal economic climate at the time, a few people moved back home and worked in unpaid internships until they found jobs. A cluster of women went into banking, finance, and management consulting; others found work in journalism, PR, or advertising; a third group headed to medical school, law school, and assorted master's degree programs; three moved to Los Angeles to pursue work in film and television. Throughout the '90s, the women earned promotions, changed careers, finished graduate programs, or headed back to graduate school. They also got married (all but two got married or are partnered, though three later divorced). Eight married their college boyfriends. Others met future spouses at work or in bars, on blind dates or online. Everyone continued to climb the job ladder, to higher-status jobs with bigger salaries and bigger responsibilities: Two of the lawyers made partner, while a third went to work for the Justice Department; a screenwriter watched an A-list movie star claim the lead in her first screenplay; a TV writer turned ad exec earned a promotion to associate creative director. As we traced our friends' career arcs, we discovered that every woman in the group followed a near identical trajectory up until the point she had her first child (nine of the women did not have children, for varying reasons). Then their lives diverged along three clear, distinct routes.

One group of women became what we labeled High Achievers. These thirteen women are C-level or C-suite-adjacent executives (as in, they describe their offices as "down the hall from the CEO"), are recognized in their chosen field, or manage large teams. The women who populate this group include the CMO of a midsize banking group, a prominent screenwriter-director, an accomplished physician at a big university hospital, the owner of a successful PR firm, a Hollywood actress, a partner in a well-known corporate law firm, and a senior rabbi with a large congregation. For these women, motherhood didn't have much of an effect on their careers. They stuck to the trajectory they'd set out on right after college graduation, and many stayed with one company for more than a decade as they made their way through the ranks.

For another group—eleven women—motherhood was an abrupt end to the careers they'd been pursuing. This group, the Opt Outers, left work after having children, though only two of them had planned to. Many had day care or a nanny lined up after maternity leave, but found they simply couldn't bring themselves to leave their child with someone else. Others asked their employers for flexible schedules, were turned down, and quit. Many also said that they'd done the working-mother cost-benefit analysis and the math just wasn't on the side of their careers—their spouses earned more than they did, day care or a nanny would eat up a sizable chunk of their earnings, and therefore the reasonable thing to do was to leave work and become a full-time caregiver. Some simply didn't like their jobs and had spouses who could support the family, so they decided to stay home. One of the women was laid off from her corporate-track job and subsequently decided to stay home, and a second chose to leave work after her fourth child was born. Today the majority of them have been out of the workforce for an extended period of time, though some take on occasional part-time or freelance work.

The remaining nineteen women continued working but chose to move into jobs that allowed them some schedule flexibility, or stayed at jobs that let them leave early enough to be home for the school bus, in some cases, or dinner, in others, or to work from home some days. We called this group the Flex Lifers. A pediatrician began job-sharing with another physician so she could be home with her children two days a week. A sales-training executive whose husband had been a stay-at-home dad decided her job was too stressful, quit, moved to a cheaper city, and now sells crafts and art on Etsy. This group also includes four women without children who opted to scale back their career tracks; these women have all chosen not to have children not so they could focus more on their careers, which have been indeed fulfilling, but so they could foster more satisfying personal lives.

High Achievers

In labeling this group "High Achievers," we are not inferring that women who are Opt Outers or Flex Lifers wanted for achievements, or that this group has the best lives, or are the richest, or the smartest, or the happiest. We call them High Achievers based on a mainstream societal definition of professional success—a "big" or "important" job, high salary, prominence in their field—combined with the way that the women themselves talk about their own careers. These are women who were bursting with pride at their work-related accomplishments, who described career arcs where they said yes to every opportunity to move up in their chosen field, and who prioritized their careers above many other areas of their lives (exercise, for example, or home-cooked family dinners, both elements that many women outside of this group felt were essential to their daily functioning).

High Achievers have a number of life elements in common:

- *A demanding job that brings professional validation and/or financial reward*

- *A hard-driving work ethic with little desire to reduce commitment to or hours at work*

- *If married or partnered, an identification as the primary or equal financial provider*

- *If a parent, a willingness to cede primary child-rearing to either their partner or another caregiver*

- *A commitment to doing what it takes to move ahead professionally (moving to another city, for example, or traveling frequently), even if it means personal sacrifices*

The High Achiever is an archetype we are familiar with. Growing up in the '70s, '80s, and early '90s, it felt like there was a binary choice for women, or at least that's how life was on TV and in the movies: You could stay at home and be a mom, or you could go off to work and be wildly successful there. You could be *The Brady Bunch*'s Carol Brady, or you could be *The Mary Tyler Moore Show*'s Mary Richards (but you couldn't be both). And off-screen, the era was filled with women making a name for themselves through sheer force of will, intelligence, and grit: Billie Jean King, Indira Gandhi, Margaret Thatcher, Barbara Jordan. We had a template for working hard, being determined, and achieving success, for being the first and often the best. And closer to home, we personally knew women who were High Achievers. Liz's mother immigrated to the United States from Vietnam in the '60s and became an executive in the very white, male-dominated biotech industry, setting the ambition and achievement bar high for her daughter. Hana's grandmother inherited the family's wholesale bead business from her father and grew it into a company with international reach, supporting her family with her earnings; she frequently took buying trips to Japan and Europe at a time when transcontinental air travel was still new and uncommon.

When we graduated from Northwestern, we assumed many of our friends would take high-achieving paths, and each time we spoke with someone who had, we were proud to hear about her successes. We initially undertook this project hoping to encounter a large percentage of High Achievers, as if each interview that yielded a High Achiever could serve as a salve for our own perceived professional flounderings—see, it *could* be done! Women could conquer the corner office, save lives, support their families, go home and help their children with long division and be happy. It was just us—we couldn't do it. But others could. So initially, every High Achiever we encountered felt like a global high five for women, and left us feeling like we'd checked off another box: Feminist dream of our foremothers: check. Woman who supports her family and feels good doing it: check. Friend who became some version of the person she'd hoped to become back in college: check. The High Achievers were indeed a group to be proud of—but not falling into the High Achiever category, we would come to learn, was not cause for disappointment. We would discover that all three designations were much more complicated and nuanced than that.

The High Achiever: Leilani

Leilani came to Northwestern from a medium-size city in Idaho, where she had been a varsity captain of her cheerleading squad and an alpha girl at her high school. She was gregarious, always ready for a party, with a big, blond, late-'80s perm. She lived in our dorm freshman year, but didn't rush the Greek system until sophomore year. She was tight with a group of girls from the dorm who pledged a different sorority but friendly and outgoing with all students, stopping to chat at the dining hall and introducing people at Wednesday Munchies nights. Though we wouldn't have articulated it this way back in college, she was a born leader, the kind of girl who might someday run for office or lead large groups of people toward innovative solutions with a whiteboard and boss-lady attitude.

We didn't discuss ambition or career plans with Leilani much in college. She was often racing through the sorority house en route to the north end of campus, where the fraternities resided. Her boyfriend was a swimmer, and as a result there were usually a few other swimmers dotting our formal parties, setups engineered by Leilani to help out her dateless sorority sisters. But when we reconnected with her decades later, a much more determined picture began to crystallize, one of a woman who had not only embraced the social aspect of college full on, but who pulsed with ambition, who had come to Northwestern to succeed. "I was going to be the best prosecuting attorney anybody had ever seen," Leilani told us. "I was going to be Atticus Finch from Idaho. I was going to be the ruling DA of my county, and I was going to end up on a court bench at some point."

Leilani declared a political science major, in preparation for applying to law school. But a couple of years in, she began to rethink that path. "I paid for my own education, so there were student loans hanging over my head," Leilani recalled. "The thought of having more student debt and going to school another three years, at a time when there was a glut of lawyers on the market, made me revisit my plan." Meanwhile, Leilani had registered to be a bone marrow donor. Junior year, she learned she was a match for a leukemia patient in need of a transplant. She went through with the donation senior year, an arduous and painful process, and it upended the way she had been thinking about her career plans. "I had my world rocked, and it left me unsettled. I started to see my priorities in a different light: Life could be short, and I knew that eventually I had to follow my passions."

Leilani was a pragmatist, though, and with college loans looming, she also knew she needed to prioritize earning, at least for a few years. She'd started to schedule interviews with business recruiters on campus when she received "the chance of a lifetime." She was one of fifty students from four colleges across the country that year to be selected by a national bank for a twelve-month management training program to learn the fundamentals of banking, with rotations in trading, the stock market, and managing money. Best of all, for Leilani, the trainees would be compensated for their crash course in the finance world.

"Honestly, I didn't think I would be very good at banking," Leilani admitted. "But they paid you to learn the first year, so I thought of it as an opportunity." The investment yielded returns. The firm assigned Leilani to a position in New York City, working in marketing within their private banking practice. She stayed for four years.

Leilani's fourth year at the bank, the head of private banking approached her and said, "We think you're talented, you've got great ideas, we want to send you to Columbia Business School." She was torn. She knew that earning an MBA from Columbia, financed by her employer, would secure her rise to a vice presidency at the company, and her rise more broadly in the financial industry, without leaving her with future loans to pay off. But she was also conflicted about the culture and ethics of her industry.

"It's a business where people will do almost anything to get additional assets under management. They'd sell their grandmother to get extra money. I was asked to write the college entrance essay for one of our clients' children. Some people I worked with had their kids walking their clients' dogs. And I would be like, 'We're a bank here, we're professionals, we're not dog walkers.'"

Leilani had been working with high-net-worth private-banking clients from the United States and Latin America, and wanted to become fluent in Spanish. Some of her clients had mentioned a bilingual MBA program in Barcelona, which appealed to her. She could finally master Spanish, earn the MBA she felt she needed to get to the next stage in her career, and live overseas. She applied and was accepted into the program sight unseen. She hadn't visited the school, and no one there had met her, either. She had a decision to make.

"Do I go to Columbia, signing on the dotted line for five years with my blood to say I'll stay at the bank and they'll pay for everything and I'll work my butt off six days a week and have to stay five years in this environment that I'm not very comfortable with from an ethical standpoint, or do I just throw it away?" She'd paid off her Northwestern loans during her first couple of years working at the bank, and wasn't sure if she'd have another chance to live abroad. And that tug of passion remained. Life could be painfully short, as the memory of her bone marrow donation reminded her. It felt a little risky, but she packed up two suitcases, took out additional student loans, and committed to Barcelona—4,000-plus miles from her hometown. She had never been to Spain. She had never even been to Europe. She told herself, "It's now or never. It's just one of those times in life."

Leilani thrived in the international business school setting. But when the two-year program was nearing completion, she wasn't quite ready to leave. "I thought I would see more of Spain during business school than I actually did. On holidays I would whisk away to somewhere, but I didn't really get to know the true Spain. So I thought, 'Let me stay for two more years. I'll work here, master Spanish like a rock star, and go back to the US totally bilingual.'" Plus, she thought the international business experience would be a boon in her next job in New York.

One of Leilani's friends in Spain had worked at a fashion and luxury goods company and told her about an opportunity there. Her marketing professor gave her a great recommendation, and she walked into her first job in Barcelona at age twenty-nine. She was still at the company sixteen years later, when we first interviewed her. Leilani started as a product manager for an international fashion designer and eventually moved into the parent company's travel marketing division, before being promoted to international retail development director of the parent company.

Professional success never seems to have been a question for Leilani. The personal side of things came along a little later in her life. In graduate school, "I had the picture-perfect boyfriend with the ideal curriculum vitae: big Austrian guy, blond hair, blue eyes, worked in private equity, skier, family went yodeling—it was my dream." The boyfriend moved on to a job in Munich after finishing business school. Leilani stayed in Spain. "We did the long-distance thing for three years, he put a ring on my finger, we continued the long distance for a fourth year, and nothing happened. We were long distance for five years, then six, then: implosion." He didn't want to move back to Barcelona, and Leilani didn't want to leave her job, where she was enjoying success, validation, intellectual stimulation, and financial reward.

"Clearly, at that point, I chose my career over him. And I must have known innately that there was something not right with that relationship because I was smart enough not to leave this great job opportunity." So Leilani ended it, heartbroken but resolute. She spent the next year alone, coping by "working like a crazy woman and watching every episode of *CSI* in my little cave." A year later, emotionally healed, she started going out again, visiting the gym, meeting people. Then, after an inspiring Spin class, Leilani spotted someone new. "I went for a totally different profile. He had blue eyes but dark hair. A sweet Spanish guy. He was my Spinning instructor." Rafael had trained as a professional cyclist and taught Spin classes at night for extra money. "So then I had to be in the front row Spinning three nights a week," taking as assertive an approach to her exercise and dating protocol as anything else she did. "It took me two and a half years to land the deal before I finally got a date." That was twelve years ago, and though she and Rafael have chosen not to marry, they've been inseparable since.

A couple of years into their relationship, the question of kids arose. Leilani didn't feel a strong maternal pull, she had a lot of friends who didn't have children, and her career was going so well—would it be wise to disrupt it? "I didn't feel this overwhelming desire," she explained. "You find as you get older that there are many ways to make a very full life, with friends, with work, with dedication to charities or other things that you believe in. We're taught to think you must have children to fulfill your purpose on this planet, but today there are many other ways of having a very grateful life." But Rafa, as he is known, really wanted kids. Leilani was thirty-seven, and she knew it was now or never, so they went for it. Their son, now nine, was born at twenty-seven weeks, weighing just over two pounds, "so he had to stay in the little oven in the hospital for two and a half months. The whole experience was quite traumatic." That, along with the cost of having a child in Europe, with only one secure income, plus the high demands of Leilani's job, led Leilani to decide that she'd be a "unibreeder." Rafa, an affectionate and very present parent, would love to have more children, but Leilani is pragmatic about her parenting bandwidth: "When I'm traveling and working this way, I would rather do one thing very well than disperse myself in multiple ways and not do it as well. I'm realistic about what I can give."

Since partnering with Leilani, Rafa has developed a career as a freelance producer of computer-generated special effects for movies. Typical of freelance workers, Rafa's gigs are project based, so his work ebbs and flows. He gets hired for two, three months at a time, then looks for the next project. Leilani's income, as a very full-time exec, is fixed. "I'm the chief breadwinner of the family. I am the *bono*, the bond of the family. I would say that we have the least typical Spanish relationship." Leilani's partner is the one home with their son more, and they also have a full-time nanny. That's a setup that works well for Leilani. Her own mother stopped working for about seven years after Leilani and her sister were born and then returned to work part-time. "What a sacrifice, what a beautiful thing. Sometimes that guilt slips into me," Leilani said. But she can't see how that arrangement would work for her family. In her career, her company, and in Spain, "you need to be constantly pushing forward. Staying flat, saying, 'I want to stay in this position because I like it and I dominated it for twenty years' would not be possible." Scaling back, Leilani fears, could also be detrimental to her job skills, especially at the speed that today's world moves. "My company is growing and changing so often that you've really got to keep yourself at the forefront—or at least that's the pressure I feel." Plus, personally, Leilani said, "I need to be growing mentally, always having new challenges."

After sixteen years at the luxury goods company, Leilani left last year. She was ready for a change professionally and willing to take another risk in her career. She accepted an opportunity as the marketing and business development director in the travel retail division of a liquor conglomerate. The job is in Singapore; the family moved last summer. She's excited that her son will become trilingual, that the family will experience life in Asia, and that she'll master marketing in a different industry. Since the move, Leilani has realized, "There are so many interesting companies, roles, and people out there in the world. I never need to fear change again. That's the most valuable lesson I've learned." Leilani is still assimilating to the new corporate culture—a very male-dominated one in Asia, and an industry with a different focus than where she spent the bulk of her career. It's a challenge, she told us, but "I am up for it!"

Leilani was a textbook High Achiever from the get-go: She pursued a competitive, lucrative industry and was cherry-picked for a coveted program by a prominent company early on. She prioritized her career as equal—and then above—her business school boyfriend's, and eventually even over the boyfriend himself. She labored hard, often putting in long hours to get the job done, and ascended to the top brass of her multinational company. As a result, she's enjoyed handsome financial compensation, extensive global travel, and a well-earned reputation as a valued leader. She consciously limited the number of children she had as a concession to her career demands. And like many of our High Achievers, she took responsibility as the primary earner for her family and expected her partner to take on more of the at-home parenting. For many women like Leilani, who have achieved tremendous success in traditional business spheres or other industries, career came first and was never on the table as an element for compromise.

Here's What We Know About High Achievers

▶ **Those who have kids rely heavily on paid childcare, spouses, and/or family members.**

Nearly all our High Achievers told us how important it is for them to have childcare that not only allows them to be at work for set hours, but also has them covered when they need to attend a seven a.m. business meeting, or stay late to work on a project, or take a last-minute business trip. In Leilani's case, her partner's adjustable hours (and the clear prioritization of her career over his) grants her that flexibility, and by extension also helps her succeed in her career.

While the need for High Achievers to be comfortable with external childcare seems an obvious point, it is noteworthy because many of our friends who were High Achievers *prior* to having children were decidedly not comfortable with it, leading them to opt out or find more flexible work arrangements. A significant number of our High Achievers who stayed in their positions at work after becoming mothers solved this problem by relying on their spouse or a relative for childcare. The remainder paid someone outside their family for childcare, understanding that the cost, both financially and emotionally, was a necessity for their continued career success—and their continued career success was a foregone conclusion for a number of reasons. In addition to their incomes being gratifying emotionally and socially, most High Achievers rely on that income to support their families, either as the sole breadwinner or part of a household that depends upon two incomes. And for many of them, their careers are an opportunity to show their children what it looks like to be a working mother with a rewarding career. When one of our C-suiters' tween daughters was asked what she wanted to be when she grew up, she responded, "Either a professional basketball player or a successful businesswoman." (We all collectively beamed across our Skype connection when we heard this.) Which is not to say that our friends don't feel guilt or misgivings over the hours they have to be away from their children—of course they do—but they are able to resolve that guilt, and that desire to be a present mother, in other ways.

▶ They miss some events in their kids' lives, but they get over it and get on with it.

Just as Leilani described feeling some remorse over missing moments in her son's life, or not being fully available to him the way her mother was for her, we heard time and again from other High Achievers that they understood from the inception of their working lives that this was what was required of them to move their careers forward, and it is a compromise they are able to live with. One C-suite friend feels resigned to occasionally "attending" her daughter's basketball games through the magic of FaceTime, but is also insistent that she be home every night she isn't traveling for work to tuck her daughter in to bed and download the day's events. An insurance executive whose husband is a stay-at-home parent told her two children when they were in elementary school that they could each pick one school event for her to attend over the year; she sets expectations early about what her schedule will permit. A few high-achieving women noted that, either due to their status as the boss or the family-friendly culture of their companies or both, they are able to carve out some schedule flexibility for important events. Our friend who is the chief marketing officer at a bank told us that when she worked as a management consultant, a "very hectic and intense job," she had enough schedule control to make 90 percent of her children's Christmas pageants. That was only possible because her office had a number of senior women in charge, who were more understanding when it came to cutting out of work early to see her fourth grader sing "Let It Snow."

▶ **Most struggle to find time for exercise or other self-care.**

Even though she met her partner in Spin class, Leilani echoed what we heard from nearly all our High Achievers when she told us she rarely gets to a Spin class these days (though she is attempting to follow through on a New Year's resolution to attend circuit training sessions—for now). Most of our High Achievers mentioned in passing that they never get to the gym, usually with a guilty shrug of their shoulders, as though college-age us might judge them for not logging enough hours on the StairMaster in between business deals. But they also understand that this is part of the deal with the lives they've chosen. For one of our High Achievers, who was a former Big 10 field hockey player, this was a tough realization. For others, not making it to the gym is just a necessary part of life.

▶ **Work schedules are rigid, especially early on, and may include frequent travel.**

Many of our business-focused High Achievers don't make it home for dinner most weeknights, and they may not even make it to their own beds every night—because being an executive in today's working world typically means being available for a meeting in Dallas tomorrow when you're in Chicago today. One High Achiever told us about a particularly demanding time at work when she was "literally in three different countries in twenty-four hours." Her story wasn't atypical. One comment we heard frequently from our non–High Achievers is that they enjoy having control over how they spend their time, the flexibility to leave work early and pick up their kids or go for a run or buy cereal at the supermarket during off-peak hours. Conversely, High Achievers' demanding work schedules mean they need to be where the meetings are: "If you're meeting with the CEO, you can't tell him that such-and-such time doesn't work for you." This extends not only to seven a.m. breakfast meetings or last-minute trips across the country, but also to the willingness to pick up and move as their careers demand. One friend of ours spent a year commuting back and forth between Vancouver and San Francisco so her daughter wouldn't have to relocate. Another, a broadcast journalist, followed her job to five different states before she settled into her current position, got married, and started a family. And Leilani moved her partner and child to another continent, nearly 7,000 miles away, for a better career opportunity. The whole family was game for a new adventure, but it was her professional life that made the move happen.

▶ **Those who are married earn salaries equal to or higher than their spouse's.**

Every High Achiever we interviewed is at least a nearly equal earner to her partner, and more than half of them are either the primary or higher earner. Accordingly, the economic contribution of every woman in this group is integral to her family's quality of life, and those who are the primary or sole earner have that pressure as both a driver for their continued professional success and an impediment to scaling back or plateauing their careers. As Leilani put it, "I haven't scaled back, and where I am, I can't scale back. It wouldn't be possible."

▶ **High Achievers derive deep pride and satisfaction from their work.**

As with all our High Achievers, Leilani is clearly energized and excited by her career. Her Facebook feed is an endless series of photos from exotic work locales as she travels through Asia and Europe, often kicking back in first class on long-haul flights en route to distilleries and star-studded marketing events. Leilani's long hours of work also provide financial support for her family—she is clearly gratified to be its *bono* in many ways. Every High Achiever we interviewed bubbled over with an enviable level of pride in their abilities, confidence in their position in the world, and a glow of accomplishment. Whereas many of our non–High Achiever friends seemed to wrestle with some inner conflict about how much time they should devote to what, the High Achievers appear to have that all figured out. Work takes priority for them, period, end of story. Their careers are nonnegotiable, and as a result, the other pieces of their lives fall into a logical order, taking precedence over how much to volunteer at school or whether they should handcraft Valentines for the entire class or just suck it up and do store-bought—conundrums that keep our other two groups of friends up at night.

▶ **Some High Achievers purposely had fewer or no children. Those with three kids felt a bit overwhelmed.**

Several of our High Achiever friends have no children, and others, like Leilani, are "unibreeders." Our friends who prioritize demanding, growing careers simply have fewer hours remaining for "present" parenting. Many of them considered that at the outset of their careers and their marriages, and made decisions accordingly about how many children they wanted. This isn't to say that it's not possible to have a big career and also have a big family—plenty of women are able to do both—but among our friends, the two High Achievers with three kids mentioned repeatedly how tough it was. Both joked that "I don't know how we do it," "Things are always chaotic," and "We are either super awesome, or crazy."

Opt Outers

Our next group of friends also graduated with much promise and poten- tial, which they pursued toward a very different outcome than the High Achievers. We heard from a significant number of friends who had relin- quished their careers, some briefly, some longer term, after having children—and admit we were initially taken aback. We remembered the women we'd known in college as poised to become the Supreme Court justices, foreign correspondents, emergency room surgeons, and Fortune 500 CEOs of our generation. Only about a third of us seemed to be on this path. At the end of a good number of our interviews, we struggled to make sense of the women who had excelled at Northwestern, earned ad- vanced degrees, achieved their dream jobs or were well on their way— and then stepped aside when they began having children.

Were all those infuriating essays about Ivy League–educated women dropping out of the workforce to be mothers actually right? Were we horribly judgmental, self-righteous mean girls for wondering how someone who had the potential to be wildly successful in her career had shelved her ambition in exchange for overseeing playdates and driving the carpool? Did our friends have any regrets about what they had given up, and if so, would they—or could they—be honest with us about them?

In keeping with what we heard from our High Achiever friends, the answers were more complicated than a simple yes or no. Most of our stay-at-home-mom friends are satisfied with their choices, sure that they have what they want, but as with so many of our friends, they also acknowledged having to compromise. Some of these women are envious of their "high-achieving" friends with their demanding office jobs and dinners with clients, some miss earning a paycheck and are ambivalent about what their own professional futures might hold. And while the minutiae of stay-at-home parenthood wears on some of them, prompting emails with exasperated-mom GIFs and memes about playdates with wine, the overwhelming majority of them are confident that what they offer their children, their larger family unit, and society is well worth what they have sacrificed by opting out. Their often invisible and always unpaid labor allows not only their children and homes to function smoothly, but their schools, local community and political organizations, and neighborhoods to thrive as well. Once we thought more deeply about their stories, juxtaposing them with our own struggles around work and parenting, we began to understand that these women were, in fact, empowered by their life choice. The majority of them viewed their situation as temporary (in this they're not alone—one study found that 93 percent of highly educated women who leave work plan to return[1]), engaged in work that, while unpaid, was valuable and necessary. As we dug deeper into this group of women, we learned that their stories, like their decisions, are much more complex than the narrative of, as one woman put it, "I gave up!"

The group of women who left their jobs to become full-time caregivers to their children had the following in common:

- *A deep desire to be primary caregiver to their child*

- *A childcare-cost calculus that meant job retention didn't make sense*

- *A partner who was not available to equally share the childcare responsibilities*

- *Not enough flexibility in their job to be the kind of "present" parent they wanted to be*

- *An inherent unwillingness to sacrifice parenting for career*

- *Some sense of loss at giving up their career*

- *A desire to return to the workplace in the future*

Many of the Opt Outers wanted to keep working, but their job didn't offer enough satisfaction to warrant staying, given the financial and psychological cost of childcare and the chaos they felt a two-career household brought to their lives. Paramount to our Opt Outers' career trajectories is that almost all of them consider opting out to be a career rest stop, not a final destination. For them, the decision wasn't stay at work vs. never work again for the rest of their lives. Instead, they saw it as a choice to pause their careers in order to achieve family-focused goals like being actively involved in their kids' schools, or keeping their household humming along smoothly. Once their children are older, all of them plan to return to their career ambitions, though not always in the same way they'd pursued them pre-children. Accordingly, nearly all of them have toggled from stay-at-home parent to some type of work outside the home since they've had their children—and a number of them are presently in the process of reclaiming career paths and reshaping their lives, which we will discuss more fully in chapter 6.

The Opt Outer: Sandra

Sandra applied to the engineering program at Northwestern, within the school of technology, which everyone on campus referred to simply as "Tech." In accordance with the stereotype of the day, Tech was heavily male-dominated, and students were known for being bookish, serious, and academically intimidating—this was pre-Internet, so Tech meant long hours spent in chemistry labs or studying electrical engineering. Sandra passed a lot of time in college running around the sorority's study lounge in boxer shorts (a lot of us wore college-logo-themed boxer shorts as loungewear in the '90s) holding a stack of thick books with intimidating titles like *Intro to Thermodynamics*, hair slightly disheveled, a cloud of panic hanging over her, as though she wasn't quite sure she would make it through the night. Sandra was the only Tech student in our class and her stress-laden sweep through the kitchen for more coffee at all hours of the night often provoked whispers, as other women wondered why on earth she would bother with such an impossible major.

"I knew I was interested in getting an engineering degree if I stayed in Tech, or if not, doing something in science," explained Sandra, who grew up in a suburb of Omaha. "And I knew there was a good chance I wanted to go to law school. I was keeping the idea of getting a science degree before law school in the back of my mind because I knew I might want to be a patent attorney. My dad was a patent attorney."

Part of Sandra's stress may have arisen because she wasn't sure how she was going to manage a career with being a parent. "I remember thinking, back when I was at Northwestern, the whole conflict of, 'Gosh, I'm working so intently, I'm trying to get good grades so that I can get this job. And I don't know how in the world I can have this job and have kids, and I know I want to have kids.' I think I was a little conflicted even then."

After graduation, Sandra went to law school in her home state, with the goal of following in her father's footsteps and becoming a patent lawyer. The summer between her first and second years of law school, Sandra got several internship offers, one of them at the corporate firm where her father worked. By the time she finished her internship, she knew she wanted to pursue patent law. After law school, when the same firm offered her a job, she jumped at the chance to work not only at a prestigious company, but side by side with her dad. "He's my favorite coworker," she said, completely seriously. Her dad never directly supervised her, but they sometimes worked on the same cases, along with a team of people. "We could definitely talk shop, like, 'I just had a call with so-and-so about this aspect of the case,' and he'd tell me, 'I was doing these motions,' and it was a fabulous experience." She worked at the firm for ten years, thriving and eventually making partner. In that time, she met and married her husband, a marketing and communications executive at a large company.

Then Sandra and her husband learned they were expecting their first child. She had always dreamt of being a mother and was thrilled to be pregnant, but also began to think seriously about how it might affect her career, which she had so thoughtfully plotted and earned. "I was hoping to reduce my hours at work. I was a partner, and they didn't have any part-time partners at the time. I think I probably could have been the first one, and they would have worked with me to make that work." But as Sandra explored childcare options, she felt increasingly conflicted about leaving her soon-to-arrive infant. "I interviewed some nannies, some nice, quality people," Sandra remembered. "I was happy to have them in my home, but just thinking of having a little baby and handing him off, visualizing in my mind, 'What if something goes wrong? Do I feel comfortable with this person that they're going to make the right call with my kid? And is my kid going to be raised in as stimulating an environment as I would be able to provide myself?' I was hesitant."

Complicating her feelings about hiring a caregiver was another family member who needed care: Sandra's father-in-law. He had struggled with a few different health issues, including dementia, all of which ramped up during Sandra's pregnancy. "You name it and he probably had it. He would end up in the hospital all the time. I think our craziest year was maybe nine hospital stays and each time would be for a week." For five years leading up to Sandra's pregnancy, she and her husband had accompanied her father-in-law to the hospital multiple times in a year. "My husband's an only child, and his mom had already died, so we were the only support for his dad—and he couldn't even check himself into the hospital because they ask you all those questions like, 'Tell me about your medical history.' Well, when you have dementia, you don't really know."

Sandra also had a full plate at work. "There were so many nights when I'd be at work until seven o'clock because I needed to get something done. And I realized I wanted to be there for my clients and be a good attorney, but at the same time I didn't want to just be leaving my baby." Sandra felt she couldn't fully succeed at work without basically hiring round-the-clock staff to help care for her family. Even before Sandra gave birth to her first baby, she sensed an imminent trade-off. "I'm better at focusing on one thing, so my priority was, I want to take care of my kid."

Sandra had her baby and went on maternity leave, though as a partner, it was the kind of maternity leave where she still went into the office once a week. Three months in, Sandra was preparing to return to work full-time and had narrowed her list of nanny candidates down to her favorite. Then that nagging feeling returned. "It's that time where I'm supposed to come back to work or I've got to quit my job. I've picked a nanny and I've got to decide, do I hire this person? Finally, I decided, I don't want her taking care of my kid. *I* want to take care of my kid. So that was it." Sandra went into her managing partner's office and resigned. "He was very supportive and nice, but I cried. It was very hard, walking away, going down that elevator."

Even though she believed she had the option to potentially scale back her job to part time, Sandra chose to leave it altogether. She realizes she gave up a lot in professional satisfaction, validation, and financial security. "I knew that I was walking away from something. I'd gotten to the point at my practice where I had a pretty nice book of clients, and I knew that the second I walked out the door, I had to hand my clients off to other attorneys." But she also says she knew on a gut level that this was the right choice for her, that even working part-time as an attorney was too great a compromise for the kind of life she wanted, for the kind of parent she wanted to be. "Being a partner in a law firm isn't one of those punch-in, punch-out jobs," Sandra explained. If she had scaled back to three days a week—an option she thinks her employer might have supported—Sandra didn't feel that under those parameters she could deliver the quality service she insisted on giving her clients. "When your clients have something come up, you can't tell them, 'I'm sorry, I'm off at three today, so good luck getting that done, because I'm not coming back until Tuesday.' I don't want to be like that. I'm more like, 'If I put in five extra hours right now, you're going to be set.'" More than that, Sandra knew she didn't want to leave her baby for even three days a week. She also had a gut feeling that her husband wasn't going to share the caregiving equally with her during the times their nanny wasn't there—not that they discussed it explicitly— and her husband earned enough money to support the family without Sandra's salary. While he supported whatever decision she made, Sandra says he was clearly happy when she decided to stay home with their baby.

Sandra struggled at first with her total change in lifestyle as a stay-at-home mom. Days filled with long bouts of solitude interspersed with different types of newborn cries (hungry? wet? tired? gassy?) and diaper changes eventually left Sandra feeling bored and lonely. "I kept hearing about these mommy-baby yoga groups that go get coffee, but I didn't know anyone who was actually doing that. It was a very hard transition."

A year and a half later, Sandra got pregnant with her second child. For most of her pregnancy, she thought about how grateful she was that she had gotten to stay home with her first baby, how important it was to her to be there for every milestone, and how she also wanted to give that to baby number two. But she also missed her job, and figured that after another year at home, she'd go back to work. She missed the intellectual stimulation, the challenge of finding solutions for clients, interacting with other lawyers. Then, shortly after her second child was born, Sandra was dealt unexpected news: her two-year-old was diagnosed with type 1 diabetes. The disease requires constant care, and for a while Sandra struggled just to learn a new daily routine to keep her son healthy. Then, two and a half years later, Sandra's second child was diagnosed with the same disease. "That was a game changer," Sandra said. If she'd been nervous before about entrusting her children's care to someone else, now it seemed like an impossibility, in part because managing her children's disease has become a 24/7 job. "You can never really totally focus in on something else, because their health is always in the back of your mind. That's the number one priority."

As her children have gotten older and more self-sufficient, and Sandra has become an expert at managing diabetes, she's begun to wonder about what she should do next, once she has more time and mental space. "Right now I'm intensely doing everything for my kids. What am I going to do when I don't have kids? But I'll figure out what to do when that time comes." A couple of years ago, she and her husband bought a farm as an investment property, and Sandra manages it—a job she says consumes about five hours a week, more during tax season. In the past year, she has contemplated going back to work in a fuller way, but only for the right job. By that, she means working with "nice" people. "I don't need to go back into any kind of stressful, awful environment. But if the right position doing the right thing came along, I'd take that in a second."

Sandra realizes that just-right position might not be a reality. "If you're out of the workforce for fifteen, twenty years, who wants you? And do you have to come back in? Or is that the time where you need to be entrepreneurial and start your own business?" She's thought about how to expand her farm business, and about whether she should go back to school and get an MBA. On the other hand, graduate school costs money, and Sandra and her husband aren't sure the cost would be worth it—a refrain we heard from many of our friends who considered pursuing additional degrees later in their lives to extend or reroute their careers. Sandra's next act remains to be seen.

S andra's story illustrates the big-picture issues we heard about from most of the Opt Outers we interviewed. She had nabbed the job she desired, been promoted to partner, and enjoyed her work—just not so much that she could give up being the one to care for her baby 100 percent of the time, at least for the first couple years of his life. She could visualize having a flexible schedule at her job, but didn't even inquire about the possibility because even that was too great a compromise. Sandra knew herself, knew she performed at her best when she could be completely available—either to her clients or her children, but not both at the same time. "I wasn't planning on staying home with my son after he was born," Sandra said, "but once he was born, I realized something had to give, and I needed to figure out what." Sandra's desire to be there for her child, at any cost, outweighed her drive to continue working. Another friend who, during her maternity leave, unexpectedly left behind a glamorous career in public relations echoed that sentiment: "Once [my daughter] was here, it shifted everything. I knew I wanted to be with her more than I wanted to be going to that office every day."

Just as career is nonnegotiable for High Achievers, childcare is nonnegotiable for Opt Outers. All of them feel that their physical and emotional presence with their children is simply richer than what a paid caregiver could provide, though many note that they would have happily left their baby with a family member. As most of them had no family members nearby or willing, choosing to leave work and take on caregiving full-time was the only logical option. While some of the Opt Outers were married to men who were already the primary wage earners, others, like Sandra, contributed significantly to the household income. But even so, they were willing to walk away and take the financial hit to provide the kind of care they wanted for their children. Some of our friends in less lucrative fields than law, or in jobs they loved less than Sandra loved hers, did a childcare-cost calculus that revealed their income would barely cover a nanny. If these women were already feeling conflicted about not being the ones to physically care for their babies, their decision became obvious: they left their jobs. And some women didn't necessarily feel, as Sandra did, that there was a push-pull, that something had to give—they just felt, on a core level, that they did not want to leave their child, that they could not. So they didn't.

Here's What We Know About Opt Outers

▶ **Opt Outers take on all the childcare and also all the household tasks.**

Not surprisingly, given that they left their jobs to take care of their children full-time, all the Opt Outers we talked to are responsible for the majority of childcare within their marriages (a good number of them also made a point of telling us that their spouses are great dads). Also unsurprising: All the women in this group take on the vast majority of housework, grocery shopping, and errands. All our Opt Outers are married to men who head off to traditional office jobs every day. Since the women opted out, and are the ones who are physically present, nearly all the tasks required to run a family are allocated to them.

▶ **Opt Outers have the economic luxury of being supported by someone else—and not supporting the family financially comes with a mixed bag of emotions.**

Our Opt Outer friends' spouses all work in high-paying jobs—finance, law, commercial real estate, sales—which allowed these women to leave their own jobs while keeping the security of health benefits and a predictable household income. Every one of them acknowledges that they are "fortunate" or "lucky" that their families can thrive on just one income, and many of them feel pride at being able to make their primary occupation raising their children and creating a comfortable home life for their families. Yet some of them also express internal conflict about abandoning their career dreams to become stay-at-home mothers and allowing their husbands to shoulder the family's financial burdens.

▶ They're still ambitious, and channel that energy into volunteer work and self-care.

This group of women left behind their careers, but not their ambitions. Those who were go-getter types in college remained so after having children, many pouring hours into volunteering at their children's schools and other organizations. Several of our friends have served as PTA president or school committee chair, and one told us she has been "the president of everything," from preschool to church to sports organizations. These women, by and large, also manage to find more time for self-care; several of them mentioned being in the best physical shape of their lives, and two recently earned their yoga teaching credentials. Both of the newly certified teachers have begun teaching professionally and love it.

▶ They worry about not being able to advise their daughters on how to balance career and child-raising.

Struggling in real time with the double-edged sword of expectations for women, several of our Opt Outers are concerned that they're not setting a good example of working motherhood for their children—specifically for their daughters. One friend who left a career on Wall Street for graduate school in physical therapy, and then opted out midway through school to raise her three children told us she worries that "I'm letting my girls down in some way by being home." She feels it is important for girls to have a woman with a successful career as a role model, but, she said, "I just don't know how that could happen with the hours in the day." The stay-at-home mom who left her career in public relations is now advising her oldest daughter on her college and career options. Still busy raising her four younger children, our friend told us, "My biggest fear is that I'm not equipped to help her pursue all these lofty dreams and ideas she has."

▶ **They relish having a well-organized home where things run smoothly for the family.**

All of our Opt Outers serve as the CEO of the house, a role that brings a swell of pride for many of them. (The former Wall Streeter told us that her managing the household allows the family's weekends to be fun, instead of crammed with grocery store, dry cleaning, and drugstore runs. "It's mostly on me to make a home. I don't know how we would do it if I went back to work," she said.) Several women explained that keeping a tightly managed ship at home allows their husbands to stay focused at work, thereby better achieving professional goals that benefit the whole family.

Flex Lifers

As we made our way through our interviews, we heard from more and more women who didn't quite fall into the High Achiever category but who also hadn't become stay-at-home mothers. At first we didn't know how to categorize these women—which path were they pursuing? But after much sketching and plotting of individual life trajectories, we began to see a third path emerge, one that was inherently familiar to us but that we hadn't seen articulated before. This third group of women, the largest, comprising 44 percent of our friends, was not easy to sum up tidily—these women wanted to be very present with their kids, but they also wanted intellectual stimulation, income, professional accolades, and—wait!—they also wanted to join a drum circle or play board games with friends in the evenings or volunteer at an animal shelter. It took us a while to recognize that this wasn't just a random amalgam of women who didn't fit into either of the other two groups, but rather a group of its own, reflecting a conscious life choice. It was a choice that, at the time we were conducting these interviews, we had both gravitated toward. We kept coming back to the fact that we didn't arrive at this liminal ambition space by accident—along with so many of the women we'd graduated with, we had chosen this life path intentionally. The more time we spent thinking about this group of women, the more we realized it was not coincidence that we'd encountered so many women who had downshifted their careers a bit (or at least hadn't floored the accelerator) in favor of family dinners, homemade bread, and a truly staggering range of extracurricular activities. This life path isn't a recognizable archetype in the same way that being a High Achiever or an Opt Outer is. Perhaps it took us a moment to identify it in part because we are used to the binary decisions of previous generations: achieve in the workforce, or stay home. This path was neither of those. But for us and all of the women who described it to us, it's not just an equally legitimate life choice but a desirable, rewarding one that many people have carved out for themselves. We've labeled this path the Flex Life.

Flex Lifers have one core element in common: They have all consciously scaled back a rigorous career, or chosen not to actively advance their careers, for a few primary reasons:

- *They prioritized spending time with family, or leisure or volunteer work, over an all-encompassing career.*

- *They were bothered that they couldn't "give 100 percent" to everything in their lives, most often parenting, so they chose not to expand their professional arc in favor of spending more time with their children or pursuing other activities.*

- *They wanted to pursue more "meaningful" work in place of a previous hard-driving corporate or business-focused career.*

- *They had seen what being a High Achiever looked like, specifically the hours and stress that it often requires, and that life just didn't appeal.*

- *They had a partner to share the economic burden that scaling back can bring, or they were willing to pare back their own economic expenditures in exchange for greater life flexibility.*

As we heard from more Flex Lifers and began to talk and write about this path, we learned how much this choice also appeals to women outside of our interview set. Workers who have control over when and where they work feel better about the amount of time they get to spend with their families, while also feeling more satisfied with their jobs.[2] Women are also more likely to stay in the workforce when they can have more informal hours or work reduced hours or part-time.[3] The arguments for the benefits of the Flex Life to larger society are many, but this path also comes with its challenges.

The Flex Lifer: Marly

Marly knew even as a child that she wanted to be a businesswoman. "I have always been interested in investments, ever since I was ten years old," she remembered. "I had been getting *Money* magazine and other investing magazines, which my mom thought was an unusual thing for a ten-year-old." What had started as a passing interest deepened when her father died suddenly when she was fifteen. Marly's mother, who had never held a job outside the home, now had to support three children alone. Even without work experience, Marly said, her mother "was a sharp woman with a lot of skills." She got hired by an old friend from high school to help manage his business, and after getting pretty good at that, she started her own. Her widowed mother's grit made an impression. "I saw what she went through, all the hard work, but with creativity and some freedom. That first week her business was open, I saw the money starting to roll through the doors. That helped inspire my entrepreneurial bent, seeing that hard work oftentimes equates with financial success."

By the time she got into Northwestern, a few hours away from the Indiana suburb she'd grown up in, Marly knew she'd go into something finance related. On the quieter side, but friendly and level-headed, she majored in economics because it was the closest business-related major Northwestern offered at the time. As graduation neared, Marly attended the job fairs on campus. She landed a couple of interviews with consulting firms and got hired at a benefits consulting house outside Chicago. This was a fairly standard track for many Northwestern graduates, but Marly didn't particularly enjoy the job. "It was a grind. They liked the people who were willing to work from five a.m. until ten at night. I didn't want to do that." Even in her early twenties, Marly knew that being stuck in an office all day wasn't going to work for her. She was living in Chicago at the time and wanted to be able to enjoy the city, to be young and go to bars and hear music and do things outside the four walls of her office. Marly stuck it out at the company for three and a half years, paying her dues, which was understood to be a requirement for anyone who wanted to be successful in the late '90s. Next she took a position in a telecommunications sales company, making good money, but didn't find it exciting or challenging. She left after a year.

In the meantime, Marly had met her future husband and gotten engaged, and, at twenty-seven, was beginning to think about starting a family. She thought being a teacher seemed like a good balanced-life career: "I thought, as my kids grew, my schedule could grow with them. It was purely a lifestyle thing." She earned her master's degree in secondary education and got a job teaching history at a high school. She loved teaching and had fun doing it, and developed rewarding relationships with her colleagues. With her career set, she and her husband began trying to have children, but they struggled with fertility issues. Finally, after her second year of teaching, Marly got pregnant, and already knew she didn't want to continue working full-time with a newborn at home. She asked the school principal about job sharing, and he said no. Marly felt she'd worked so hard to get pregnant, she couldn't imagine delegating the childcare responsibilities to someone else, at least not right away, and certainly not full time. She left her teaching job before giving birth, had her son, and stayed home with him. A year later she got pregnant again, with twins, and stayed home with them initially as well.

Marly loved her time at home with her little ones, but longed for something more. She wanted work that would allow her to be home some with her young kids, but that also offered professional stimulation and some needed income, now that she had three children. And she was still interested in business and investing. Partnering with a friend who had just earned an MBA from the University of Chicago, Marly bought a small marketing company to run out of her home. "It was fun. But hard work. My babies were two and I had a three-year-old. And I was working ungodly hours. It was supposed to be a part-time thing, that's what I had wanted. But what I found out is, with business ownership, there's no such thing as a part-time business owner. You're on twenty-four/seven." And then, the economy tanked in 2008, and most of her clients tanked with it. Marly and her partner sold the business, or what was left of it, and managed to get out with minimal financial damage.

Marly felt burned out and was sick of constantly juggling her work and kid responsibilities. "I'd shed many tears over having to work sixteen- to eighteen-hour days while my kids were shipped from person to person or just pulling at my jeans and I had to say, 'Go away, Mama's gotta get the work done.'" In a stroke of excellent timing, Marly's husband had just undergone a career change, moving into software sales, that had conveniently doubled his income. Staying home with her young children for a couple more years wouldn't have much of an economic impact on the family.

After five more years at home, Marly again was "itching to get something of my own going, something creative and challenging." She took a self-study course to get her real estate license. Real estate appealed to

Marly's interest in sales and investing, and also meant she could effectively run her own business while still keeping a flexible schedule. Her original plan was to work part-time as a real estate agent and then spend afternoons with her kids, but Marly discovered she's pretty good at real estate, and her business has been booming. She's parlayed what was initially supposed to be a part-time gig into nearly a full-time career—but she's still able to spend a good amount of time with her kids and, if needed, even pick up a few more showings in the evenings. "I'm happy with it. And my kids are now fifteen, thirteen, and thirteen, so they're pretty self-sufficient. I can work around their schedules." She crams in as much work as she can before the kids arrive home from school between two thirty and three thirty, and then shuttles them to sports and piano and other activities. And then at night, when the activities slow and her kids are cranking through homework, she'll get on her computer and work two or three more hours. "I love to multitask and I love to be a crazy woman with, like, forty balls in the air—that's how I thrive."

Marly laments that she doesn't have enough date nights or random fun nights out—who has time to plan them?—but on weekends, she does carve out time in between her business calls to take out the boat she and her husband bought for family rides on the lake adjacent to their house.

Marly's life is a hustle right now, but she wouldn't have it any other way. In fact, she plans to work on developing her career even further when her kids leave home. "I see myself growing my real estate business while my kids venture off to college. If it's done the right way, it could be pretty lucrative, and it's very flexible." She also sees herself wanting more income to pay for her three kids' educations. Having now successfully executed several different job transitions, Marly knows she doesn't have to settle for something she's not really excited about. All she knows for sure about the future is "I never want a nine-to-five. I will never sit behind a desk again."

T he driving force for most of our Flex Lifers, like Marly, is their pursuit of a flexible work life. Many of these women have tested out different work scenarios to figure out what's best for them and their families. Marly moved from full-time finance jobs to teaching in a public school to being a startup small business entrepreneur clocking seventy or eighty hours a week to a real estate career where she could make her own hours and spend some afternoons helping her kids with homework. She has been successful at all these jobs, and ultimately chose the one that let her prioritize time with her family while also keeping her brain busy and her bank account refreshed. She admits to a little insecurity over feeling as if she may not be the most successful person who graduated from Northwestern, but she has created the life she wants. "I get the alumni magazine and I see all the people doing all these cool things, and I feel like a loser. But I'm not a loser, because I'm happy."

Here's What We Know About Flex Lifers

▶ **Most feel pushed to the limit, but also feel this is the life that works best for them.**

While Marly seems fairly nonchalant that her desire to run a business and a family all at the same time means cramming work into the corners of the day, in between travel soccer games and homework and dinner, most Flex Lifers admit to feeling spread thin many days of the week. Many of them short themselves on self-care, never getting enough sleep or exercise or time with friends. A part-time pediatrician friend told us that between her three days of work and raising three active preteens, life feels constantly chaotic. "I find once I try to carve out time to exercise, something else falls apart. Like we end up not having any food in the house for the week, so there's nothing to pack for lunches, or I'm having to stay up late in order to finish sewing some costume that some kid needs for some performance, or I'm just not sleeping. I'm always telling myself, 'Maybe next year it will get better.'"

Another friend, a middle school teacher, complained of "never feeling caught up on anything," citing so many nagging piles: unopened mail, unfolded laundry, unwritten thank-you notes. Yet she, and many Flex Lifers like her, doesn't want to sacrifice attending her children's sporting events, or any of the other seventeen important commitments she has shoehorned into a day, just to stay home and take care of those piles. Our friends all feel the guilt of not being present enough with their children when work calls, and at the same time feel guilty about not giving their all to their work because of the demands of parenting and running a household. The Flex Life leaves many of its proponents frazzled, but they soldier on, undeterred enthusiasts of their life path. Most of these women, when asked what they would change about their lives, said they were happy with their current configuration—but that they could use a few more hours in a day.

▶ Most try to do it all anyway.

Our Flex Lifers all said that while they understand they can't give 100 percent to everything, they try their best to do so nonetheless. One woman who works in health care sales sets her alarm for 4:10 every morning so she can exercise on her treadmill in the basement. Would she love another hour of sleep? Certainly, but she also feels she might unravel without the stress relief of her exercise routine—she can't give that up! She then works on her laptop for two hours every day before her children wake up, gets them fed and ready for school, works six more hours from home, picks up her children after school, drives them to swim practice, and crunches numbers on her computer while her kids do laps. She has dinner with her children and husband most every night, and often dozes off while snuggling her kids before bedtime. Another Flex Lifer, a lawyer, told us, "There are weekends I'll be at my daughter's volleyball game on a conference call the whole time," and most of our Flex Lifers concurred that multitasking is their baseline—and they couldn't imagine life any other way. The two of us plead guilty, too: We have regularly filled our days with a steady stream of freelance work that bleeds into the hours after school pickup and often after the kids' bedtime, a quick trip to the gym while simultaneously checking email, a few hours with our children most afternoons, a homemade dinner with our families, and never being fully caught up on the mail or the laundry or the eighty-nine-plus unwritten thank-you notes dating back to 2013.

▶ **Flex Lifers love the flexibility their jobs give them, even if it means earning less or turning down promotions.**

A legal director for a nonprofit told us she has stayed at the same job for more than a decade, not pursuing an executive directorship elsewhere, because of the flexibility her current job affords her. "I get paid for shit, but I have a lot of work-life balance, so I don't feel I'm sacrificing my parenting the way I might at other jobs." Our part-time-pediatrician friend took reduced hours and salary in exchange for the two days she is now able to be with her kids and do all the necessary tasks required for a family to function. Her job comes with some tiresome admin tasks and isn't always the most exciting, but it's worth it for the personal freedom she receives in exchange. A nonprofit health care advocate has eschewed promotion at her current job because with promotion comes "the expectation that I'm working sixty-plus hours a week, and I don't want to give up that time with my family. It's not worth an extra $30,000." Most Flex Lifers in this group have the economic privilege of being able to scale back their jobs in this way, but most of them also said they would make a reduced income work because they value their time more than a bigger income.

▶ **They plan on working harder or changing careers entirely down the road.**

The nonprofit legal director told us that because she has enjoyed so much flexibility from her current employer, she feels that, once her children are older, she'll be karmically paying back that flex time by clocking in many more hours than she currently does. Several other Flex Lifers told us that once their children are older and more self-sufficient, they would like to refocus on their careers or change them entirely. Our friend the utilities executive is counting down the years at her corporate job until she can retire and start the animal shelter she has long dreamt of. The two of us are at transition points now that our children are getting older; we are both assessing our ambitions, our options, and our next steps, with the understanding that we may not enjoy this kind of flexibility for the remainder of our careers.

You Have Choices!

While we've described the three paths our friends' lives have followed, perhaps our most important finding from their stories is that selecting a path is not a finite choice. Their life trajectories are not straight lines from college to job success, end of story—rather, they are fluid, elastic narratives shaped around desires and circumstances that shift over years and decades. In fact, almost everyone in our group toggled successfully across paths over the twenty-five years we have known them—some of them even in the duration of our first, second, and third interviews over three years' time. High Achievers became Flex Lifers after having children, Opt Outers took years off from paid work, then returned to fulfilling part- or full-time careers, and Flex Lifers put in the hours to become High Achievers years or even decades into their professional lives. As you'll discover in the stories to come, women move across paths regularly in a lifetime.

One woman who had never intended to stay home was blindsided when she gave birth to her first child on 9/11. She quit her job and stayed home with her new daughter. Seven years later, she was the mother of three young children; when the financial crisis hit, she decided to return to work to help provide more economic stability for her family. She's been with the company for ten years now and is once again a High Achiever.

Another friend was the junior rabbi in a New York City suburb enjoying work-life balance as a Flex Lifer, and then, tired of "making things happen for other people," she decided to go for a bigger job. A year later, she became the senior rabbi at a large synagogue, moved her family to the Midwest, and is now the primary earner, albeit with a lot less time to herself.

And, of course, it is possible to move in other directions as well. Our friend who was a health care sales rep, working all hours as a high-achieving half of a dual-income family with two kids, switched to job-sharing so she could enjoy more hours with her kids as a Flex Lifer. Years later, still feeling constantly pulled by both family and work commitments, she left work entirely and became an Opt Outer. (The company continues to suffer her loss and has attempted to hire her back twice already.)

The only women who didn't stray from their early chosen path were the High Achievers who did not have children, as well as those who were the sole or primary earners and whose partners had left the workplace to raise their children. Some of these women either couldn't financially afford to scale back or had created a life where they just couldn't imagine it, for both professional and personal reasons; some of them enjoyed their high-driving career success and had no desire to curb it.

This realization that women's life choices are fluid and flexible seems a radical departure from the previous generation of ambitious women. Riding the success of Second Wave feminism (and driven by immigrant ambition), Liz's mother entered the workplace, ascended the ladder in her chosen field, climbed to an executive position, and didn't cease climbing until retirement. The previous generation of women had fought for, and won, revolutionary gains in the workplace, and those successful working women didn't intend to cede an iota of those gains by opting out, transitioning to part time, or fantasizing about a different career altogether. Conversely, most of the mothers we observed growing up, Hana's mother included, viewed staying home as a permanent life choice. The terms *housewife* and *homemaker* aren't used much anymore, but they conveyed a finite decision. One rarely moved from being a housewife to being an executive, and obviously the options to work part-time from home were limited. Our generation, by contrast, inherited not only the potential to be kick-ass working women, but also something equally valuable: the luxury to reshape our work lives. Our friends have realized over the course of their lives that their career paths don't have to mirror their mothers'. They have more choice and flexibility than their mothers did, and accordingly, they've been High Achievers, Opt Outers, and Flex Lifers all in one career lifetime.

The next generation of women—millennials and younger—will inherit that work-life flexibility and more. Opting out when you have a child no longer means you are a stay-at-home mom for eighteen years and your work options are done; now staying home can be a temporary choice that feels right for you and your family one year, a choice that isn't a career-ender the way it might have been just one generation ago. Perhaps for the first time ever, women's career trajectories are no longer rigid, fated upon one decision made at one milestone point in life. Use this knowledge—that not just one major decision, but many micro decisions, comprise a life path—as your guide, and let it shape your life in transformative ways.

CHAPTER 2

AMBITION

We started this project with the underlying assumption that all our friends from college, or nearly all of them, were ambitious. They'd gotten into a top university, which meant that, at the very least, they were people who had achieved a high degree of academic distinction in high school. One of our friends recounted an anecdote about her first day in Northwestern's undergraduate journalism program: "They asked everyone who had been editor in chief of their school newspaper to raise their hand," she said. "And every single person in the room raised their hand except me." She'd been the most ambitious member of her high school's graduating class, but now she was in a class full of people at least as driven as she was, if not more.

As with any group, we remembered some of them being more ambitious than others—one woman seemed to permanently live in the Smoking Room at the sorority house (yes, in the '90s many sorority houses had a dedicated room for people who wanted to smoke and study at the same time), nose-deep in thick textbooks. Many were enrolled in one of Northwestern's selective majors—small programs where undergrads competed for spots and typically graduated with honors. Others were there, in the words of one of our friends, "to just do college." Some hit the tailgate parties religiously, or refused to enroll in any class that met before noon or attend any lecture that required more than a fifteen-minute walk in winter (hey, Chicago is cold in February!). And then there was the ritual sharing of GPAs. Once a quarter, as part of our weekly sorority meetings, the chapter president would announce the average GPA for our sorority as compared to other sororities on campus, as well as who had made the dean's list. The list was always long.

So when we started interviewing our friends, we expected to be speaking to women who had continued right along the paths they'd charted in college. The woman with the fancy Chicago ad agency internship senior year, who was constantly rushing in and out of the sorority house in a suit, was surely an advertising VP, working out of an office overlooking Lake Michigan. Our friend who had planned to open a progressive school was probably busy *this minute* securing equipment and mentors for the hands-on STEM curriculum she'd designed. And as for our former classmate who had left Northwestern and headed straight to Harvard Law, we imagined her mere minutes away from a Supreme Court nomination. As soon as there was an opening.

We were a bit taken aback, then, when we interviewed four stay-at-home mothers in a row. The two of us paused our interviews, trying to reassess what we were after. What if we charged on through our interview schedule only to discover that a majority of our friends had abandoned their career dreams? There would no doubt be plenty to write about there, but we couldn't help but feel disappointed that we weren't encountering more women marching over the patriarchy, seizing CEO jobs, filing patents, and curing diseases. We'd started this project hoping to find women who had figured it all out; instead, we discovered that a lot of our friends had lives more or less like ours and were figuring it out in real time, day after day. There's no cheat sheet for how to be a woman in the modern world, and we all struggle, no matter which path we're on or how we channel our ambition.

As we talked through what we'd heard, we began to wonder what we were missing. Why, exactly, had so many women who had not planned on becoming stay-at-home parents traded promising careers to do precisely that? Why were so many of our friends idling in good-enough jobs year after year instead of chasing promotions? How could we reconcile the women we'd known in college with the full-grown adults they'd become today? An easy explanation is that maybe these women simply were not as ambitious as we thought they'd been. The reality, of course, is something entirely different.

We would not be the first people to doubt women's level of ambition. Women have been criticized for their dearth of ambition practically since they were told they could be ambitious in the first place. A 1987 study found that women's lack of ambition prevented them from applying to medical school;[1] a 1990 study reported that women suffered diminished political ambition.[2] And even today, you don't need to look far to find research illustrating all the ways women are ambition-deficient. Studies have found that as women rise through the ranks at companies, their ambition level drops,[3] and that women are less interested than men in becoming senior executives.[4] Taken together, these findings possibly explain a third study, which found that women's ambition is slowly chipped away by unsupportive work cultures.[5] For many women, it's a tedious, difficult slog to the top, through a workplace that doesn't really want you at the top anyway.

Explanations for women's assumed lack of ambition have varied over the years, but the popular rationalization of the day is the "ambition gap." Sheryl Sandberg coined this phrase in a panel discussion at the World Economic Forum in 2012,[6] arguing that girls' ambition is thwarted from childhood: "We don't raise our daughters to be as ambitious as our sons." While this theory may hold true for some women around the globe, it doesn't fit for our former classmates, the majority of whom came to college with dreams of being the first, the best, and the boss. They told us, "I had ambitions of being the president of the Red Cross, or running for Senate," "I wanted to help people who didn't have a voice," and "I thought I was going to be the press secretary at the White House."

But if our friends were, in fact, as ambitious as we remembered them, why wasn't that reflected in our conversations? If these women had been bursting with ambition when they got to Northwestern, why weren't we looking at twenty-two or thirty High Achievers instead of (what felt like a paltry) thirteen? If they had planned to rule the world, why weren't they doing so? We thought about the elements that hold women back—sexism! unconscious bias!—and more circumstantial obstacles: the natural course of events, the outsize dreams of youth curbed by how things actually happen in the world. Any of these were possible explanations for our former classmates' life trajectories. By extension, these are possible explanations why, as of 2017, only thirty-two of the companies in the Fortune 500 are run by women (an all-time high),[7] why only around 11 percent of Nobel Prize winners are women,[8] why only one of the eighty-eight people with Best Director Oscars sitting on their mantel is a woman,[9] why only one of the nation's largest art museums is run by a woman,[10] and on and on and on. But again, the answers weren't that simple.

Nearly all the women we spoke with, whether they spend their days chasing kids around the playground or chasing C-suite executives around a meeting room, still radiate ambition. Almost all the Opt Outers we interviewed spend large chunks of their time doing things on top of childcare or housekeeping, and they pursue those activities with as much ambition and dedication as they had previously pursued high marks in college or promotions at work. One woman noted, "I wasn't working for almost two and a half years. I struggled with that and overcompensated with volunteering. I did the yearbook and was PTO copresident." Once she returned to work, she scaled back her school leadership involvement, but mentioned, as an aside, that she had recently solicited a large donation of bottled water for the school carnival, as though she couldn't help herself. Another woman who left the workforce after her kids were born is on the board of multiple charity organizations and maintains a contacts list full of powerful, accomplished women. These are not women who lack ambition, waiting aimlessly for the moment their children return home from school. They have chosen to leave the paid workforce, but still want to be out in the world, contributing in ways that feel meaningful. They volunteer for nonprofits, advocate on local issues, raise money for their children's public schools, figure prominently in their communities. They may not be writing the nation's foreign policy or negotiating billion-dollar mergers, but they are also not content to live without goals and recognition.

The recognition portion is key here. In a seminal study on psychological development, Jerome Kagan and Howard Moss followed a group of eighty-nine people over a twenty-nine-year span, from childhood to adulthood, and found a high correlation between the desire to master a specific skill and "social recognition through acquisition of specific goals or behaviors."[11] Psychiatrist Anna Fels took this finding a step further. While conducting a study on women and ambition for her 2004 book, *Necessary Dreams: Ambition in Women's Changing Lives*, Fels received some puzzling responses. None of the women she was studying would admit to being ambitious. In fact, they seemed to hate the word. (It's interesting that we encountered the opposite—nearly all our friends prided themselves on being ambitious, which could indicate a generational shift, or could be related to the fact that we were interviewing friends, who perhaps felt more comfortable sharing their ambitions than women being interviewed by strangers would.) Fels decided to conduct a literature review on what others before her had found about ambition. "Looking through studies on the development of both boys and girls, I noticed that they virtually always identified the same two components of childhood ambition. There was a plan that involved a real accomplishment requiring work and skill, and there was an expectation of approval in the form of fame, status, acclaim, praise, or honor."[12] As hydrogen and oxygen must both be present to make water, so must mastery and recognition converge to enable ambition. That is, in order to be ambitious, you must have a burning desire to master something, anything, be it juggling or big data. The seeds of this desire are planted in childhood, and the object of ambition may shift over time or may span multiple topics (in our cases, we wanted to master ballet, writing, field hockey, speed walking, and social graces). But it is not enough to simply *like* juggling, for example. You must be the kind of person who annoys everyone by juggling in the hallway, at dinner, in your room after your homework is completed, driven by an innate desire to get really, really good at juggling simply because you must. You're not sure why, but you're going to manage to keep four balls, or bowling pins, or potatoes, going at the same time if it kills you.

The true driver for most people, the thing that keeps you going back time and again to improve your skills, is the goal of being recognized for your achievement. It is not enough to be a secret juggler, lofting potatoes into the air in the corner of your bedroom. An ambitious person is not sated by having mastered something simply for the sake of achievement and self-satisfaction. Those of us driven by ambition need to take our juggling act on the road, to perform in the school talent show, for parents, for neighbors, for strangers on the street. For those whose interests lie in something less performative—math, writing, problem solving—recognition comes in the form of awards, publication, high grades, coveted jobs, flawless performance reviews, promotions. As Kagan and Moss noted, "It may be impossible to measure the 'desire to improve a skill' independent of the individual's 'desire for recognition.'"

Using this definition of ambition, there is no doubt that our former classmates arrived at Northwestern with both the desire to become great at something and the need for the world to know they were great at it. So what happened next? Here come the complications. For some women, who had come from small towns or suburban enclaves where they'd been the stars of their high schools, finding themselves at Northwestern in a sea of other high school superstars was a splash of ice water to the ego. They arrived certain of their place in the world, but a year or two—or for some, even just a few days—in, they weren't so sure they were that special after all.

One friend from a small town in Ohio told us, "I was a little star in my high school. Back then I had my eyes set on being a real star, onstage. It was like a slap in the face when I got to Northwestern. Because honestly, everybody was talented when I got there, and I felt like most people were better than I was."

Not only did a number of women we went to college with recount feeling a bit unmoored after arriving on campus, but so did the majority of the current students in our sorority at Northwestern. In a survey we conducted with our current sorority class, 80 percent of the women gave themselves the highest or second-highest rating on an ambition scale at the start of their college career. But when we asked about their current level of ambition, these women, mostly sophomores and juniors, reported that it was lower than it had been a year or two earlier. Given that ambition must be fed continuously with recognition, this makes sense. Northwestern is a place where there are plenty of opportunities to be recognized, but also plenty of opportunities to see just how great everyone else is doing. You can be president of the student government or editor in chief of the campus newspaper or selected for a competitive major, or you can watch everyone else do those things while you "just do college."

But, ever ambitious, even the women who struggled through Northwestern continued to look for ways to achieve and gain recognition. A friend from a midsize town in Florida, where she'd been on her school's highly selective cheerleading team, found her ego bruised when she applied for one of Northwestern's majors with limited slots and didn't make the cut. But she quickly recovered. "I wanted to be in the writing program in the English department. Even though they only took fifteen people, I thought for sure I would be one of those fifteen—how could I not be? But I wasn't. And so when I got rejected from the fiction track, I wasn't really sure what to do. The fiction professor told me that the poetry professor had blackballed me, and that if I waited a year I would be accepted because she wouldn't be on the committee anymore. By the time that rolled around, I had talked my way into taking screenwriting classes, and I didn't want to be in the writing program anymore, so I didn't apply. Which made that professor really angry, and he was like, 'Well, you just go to Hollywood and make lots of money.' And I'm like, 'Okay, sounds good to me.'"

Once they moved out into the world, our friends' desire took them in a range of different directions. On the surface, some of these directions made it seem that the women's ambitions waned, that they had lost their way. A few of the women themselves wondered aloud to us where their drive from college had gone. But as we interviewed more and more of our friends, we began to see an increasingly nuanced, complex portrait of ambition—a sort of ambition that can shift over time and be directed into many different streams of life. Ambition needs to be continuously nurtured and rewarded, and these women found ways to do that that were as varied as the goals to which they had initially aspired.

Redirecting Ambition into Lifestyle

For many of our college friends, having children was what spurred them to redirect their ambition away from their careers and toward their families. This aligns with an encyclopedia's worth of studies that have found that becoming a mother negatively impacts women's career progression and compensation.[13] For others, though, the decision to take a few steps back at work had nothing to do with kids, but instead with the desire to live a different kind of life. These women spent time working corporate jobs and earning promotions only to take a look at where they were, or where they were headed, and decide that the life they were chasing was not the life they truly wanted. Once these women identified the ways they wanted to channel their ambition, they moved toward happier and more fulfilling lives. While some of our friends strived directly to succeed on the CEO track, others found themselves there unwittingly, realized that wasn't what they wanted their lives to look like, and made dramatic changes. Much of the writing around ambition, and women's lack of it, focuses on these common professional success end states—and how women are failing to reach them. CEO. Senator. Big jobs with big titles. High incomes. Career tracks that let you know someone is a superstar. But what these studies, books, and essays fail to address is that ambition doesn't look the same for everyone.

Emily's Ambition:
A Stimulating Career, plus Mountains and Dogs

When she was growing up in Kansas City, Emily's parents instilled in her the value of serving others. She was always required to do community service in some way, shape, or form. Emily became a Girl Scout, and to this day describes herself as such. A huge part of Scouting for her was the service aspect, and she always felt the obligation to be involved in her community. When she got to Northwestern, Emily chose an economics major. "I am generally a quantitative, analytical person who is also a helper," she said. "Economics is a good way to combine those things with a social science component. There is a lot of asking and understanding why things happen and modeling what could happen—and how could all that help communities improve." To that end, she set her sights on working for the World Bank. Landing that kind of job required a business degree, so after a year spent in a standard-issue first-year-out-of-college job at a marketing firm, Emily headed to Thunderbird, a business school in Phoenix with an international focus. Emily had always excelled academically, and B-school was no different. When she graduated, her hard work paid off with three job offers: one from a large global technology company, one from Citibank, and one from the MBA Enterprise Corps, an organization Emily describes as "the Peace Corps for people with MBAs." The Enterprise Corps was exactly what Emily had envisioned herself doing, but the low pay, combined with her business school loans, made her think twice about taking the offer.

"I looked at it and thought, 'If I do this, I am going to go way into debt, and I will never own a house.'" She took the job with the behemoth tech company instead. It was in corporate finance, which wasn't her first choice, but Emily hoped she'd eventually find her way around to work that was more personally meaningful.

"I thought, 'All right, I'll do this two, maybe three years, and then I'll go back and do something more aligned with what I'm interested in,'" Emily explained.

But after a short time at her starter job, Emily found herself growing restless. She was at the company's headquarters in Paramus, New Jersey— a bedroom community best known for its hulking mall, and not the type of town a lot of twentysomethings fantasize about living in. On top of that, the work came easily to Emily—too easily—and she was ready for more of a challenge.

"I was like, 'Okay, I got this,' and that was one month in. I'm thinking, 'What's next? I'm in Paramus, and I have to do something to move this along.' I was trying to do anything to move my career faster."

As soon as she could, Emily switched jobs, moving to J.P. Morgan and into an apartment in Manhattan, which suited her single lifestyle better. But a few years later, her former boss at the tech company called with an offer. The job was a big leap forward for her career, and not only that, it was in utilities, an area that satisfied Emily's social conscience. "This was right around the same time that there was a lot of focus on green energy— trying to bring in wind and solar, energy reduction, energy efficiency. That appealed to that social element for me. There was a connection to doing some sort of public good as opposed to just working for a giant cash machine." Utilities was a male-dominated field, but Emily wasn't bothered that she was frequently the only woman in the room. Instead, she made it an opportunity to foster close relationships with the few women in the field. "There aren't very many women in utilities, so there's an instant bond. I connected with almost all of them, mainly because they're like, 'Oh my God, a woman!' They're so excited to see any other female around."

Emily stayed with the company for another six years, following her job from New York to Boston, marrying a startup entrepreneur whom she'd first met at Thunderbird, and climbing the ranks on her way to a management position. Before they married, Emily and her husband had agreed that they wouldn't have children, in part because she knew she didn't want to be a stay-at-home mom but also couldn't imagine simultaneously being a hands-on parent and pursuing a career. "I wanted to have a career. That was important to me, it was interesting to me, it was what I wanted to do more." And when she really thought about it, Emily realized that she preferred puppies to babies.

"If we go out to the park and there's a baby and a puppy, my friends would always be like, 'Oh, look at the cute baby.' I don't see any baby. I see the puppy and I'm like, 'Oh, oh, the puppy.' I love animals. And I thought, 'If I don't see the baby, maybe I'm not interested in babies. And if I'm not interested, then I'm not going to make a good parent.'"

Emily is someone who knows her own mind, and she had a perfect setup to claim a leadership position at a Fortune 500 company. Smart, motivated, with a take-no-bullshit style, Emily is the kind of person you can easily imagine commanding a room of gray-haired men who have been running family-owned utilities organizations for generations. And for a while, she eagerly climbed the corporate ladder. But over the years, she became bothered by how miserable the people in leadership positions at her office seemed. "Most of them were divorced, grossly overweight, exceptionally ill, constantly drank. They were good at their jobs, but that's all they did. They had no other hobbies. They never went on vacation because they didn't know what to do when they had free time. They did nothing but work, at all times of the day, every day, and thought nothing of asking everyone else to as well. They were the most boring and sad people on earth, and [ultimately] I could not stand the thought of being one of them."

Many of our friends cited today's toxic work culture and the hours they would have to devote to work if they landed leadership positions as reasons for channeling their ambition away from work and into other areas of their lives. When we asked a lawyer at a women's legal aid nonprofit if she had dreams of being an executive director at a large legal nonprofit, she answered, "Not really, because I would be working all the time and you're going to get emails from me at two a.m. I totally don't want to do that."

We also heard from many women that day-to-day job satisfaction was more important to them than long-term career success. A friend who is a sought-after Silicon Valley marketing guru recounted a conversation between herself and her boyfriend, in which he pointed out that people are always telling her she's a leader and wondered aloud why she didn't go for a C-suite position. Her response: "Because that's not fun for me. It's important for me to be happy in my job, to solve really fun, intellectual problems. I get up at five thirty in the morning and go to my job and I'm excited to go. I love the woman I work for. I love my team. Do I need a title? I don't think so. Do I need to lead an entire group? Not so much."

And Laurel, an in-house lawyer at a furniture company, noted that back when she was an attorney in a corporate law firm, both she and her husband had agreed that they had zero interest in making partner. "In the law, there are a lot of people, in particular men, who judge their success as lawyers on whether or not they make partner. That is their measure of accomplishment. That was never my measure."

Once Emily determined that rising further up the ranks wasn't for her, she thought about what she did want from her life, and the answers came easily. She'd loved the accessibility to the outdoors she'd had back in business school. She'd begun to find the East Coast "crowded," and too far away from her family back in Kansas City. She wanted to live in a beautiful place where she could climb mountains and ski, and on top of that, while working in utilities met some of her need to do good in the world, it wasn't quite enough. She wanted more time to volunteer, and to think about a possible third act. Over the course of her life, she'd amassed a menagerie of animals, and her love of dogs had grown into a passion. She wasn't ready to abandon the business world yet, but she wanted to start putting the pieces in place that would, down the road, allow her to work with animals full-time.

And so she stepped off the leadership track and transferred to a position in Colorado, knowing full well the decision she was making. "Moving away from New York meant you were not going to be any kind of senior executive. You've got to be in New York if you really want to be CEO or CFO or any of those things. I decided I just didn't want that life. It was not for me. I do not aspire to that. I aspire against it."

Nearly a decade later, Emily left the company. She found a new position as a utilities manager for a Chicago-based firm that would allow her to work out of her home in Colorado. She remains the primary earner in her household (her husband's salary fluctuates depending on where he is with his current venture), but enjoys much greater schedule flexibility than she had before—which allows her to volunteer for an animal shelter; hike, fish, snowshoe, and ski with her husband; and play with their four rescue dogs.

Even with her shifted career ambitions, Emily can't help but excel. She was recently promoted to vice president and now manages her former team. She was ready for a change (ambition never sleeps) but also isn't interested in climbing up yet another corporate ladder. "With my previous role, I felt like I wanted to do more, but I don't see myself sticking around for ten years and being their CEO, either. I just don't want to do that."

Having scaled back her lifestyle in a cheaper locale, Emily and her husband have been able to save enough money for her to look toward an early retirement from the business world and her plans to open an animal shelter, fully shifting her career toward work that is deeply meaningful to her.

"My business career will end long before the average retirement age, and I will move on to the next thing. While I was once on a path that I might not have chosen entirely of my own accord, I will get to do more of what I would like to be doing sooner this way. Financially, I've been able to do more. My salary has been higher. I've been able to buy a nicer house, which I'll be able to keep down the road when I'm doing something less lucrative."

Emily doesn't see her time in the corporate world as a waste. She enjoys her current job and finds it intellectually challenging, and likes working with clients, solving problems, and managing a team. She sees the pieces falling into place for her next path—her husband recently started a small business that is doing well, putting less pressure on her income—and she's been taking notes in her work with the animal shelter, studying how best to position herself and her next career idea.

"You can't have everything you want at the time you want it," Emily told us. "You have to figure out why you're going to do something and how it fits into your overall goals—and understand you might not achieve them all every day. But it's important to do something every day that helps you remember what you want to be doing. That's why I started volunteering at the animal shelter. It honed in on how I could do something more meaningful."

No one could rightfully look at Emily's path and argue that her ambition has diminished. If anything, she's become more ambitious over time as she's been rewarded for both her corporate work and her volunteer work. Instead, Emily carefully plotted how to accomplish everything she wanted—not, as she notes, all at the same time, but over the course of a lifetime. She didn't step off the leadership track because her ambition waned, but because she saw what the road ahead looked like and decided it wasn't for her. When we last interviewed Emily, she seemed to be enjoying even more job success, and seemed more vital than ever before, ready to take on her next chapter.

Redirecting Ambition into a Creative Career

While Emily worked out a way to divide her time between a career she enjoys and the volunteer work that feeds her soul, it helped that she knew fairly early on exactly how she wanted to direct her ambition. She picked a career direction (business) and stuck with it. Once she realized that becoming CEO wasn't for her, she reconfigured her career into something that was a better fit. But lots of the women we interviewed weren't quite as directed as Emily. Their career paths wound around and sideways as they sought out what felt best for them. What we learned from these women is that what was right for them at one time in their lives didn't always turn out to be what was right for them ten years, or twenty years, or even just five years on. Some years they were ready to take on a grueling work schedule for the adrenaline rush, the big paychecks, or the satisfaction of a prominent job well done, and other years they found that they had different priorities, changing interests, or simply other things they wanted to do. At no point did they cease being ambitious. In Sarah's case, when we last spoke with her, she was on stage three of a career that had swung across a wide range of directions ("Go meanderers!" she cheered when we asked if she considered her career path to be meandering), each stage satisfying a need at a different transition point in her life, each stop a place for her to flex different intellectual muscles to see where they would take her.

Sarah's Ambition: Joy, Freedom, and Self-Care

Sarah arrived at Northwestern with a poofy perm and a plan to be "a poli-sci major and a super-fabulous lawyer like my dad." But toward the end of freshman year, she was at Clarke's, a popular off-campus hangout famous for all-day breakfasts that involved a lot of melted cheese, and stood up in her booth to make an important point. (Sarah tops out at a little over five feet tall, so standing up to create emphasis is a frequent occurrence in her life.) She was mid-gesticulation when a nearby stranger interrupted her to tell her she should be an English major. A week later she switched to English, though she wasn't sure where that was going to take her.

"My plan became, I'm an English major who stands up in booths and gesticulates," declared Sarah, a woman with fervent passions and the determination to turn those passions into actions. "I didn't know where that was going to go—I just knew that it felt right, that I wanted to do something involving literature."

After graduation, she followed her boyfriend to Boston and enrolled in a graduate program in English literature at Boston University, planning to earn a master's degree rather than try to gain entry into the school's highly competitive PhD program. But once she started the program, she "fell head over heels in love" with English literature, broke up with her boyfriend, and decided, "Hell yes, I'm getting a PhD, obviously." As with many of our ambitious friends, the competitive piece of the program appealed to her nearly as much as the subject matter. While lots of students were accepted into the master's program, only six of those were invited to move on to earn their PhDs. Sarah was one of them.

But four years into her PhD program, Sarah began to doubt her career choice. She was midway through writing her dissertation (a feminist take on eighteenth-century satire) when one of the two professors who specialized in eighteenth-century literature left the university. Sarah was pretty sure the remaining professor hated her, and she felt it was too late to switch time periods and topics. She sunk into a depression of sorts as she tried to figure out her next move.

"For about six months, I built Legos and chain-smoked and cried, because what was I going to do with my life and how could I leave graduate school without a PhD? That's not okay. Then one day after about six months, I woke up and said, 'Yeah, okay, I can leave graduate school without a PhD.' So I did."

Sarah knew that whatever she did next, she wanted to write, so when she was asked to be a coeditor on a college composition anthology, she jumped at the chance. The gig only paid $1,200 for a year's worth of work ("My story's full of money," Sarah said. "Get used to it."), so she took on a second job at a data-entry firm to pay the bills. Even though the second job was supposed to be just a day job, she found she just couldn't phone it in like everyone else.

"Everybody was there to do a mindless thing during the day, except that I am an overachiever and I can't help my little self, so I had to go running up to management and be like, 'More things, more stimulation please, more, more, more, more.'" As Sarah told us this story, we were reminded of all our other ambitious friends who couldn't be satisfied doing just one thing, who also had to take on more, more, more, more. "I was at that company for six years," Sarah said, "and when I left, I had been promoted to vice president."

As the vice president of training and strategic communications, Sarah earned a handsome salary, five times what she could have expected to earn as an English professor. And even though the job wasn't anything close to the career she'd planned on, she liked the work and the recognition, and quickly became indispensable to the CEO and others across the company— acknowledgment that she had once again become great at something.

"I was delivering live training all over the country, and I reported to the CEO. As I traveled around the country, people learned that I cared about them and I cared about the company and I wanted everybody to be successful. So not only was I trying to do my job and make the CEO happy, but also my phone was ringing all the time. I loved my job and I commit fully to everything that I do, so I was happy to answer that phone at nine thirty at night when somebody was calling from California in a panic."

A few years into the job, Sarah and her husband had a son. Sarah's husband, at the time also a PhD candidate in Sarah's old program, had been growing increasingly dissatisfied with his academic track, so the couple decided that her husband would quit graduate school to stay at home with their son. The arrangement meant that Sarah could work long hours, which was convenient, since she often didn't get home until after ten at night.

She liked having money to spend on her family, and she felt immensely rewarded by her swift rise through the corporate ranks, but as time went on, she also felt increasingly spent. It turned out that being indispensable was exhausting.

"It just felt like I was on a wheel, like you work super hard and then you can have the things you want, but to keep having the things you want, you have to work even harder, and I don't know how I can work any harder because I'm about to have a nervous breakdown. At one point, I just became so exhausted that I could not cross a room without feeling like I needed to take a nap."

Six years into her career, on a vacation to North Carolina's Outer Banks with her family, Sarah decided she wanted to change everything. The vacation was intended to be a respite from her frenetic schedule. She was supposed to come back feeling rejuvenated and ready to work. Instead, after a week spent playing mini golf, hiking, and making a few failed attempts at bird watching, Sarah came to understand that her job was not making her happy.

"I suddenly realized that I was feeling a sensation in the center of my chest that I had forgotten was possible. It was joy. It was freedom. It was self-nourishment instead of self-sacrifice. It was the absurdity of scaring birds and laughing on the beach and not needing to feel guilty, because there was nowhere else I was supposed to be and no one's needs I was supposed to be putting ahead of mine." On the drive back from the Outer Banks, Sarah and her husband decided to move somewhere cheaper so she could quit her job to pursue something more artistic. "I missed writing. I missed creating. I missed feeling good inside."

While Sarah was working at the data-entry company, her husband had been reading up on videography and had taken an internship at a company that shot video for legal work. He thought he might be able to find work in videography, and they agreed to move to Sarah's hometown of Pittsburgh.

At first, Sarah planned to write. She worked on several screenplays and a novel. But she found that writing stressed her out, and the whole point of downshifting her career had been to ease up on the stress, not create more. Then one Christmas, inspiration hit.

"We were broke, and I was looking for, 'How do I give Christmas presents that are super cheap?' so we were wandering through Michael's. I saw a set of rubber stamps and I was like, 'Oh, I can get a little thing of alphabet stamps and a thing of ink and I can get cardstock and fold it and I can make cards with people's kids' names on them and we can give those out for Christmas.' That, believe it or not, is the starting point for how I'm now an artist."

Sarah set aside her novel and, with another artist, began a business selling dark paintings and curios inspired by history, pop culture, and politics, like King Henry VIII and Anne Boleyn salt and pepper shakers, crocheted

Rocky Horror Picture Show characters, and paintings of female Supreme Court justices. The business took off, and soon Sarah spun her website into an Etsy store. She does enough business to keep her very busy, intellectually challenged, and creatively satisfied, though her family has significantly less income now. But Sarah is much happier with her revised life, in which she has joined a collective of artists in other states, helped transition her father into retirement, and takes an evening walk around her neighborhood with her husband and son every night after dinner. She's also able to move the pieces of her life around as her interests and needs change. Her increased dedication to activism ramped up after the 2014 shooting of Michael Brown in Ferguson, Missouri, and subsequent unrest. After the 2016 election, she began volunteering for the ACLU.

Sarah explained, "I can't be an armchair participant anymore. I can't march once a year and be like, I'm awesome! I have to get involved on a bigger level." When we last spoke with her, she had moved from volunteering for the ACLU into a thirty-hour-a-week contract job with the organization, though as before, she was finding it hard to control her desire to push harder and work more. "If I walk out the door having worked thirty-five hours, I feel good about having constrained my workaholic madness." While Sarah may no longer be racing up the corporate ladder, no one could accuse her ambition of fading. In fact, she's so devoted to her non-profit job that she recruited her politically active seventeen-year-old son as an intern last year to help her wrap up a big initiative.

"I could be an executive at a company if I wanted to be, but I didn't like that. I don't want my time to work that way. I am proud that my career doesn't conform to a capital-C 'career,' and that I've found self-definition in lots of ways that don't relate to my job."

Both Emily and Sarah found ways to redirect their ambition that didn't leave them wanting. They're both intellectually challenged by their work, receive enough recognition (in the form of promotions for

Emily, and sales—and civil rights gains—for Sarah) to keep them motivated and hungry for more, and also manage to find deep personal satisfaction in the way they spend their time. But for many women, especially
those with kids, redirecting ambition can be more fraught.

Redirecting Ambition into Family

Ambition cannot be contained neatly in a box labeled "career." One after
another, we heard from women who wanted to kill it in their careers but
also wanted to be fully present in their parenting, in their hobbies, and in
their communities. Prior to having kids, they were able to channel all
their ambition into their careers, and they rose through the ranks accordingly. But once marriage and children arrived on the scene, they found
that it wasn't enough to be a nonprofit lawyer doing important work on
women's issues, or a senior rabbi at a large temple, or making the highest
numbers in the sales department. They also wanted to show the world that
they could excel in their careers while simultaneously organizing massive
charity 5Ks or running the big school fund-raiser.

These women grew up competing (a few sample comments: "I like to
do well, I like to drive and succeed," "When you put me up against someone else, I want to beat that person," "If there's a competition, I want to
win") and know no other way. But for some women, the competition field
broadened once they had children, and they found themselves trying to
excel on multiple fronts at the same time. Given that modern-day parenting can sometimes feel like a competitive sport, it's easy to imagine how
these hard-charging women would want to dominate in that arena, too.
For our friend Audrey—who is driven to show the world that she has
climbed beyond her lower-middle-class roots, that she can compete and
win at the highest levels—redirecting her ambition didn't come easily,
and she still struggles with her choices. Audrey has this in common with
many of our friends who came from either working-class or lower-middle-
class backgrounds, or who were first-generation Americans. Many of

these women became High Achievers, compelled to strive and succeed by parents who told them they didn't have a choice but to be the best. Audrey, who grew up in a single-parent household, raised by her mother in a suburb outside of New Orleans, knew she wanted more out of life than what she saw immediately around her.

Audrey's Ambition:
Big Law and Hands-on Parenting

From an early age, Audrey dreamed of journalism, Pulitzer Prizes, and flying around the world exposing corruption. "I wanted to be the next great *New York Times* foreign correspondent, reporting from exotic yet glamorous places." She was eager to get out of a hometown she found provincial, and when she scored an acceptance to Northwestern's Medill School of Journalism, she figured she was on her way to stardom. But when Audrey arrived on campus, she immediately felt out of her league. Everyone at Northwestern seemed to be so accomplished and worldly already that she didn't see how she could fit in. Audrey hadn't grown up with a lot of money or connections ("I was the resident poor person in college"), and knew she wanted to change that for herself and her future family. But it felt like no matter what she did at Northwestern, she couldn't manage to be the academic and social heavyweight she'd been in high school. She got a C+ in one class freshman year, and as she told us about it twenty-five years later, we could hear how the memory of that grade, and how it suppressed her GPA for the rest of college, still stung, as did a number of lost elections for sorority leadership positions.

"They would talk about the average GPA of our sorority and we would get lectures to bring our grades up," she remembered. "My overall GPA was terrible because I made such bad grades, including that C+ freshman year. So I felt like I was below the mean in our sorority. And then I kept running for various offices in our sorority and losing, and I remember feeling like people didn't view me as bright."

Audrey was juggling so many things in college—a boyfriend, a work-study job so she could afford books and make her tuition payments, a culture that was alien to the one she'd grown up in, not to mention the demanding academic workload—that her ego and ambitions suffered along with her grades. One of her professors commented that half of the assignments she turned in were stellar and the others were poorly written. The ones that were poorly written, Audrey explained, were the ones she'd rushed to complete while putting in twenty hours a week at her job checking student IDs at the gym on campus. Journalism was a cutthroat major at Northwestern, with professors handing each student their individual ranking at the beginning of each class and students competing for the most coveted internship placements in a program called Teaching Newspaper, where they won assignments to newspapers around the country to learn the print business firsthand. As Audrey struggled through her demanding major and saw all the extra time it required to excel—time that she simply didn't have—she quickly abandoned her journalism dreams.

"I felt jealous of the kids that didn't have to work because they could write for *The Daily* [the campus newspaper] and get more experience, and I just couldn't manage all of that. The combination of not feeling like I was very good and like I was competing with all these people who were better than me out in the world made it clear to me that my dream of being this glamorous foreign correspondent was not going to happen. It was more likely that I was going to be working in some little town reporting on local news. And that just didn't appeal to me at all."

Audrey began to experiment with classes beyond journalism, and ultimately a constitutional law class started to turn things around for her. Unlike journalism, which was a struggle, law came to her naturally. Not only did her grades improve, but law was exciting to her. Here was an area where she could master a skill and finally begin to gain some recognition. She did well on the LSAT and landed at law school immediately after graduation. Not a top law school, she is quick to point out, but one that was good enough to get her where she ultimately wanted to go: a prestigious career, a place where she didn't need to worry too much about money, a life like so many of the other students had at Northwestern.

At law school, Audrey began to find her footing again. She liked the structure and she liked the competition. "Law school really turned it around for me; it gave me a reset button, and it reinjected some confidence back into me."

Her initial plan, when she got to law school, was to be a "do-gooder." Just as she'd wanted to use journalism to expose corruption, she planned to use the law to right wrongs. But the further into law school she got, the less appealing that plan felt. For starters, Audrey was accumulating a lot of debt. She looked at the student loan checks she was signing over each month and concluded that taking a low-paying job in public interest law didn't seem all that realistic. And also, it wasn't part of the law school game. "I got very caught up in the competitiveness of law school, partly because I realized I could be good at this," Audrey explained. "Going to a big firm was part of that. I knew it was a huge résumé booster, and I wanted to be a superstar again."

Audrey graduated from law school and worked her way up the legal ladder in Washington, DC, eventually landing at a prominent corporate firm with the promise that she would be promoted to partner within two years' time. She was newly married then, and as she watched the two people ahead of her in line for partner get promoted, she figured her promotion would come the following year. But that year, while pregnant with her first child, the financial crisis hit, and Audrey's law firm, which had seemed so stable only months earlier, suddenly found itself on shaky ground. To make matters worse, another attorney had jostled his way to the front of the promotion line, and Audrey began to worry that she wasn't going to make partner that year after all. Her worst fears were confirmed when, eight months pregnant, she was called into a meeting with several of the partners. They told her they were only promoting one person to partner that year, and it wouldn't be her. Instead, they would be promoting the more junior attorney who had made his way to the front of the line.

"I was enraged," Audrey told us. "I knew I was much more experienced than him, I was much higher rated than him, and much more respected. I was senior to him, and I couldn't believe that this cliché was happening to me. And I said, 'No, I will not wait a year. You made me a promise, I came to the firm based on that promise, and I'm not going to take no for an answer.'"

Audrey confronted one of the senior partners. She was a month away from her due date, and fueled by a powerful combination of injustice, ambition, and fury, she let him know that she was willing to put everything she had into helping secure the firm's financial future. "When I get back from maternity leave, I will do whatever it takes to make our group successful and bring in business," she told him.

Two days later, Audrey went into early labor and delivered her daughter a month early. The next week, while out on maternity leave, she learned that she'd made partner. She'd honed a skill, and here was her reward, hard fought and well earned. While this should have been a pure professional triumph, things were suddenly more complex than they'd been only days earlier. Audrey was now a new mother. And while her driving ambition to that point had been to prove to herself and the world that she could earn a powerful position in a prominent law firm, this was only part of her dream. The other piece, only slowly coming into focus, was that she also hoped to create the financially secure and emotionally stable home life she'd lacked as a child.

"I never imagined myself getting married and having kids, not because I didn't want kids, but because I came from a dysfunctional family background. I just didn't think it was in the cards for me," she told us. But now here she was, married, with a newborn and a new position as a partner in her firm, more than she had ever even dared fantasize about. Everything seemed like it should fall into place, but it didn't.

In order to spend more time with her newborn daughter, Audrey went back to work on a reduced schedule, billing only 80 percent of her time, as opposed to the standard 100 percent that others at the firm billed. But she quickly discovered that while the reduced hours made her schedule more tenable, it wasn't a recipe for career stardom. When working at 80 percent didn't feel right, Audrey tried other combinations to keep her corporate law career going and also spend time with her daughter, including the post-kid's-bedtime laptop sessions that are familiar to many working parents: "You get home at a reasonable hour, you put your kids to bed, and then you pull open the laptop at eight o'clock at night and work until twelve or one. I did that for a while, too." Audrey and her husband had their second child two years later, which didn't make the juggling any easier. Between the ongoing financial crisis, Audrey's long hours, and the stress of trying to be the kind of parent she wanted to be, she felt like she might break in two.

As her law firm began to implode around her, the choice was obvious. Many DC-based lawyers bulk up their résumés with government work in addition to law firm work. A government job would mean routine hours and less stress. So Audrey decided to move to a government agency for a few years, work her way up to a senior position, and then go back to the private sector to build her own practice. But once she landed in government, Audrey felt her inner drive toward the top of private law dissipate. She likes the lifestyle that her job permits her, the time she's able to spend with her kids, the fact that if one kid gets sick she can easily take a sick day, the federal holidays that allow her to spend entire days at home with her children. She likes not feeling crazed by her workload, not having to pull the laptop out at night and work until one a.m., not having to constantly worry about where her next case is coming from. And yet her current job leaves her intellectually wanting, so she's begun to look around at other options.

"This job has been fantastic for my personal life. For the first time since graduating law school, I have a personal life again, which is lovely, but I'm trying to find that holy grail of having a fulfilling professional career and a fulfilling personal life. I don't know if it's possible, but I want to continue to try to find as close to a happy balance as I can."

We heard this from a number of our friends: They downshifted their careers for the sake of their sanity, their children, or a healthier and calmer lifestyle, but after years of channeling their ambitious energy into their careers, they missed the thrill of competition. They missed working hard at a challenging job and being rewarded with accolades, they missed the tiny electric shiver they got when they told someone at a dinner party what they did for a living and that person paused, stood up a bit straighter, and understood that they were dealing with a successful professional. That lack, that wanting, is what puts many women in a state of constant transition. A job that ticks all the career-ambition boxes might not leave time to also tick all the personal-ambition boxes, so Audrey, like many of our friends, switched paths, moving from High Achiever to Flex Lifer, first chasing career ambition and then looking to satisfy her personal ambitions. In search of that stimulation, Audrey has poured her focus into her personal life. If ambition starts with the mastery of a skill, Audrey acknowledges that she is now focused on mastering "having a life." Yet at the same time, she feels the shadow of her career ambition lingering over her shoulder.

"In some ways, I've channeled some of that energy to my personal life. Not just taking care of the kids. I'm in two book clubs now. I did this big volunteer fund-raising job for my kids' school last year. That shows that I'm still not completely satisfied. I am definitely striving to find a job that I find more professionally fulfilling and that appeases my ambitions a little bit more."

In other words, Audrey is still as ambitious as she ever was. She misses the adrenaline rush and professional validation she got from the corporate job, so she's continuously searching for other ways to feed her ambition. Audrey is politically active, and recently added campaign volunteer work to her activity list (on top of her full-time job, two children, two book clubs, and the work she already does for her kids' school, because yay, ambition). As with many of the women we interviewed, she's still trying to find a way to "scratch that deeper itch."

One after another, our friends talked about wanting more, not being quite satisfied with just a good job and a happy marriage and healthy children and some volunteer work and a couple of vacations a year. The career ambition that many of these women had curbed managed to ooze out into other areas of their lives. Ambitious people, we were reminded, need and want more.

"I'm well paid," Audrey says. "It's not about the money, it's just about the ego and the professional satisfaction. It's actually starting to drive me crazy. [My career] is such a part of my identity that while I can make do, it's just not enough. I think that's what I've determined. It's not enough."

T his is not a woman who has lost her ambition. This is a woman who has decided, temporarily, to channel her ambitious energy beyond her career for the sake of her family. Once her children are older, Audrey anticipates stepping up to a more demanding professional life, scratching that itch. Anecdotally, this is a choice that many, many women—in fact, the majority of our former classmates—feel forced to make, to choose between being the parent they want to be and having the career they want. For ambitious women, wanting to be the best at your career and also the best parent and also the best partner or human being is the natural outcome of having grown up challenging yourself and aiming high. Some of our friends explained this conflict away by saying that they were no longer all that ambitious when it came to their careers, that they were fine with where their lives had led them.

Ashley, a health care professional who has run an AIDS study for a federal agency, told us how her priorities had changed since having kids. "Twenty-three years ago, I didn't have children. I wasn't even maternal. So the idea of just putting everything aside and focusing on my goals back then—of course I was going to do that. But at the end of the day, probably my greatest contribution to this world will be my children. I'm not going to be White House press secretary. I'm not going to be the CEO. I'm not going to be the star of any particular company, but I know I'm going to really be able to give something to my children, and that's really what's going to matter to me."

Others wrestled with the ambition conflict right in front of our eyes, live on Skype. They explained very rationally why they'd decided to downshift their careers, and then in the next breath said they felt unsatisfied, or shortchanged, or like they weren't living up to their potential. And then they'd conclude that, in the end, their downshifted career was best for everyone.

Obstacles to Ambition

So why the struggle? Why the back and forth? At first we thought that it may be hard for women to reconcile their ambition with their desire for achievement in all areas of their lives—not just career—in part due to the strides made by women in previous generations. As Gen-X girls, we were raised on stories of women overcoming odds to be superstars in their chosen fields. We heard about the first women to do one thing or another—Sally Ride, Sandra Day O'Connor, Margaret Thatcher—and understood that these were the small, starter ripples in a movement that we were supposed to turn into a full-on tidal wave. Throughout our teens we watched a trickle of powerful women who had defied the odds show up on television and film—Holly Hunter in *Broadcast News*, Melanie Griffith in *Working Girl*, Linda Hamilton in *Terminator 2*, and of course *Thelma & Louise*—not to mention a real-life woman, Geraldine Ferraro, who made it onto a major party's presidential ticket only to be clobbered at the voting booth. In college, we gaped open-mouthed at the way Anita Hill was treated by an all-white, all-male judiciary committee, and then cheered as four women claimed Senate seats the following year, some reportedly spurred to run by watching Clarence Thomas's confirmation hearing.

The world was tough for women, we knew, but things were getting better and easier, and we took seriously our generation's responsibility to turn these progresses for women into the norm. We would bring the world to a place where we could stop talking about the first woman to do this and the first woman to do that, and just talk about women like they were people. If the women who came before us could do it, with all the challenges they faced, we could, too. We were meant to be superstars. But perhaps this burden—the psychological weight of the dreams of previous generations of women—makes it that much harder for many women to step away and admit that being the first and the best and the boss isn't what they really want after all. Perhaps that is the conflict we were seeing, writ large on our computer monitors over the course of our interviews.

But the more women we talked to, the more we came to understand the churning of our friends' conflicted feelings about their workplace roles. What we were hearing is just one layer of a highly complex issue. Certainly, many of the women we interviewed felt they were letting everyone down by stepping away from their careers, or even just by stepping back. A few who had become stay-at-home mothers worried that they weren't setting good examples for their daughters, or that they wouldn't be able to advise them on their careers. But the conflict runs much deeper than simply an external pressure to achieve. Instead, we observed that for many women there are substantial obstacles to career ambition. To move up in most careers requires putting yourself out there, demanding a promotion (as Audrey did, and we heard several stories like hers), declaring that you want it, and claiming what's rightfully yours. This might be hard for anyone, but it is especially hard for women who have competing interests, like a spouse who is outwardly supportive but also clearly prioritizes his own career, or kids who want you to be there for their Friday-afternoon dance recitals, daily meals that don't make themselves, houses that aren't self-cleaning, or the school PTA members who wonder why you can't take on just one more fund-raiser.

As we watched our friends wrestle with this conflict during our interviews, we came to believe that as smart and self-aware as these women are, they often don't see the obstacles to ambition right in front of them. Some of these obstacles are universal for this socioeconomic slice of women—the trouble stretches across industries and personality types and marital arrangements, and across the country, from Minneapolis down to Dallas and out to Silicon Valley, and most insidious of all, these stumbling blocks often appear murky and undefined, originating from a combination of deep-seated beliefs these women hold about their own careers, ambition, and rightful place in the world.

Natalie's Ambition:
TV Stardom at the Network

Natalie came to Northwestern from Seattle with a plan to be on one of the news magazine shows that were popular at the time—*48 Hours*, perhaps, or *Dateline*—something long-form that would allow her to spend time telling stories and get deep into writing, which she loved. She liked the idea of being the first person to know something, of breaking news to the world and "contributing to what people are talking about, setting the agenda, holding people's feet to the fire, making sure that people know what the truth is so that they can make their own judgments about what's going on in the world."

As with Audrey, Natalie suffered some initial setbacks while at Northwestern. So many of the students in the broadcast journalism program seemed like they were born for broadcasting, and while Natalie enjoyed her major, she received some early—and unsolicited—advice from one of her professors that maybe TV and radio news wasn't the best fit for her.

"One professor called me into her office and asked me if I ever even watch the news. I said, 'Of course I watch the news, I watch it religiously.' She said, 'I think you should rethink your broadcast specialization, because you just don't get it. You're not going to be in this business.'"

Undaunted by this criticism, Natalie felt certain broadcast journalism was the right path for her.

"I felt like it was too early to quit and I should just keep trying. While I didn't necessarily believe that I would someday be a network news correspondent, I thought that it was worth at least giving it a shot to see how far I could get."

After graduation, she moved in with a cousin in Chicago and drove all around the Midwest hand-delivering her reel to every small station she could find. And then, in the fall, a station in Sioux City, Iowa, called her with a job offer. She took the job "sight unseen," packed up a U-Haul, hooked it to her little Toyota Corolla, and drove out to Iowa to begin her first job in television.

"I was a one-man band, so I shot and edited most of my own stuff," Natalie told us. Working at a small-town station meant more independence and creative freedom, but also a more provincial mind-set, including a level of ignorance about race that harked back to taunts she'd first encountered in grade school.

"That's when I started getting the Connie Chung thing. Anywhere I go, people ask me if I'm Connie Chung, and they're not always kidding. That happens a lot, especially in Sioux City. People will just roll down the windows and yell, 'Connie Chung!' or ask me, 'Hey, Connie Chung, where you going?'"

Natalie points out that being Asian American in broadcast journalism typically means being the only Asian American reporter at a station. Stations in locations with large Asian American populations tend to be more pliant in their hiring, but in the locales Natalie has worked, "I think management feels like, considering demographics, one is enough. Not only have I been the only one, but I've replaced the person who had been the only one."

Natalie pushed on and eventually made her way out of Sioux City and into larger and larger media markets. Fifteen years ago, she landed back in Chicago, where she's been the on-air financial reporter at the top station in the market ever since.

"Our station is a huge powerhouse," Natalie told us proudly. "If you add up the ratings of all the other networks at five o'clock and compare it to our one station rating, we win. We have a higher rating than all other stations combined in certain slots."

Most people, Natalie said, would be more than happy to live out the rest of their careers at a station like hers. It's considered a stable job in a fickle industry, it pays well, and it comes with a level of prestige. And yet Natalie was quick to tell us about an offer she'd gotten nearly a decade ago.

A few years into her Chicago job, the network offered her the chance to move to its New York affiliate. The only caveat: She needed to get approval from the general manager at her station first. But her general manager refused to let her go. The promise of that job, the moment when she was sure she was on her way to New York, where she would show the world she'd achieved a top slot in her field, haunts her to this day.

"I'm still pained when I think about it. I think that if I had been allowed to take that job, I would have forever felt like I made it. You know, 'I'm at the number one station in the number one market in the country.'"

Instead of moving to New York, Natalie stayed in Chicago, with a promise from her general manager that she'd find ways to help move Natalie's career along. But somehow that help has yet to materialize.

"She said, 'We have big plans for you here.' The truth is, I'm doing what I have been doing for the past fifteen years at my job. Whatever those plans were never manifested, so I'm a little bitter about that."

None of this is to say that Natalie isn't happy with her job and her life. Shortly after losing out on the New York job, she met the man who would become her husband, and soon after marrying, they had two children. She points out that if she had moved to New York, none of that would have happened. Not that Natalie has scaled back her work hours since becoming a parent. Ambitious as ever, she returned to work immediately after each maternity leave. She's got enough childcare to allow her to fill in on the morning show when she needs to, and she doesn't want to reduce her hours because she worries it could jeopardize her options for advancement.

"I have certainly had dreams like, 'Wouldn't it be nice if I could be part time, and worked three or four days a week instead of five?' but it was never a very serious consideration. I recognize that while that is very appealing to me right now, to work part-time while my kids are young, it would be hard, and I've seen it happen here, where if you step out for a little bit, even if it's just partway, it's hard to really get back in."

Natalie has what many people would consider a dream job. On some levels, it's a dream job for her—she gets to work in a field that she loves every day, and she also has a flexible schedule that allows her to drop her kids off at school every day and attend every school event. But while her job might be enough to satisfy most people, it clearly doesn't satisfy Natalie. Objectively, she still has places she wants to move her career, and things she wants to do. She longs to move past her current station even if from the outside her position seems ideal. And yet over Skype, we saw her wrestle with articulating this point. Our interview was full of justifications like, "Most sane people would just stay here" and "I can pick and choose what stories I do and when I do them." Natalie rattled off a list of the benefits of her job—"I'm home for dinner every single night, I often anchor the weekend morning shows, I get paid better than a lot of local reporters"—as though by downplaying her ambition, she could make it disappear, calm the voices telling her to reach for that next job, convince herself that where she is now is where she should be and that she should be satisfied with her position as the financial reporter for a large station in a major media market.

Why the arguing with herself? we wondered. Why not embrace what she clearly wants to do and make it happen, or at the very least simply acknowledge it and own it? What are the obstacles to Natalie's ambition?

One is those pesky internal voices. Not only does she have a chorus telling her she won't be satisfied until she lands a bigger job, but she's also got a crowd telling her she should be happy right where she is for a whole host of sensible reasons. And competing with all those voices are the same insecurities and anxieties that follow most of us around on a daily basis.

"Am I good enough? Do I deserve it? There's a lot to overcome and to take into consideration when I think about going down this road of looking to leave this place. This job allows me to be the journalist I've always hoped to be. I'm working in television news, I'm doing the beat that I love, and I get to have quality time with my kids and my husband and my friends. My husband says a lot of this desire to do something else is really ego. He's like, 'How much is that worth?' I'm trying to figure that out, too. I do think I can make more of an impact [at the network level], right? Network versus local, that just goes without saying."

Another barrier is Natalie's husband's career. He's an orthopedic surgeon. He earns more than she does (we heard from a lot of couples who prioritized one person's career over the other's based on who earned more) and feels it would be hard on his career if they relocated. In fact, when Natalie was considering a job in Los Angeles, he discouraged her. Even though it would have been a step up for her professionally, the job didn't pay enough to offset the cost of disrupting their family, Natalie explained. And ultimately, it came down to money and what was best for the family.

"He brings in more than I do, and so just on a practical level, it doesn't make sense. I wouldn't take a financial reporting job in New York because I wouldn't make that much more that it would make it worth it for our family. While it might help me feel like I achieved this ultimate thing, I don't think that would be fair to our family. I have responsibilities beyond just going for the pinnacle of my career."

Natalie and her husband agree—for now—that if she were to follow her career ambitions to a job that would satisfy her, one that would feel like a real achievement, she won't do so at a cost to the family. She can take a job in a bigger media market, but only if the family stays put. If a job opens up at the network level, she'll spend a few days a week in New York, then fly back to Chicago to join the family for the rest of the week. But that doesn't sound all that appealing, or realistic, and Natalie knows it. She's convincing herself, for now, to stick with the good things she already has going, and let the network dream go.

"I have the feeling that even if I go down this road of looking for a network gig, I will likely make the decision in the end that I am going to embrace what I already have, and make the most of it, and decide that this is actually the best thing for me. But I wonder if I need to go down this road to come to that realization in my heart."

Why, we wondered, shouldn't Natalie get to aim for the pinnacle of her career? Her kids are young, and the couple doesn't currently live near their extended family, so no one would be left behind. Even if staying put is the best decision for the family, it sounds like Natalie's career ambitions come second to her husband's, and that both Natalie and her husband accept this order without question. In this, they are not alone.

In a 2014 study of Harvard Business School graduates, over half the men surveyed anticipated that when they got married, their career would take priority over their spouse's.[14] On the other hand, the women in the survey overwhelmingly thought that career priority would be more like 50/50. Only 9 percent thought their own careers would take precedence. Unsurprisingly, this did not go well for the women in the study once they entered into relationships that were no longer hypothetical. About 40 percent of the women reported that their careers take a backseat to their husbands', which is double the number of women who anticipated being in that type of relationship. (Keep in mind, these are women who are ambitious, smart, and career-driven enough to graduate from Harvard Business School. Imagine making it to one of the most elite schools in the country, only to discover that you're married to someone who views your career as secondary to his because, well, you're not a man.) Of the male graduates, more than 70 percent are in relationships where their career takes precedence.

This attitude has been in place at least since the '70s, when the General Social Survey began collecting data on attitudes and behaviors in American society.[15] The survey found that the majority of couples believed that women should be willing to give up working in order to advance their husband's career. Quaintly, the study also found that in 1972, 67 percent of those surveyed felt it was *okay* for married women to work for pay, conjuring up conversations between spouses that possibly sounded like, "Honey, is it okay with you if I work a few hours in the steno pool? I'd love to have a little money to put away for extra stockings and a new hat."[16]

It's not surprising, then, that women raised in the '70s internalized these attitudes about their careers. They were free to drive hard at whatever career they chose—free to be business executives and partners in law firms and TV reporters—but only as long as their career needs didn't affect their husbands' careers. We will get into this topic in greater detail in the next chapter, but for now we will note that the prioritization of careers within a marriage is one more barrier to ambition that we observed among our friends, and that Natalie's struggle is not unique. We believe it is important that women recognize this phenomenon and understand that there is a deep internalized belief shared by both men and women that a wife's career is less important than her husband's (and we say "husband" intentionally here, as the dynamic within the same-sex marriages we've witnessed is markedly different). Recognition is a first step toward overcoming this belief, allowing women to ride out their ambition to whatever end point will make them feel accomplished, in the same way that men are encouraged to.

Finally, for many of our friends, their inability to clearly state what they want and go after it presents a more nuanced barrier to their ambition. A different way to say this is that they simply can't get out of their own way. This is something we've experienced in our own careers as well, so when our friends talked about all the reasons they didn't want a promotion or a bigger career, we nodded our heads and understood. The time commitment. The fact that prioritizing a career, by the very nature of the modern work world, means deprioritizing children and family. The stress that comes with a big career. The ability to buy toilet paper at odd hours, thereby saving countless minutes of aggravation standing in line and honking during rush-hour traffic. But at the same time, we found ourselves sometimes wanting to stand up in the middle of an interview and scream, "Stop saying you don't want it! You want it!"

But openly stating that they want to go all out for something they might not get is hard for many of them. Some of our friends talked about how they didn't know if they wanted to reach out and grab jobs that weren't easily on offer to them. If someone really wanted them to do the job, they'd ask, right? Others said they didn't really think they wanted to be CEO, while every action they described to us seemed like that of someone ambitious and smart enough to land exactly that type of role. And a few found their ambition waning after being passed over for promotions, opting to quietly content themselves with where they were rather than fight for what they felt they deserved.

Our friend Suzanne, who built a strong reputation for herself as a marketing executive in Silicon Valley, described how, after missing out on a promotion at one company, she began to doubt that she really wanted to move up even after switching jobs.

"I was reluctant to push for myself because I was like, 'I shouldn't have to. I set the curve. You told me my performance is extraordinary.' That's the thing with ambition. Sometimes you see the people that succeed are the loudest in the room or the squeakiest wheel, and they really, really want it. I just don't want it that bad."

Research shows that men don't have to squeak as loudly to be set up for success. While men and women both find value in being mentored by coworkers senior to them, the form of that mentorship looks different: women are typically provided with constructive criticism on management techniques or ways to change their personal work style or interactions to help them move up the ladder at work, while men are given "sponsorship." They are often taken under the wing of some higher-up colleague, who works with them to plan out strategies for promotion, bolsters their confidence, and fights for their advancement.[17]

But with no one to fight for her in cutthroat, male-dominated Silicon Valley, at a company whose culture Suzanne compares to *Game of Thrones*, it's no wonder she has decided, "I'm okay being villager number nine. I do not need to be up there running Westeros with all y'all."

Our friend Rachel, a director at a large health care nonprofit in Portland, described to us how she's consciously moved up in her career so as to increase her sphere of influence. The higher up the chain she goes, the more people she can help. She started out in the Peace Corps helping a small community, then moved to small nonprofits, where she found she was able to have an impact on larger communities.

"Then I realized, 'Wow, these nonprofits are kind of rinky-dink. What if I got into a huge system and was able to wield my influence and advocate for systems on a bigger scale and have a bigger impact?' I've been gradually pushing my sphere of influence out a little bit as I get more comfortable and more experienced."

And yet she told us repeatedly that she's not interested in becoming a vice president at her organization, despite the fact that she seems to think that type of position would give her the ultimate sphere of influence.

"I think I'm a very ambitious person. But my ambition has never been for hierarchical leadership. In fact, I don't want that. I like working hard and doing good work, but I don't care as much about title. At a place like [her current nonprofit], which is very corporate and hierarchical, not wanting to be vice president could be perceived as not having ambition."

Which is it—does she want to increase her sphere of influence, or does she want to stay where she is? Is she afraid to put herself out there for a higher-ranking role, or is it really just not her cup of tea? It was hard for us to untangle Rachel's and our other friends' seemingly contradictory statements. These conflicted feelings correlate with the very real external hurdles that women face to their ambition. One study found that women get more pushback than men when negotiating raises and promotions, are less likely to be promoted to manager positions, and have less access to senior leadership than men.[18] It's no surprise that the same study found that only 40 percent of the women surveyed expressed interest in making their way to a top executive position, compared to 56 percent of men.

We understand exactly what these women are describing, because we've experienced all these conflicted feelings ourselves. But we also observed that our friends seem unaware of their contradictory statements. They are ambitious, but not *that* ambitious. They want to win, but they don't want to win all the way to the top. They want to win all the way to the top, but not if their husband doesn't support their winning. While we would love to call for policy change, to upend corporate culture and marital norms and create a more just world where women can go as far as their ambition takes them, in the short term, women can benefit from at least knowing what kind of challenges they're likely to face. Knowing you're not alone goes a long way. If you get passed over for a promotion, or feel like you don't have a champion at work, or aren't sure you want to be the squeaky wheel when it comes to moving up the ranks, know that it's not just you. It's all of us, it's systemic, and it needs to change.

Our college friends' ambition has taken them down many varied roads, and we are right there with them, whichever path they chose. For those whose ambition has taken them on a more traditional trajectory at work, we want them to be able to follow their ambition without stigma, without being tripped up by self-imposed hurdles or hidden barriers. For those who have purposefully chosen to stay put or scale back, we want them to feel empowered, to know that they're not letting anyone down by deciding that work is only one color in the variegated pattern of their lives. We want all women to have everything they want, be it perfectly crafted homemade treats for the bake sale, invigorating hikes in the Rocky Mountains, or a coveted promotion to a corner office with views of a sky-scraper forest.

Here's What We Know About Ambition

▶ **Ambition looks different at different points in your life.**

You may start your career filled with ambition and drive, with your identity and profession so intertwined that you feel like your job *is* your identity. As time goes on, you may find yourself stepping slightly away from your career to raise children, releasing one career to pursue another dream, seeing your priorities shift due to life circumstances. Your ambition can, and very likely may, change over the course of a career and a lifetime—and that evolution can lead to a multitude of successes and experiences. All of which is to say, no judgment.

Our friends who became presidents of the PTA and everything else as part- or full-time stay-at-home parents seemed no less ambitious than those who became CMOs. Those who scaled back corporate careers and then pivoted their energy into working for nonprofits, volunteering on political campaigns, or becoming artists later in their lives conveyed a drive similar to those who stayed on the corporate ladder—the former group just coveted and pursued a life that looked different from that of the latter.

Channeling your ambition into rapid promotions and channeling your ambition into running the PTA are life choices that may suit different people at different times, *or the same person at different times.* Wanting one thing when you're twenty-five and another when you're thirty-five doesn't mean you were wrong when you were younger, or that your ambition is slipping away as you age—it simply means you're a human being adjusting to the vast range of possibilities, needs, and desires you might encounter over your lifetime.

▶ **But make sure your changing ambition is a reflection of your own desires, not others' needs or the challenges of working while female.**

As they moved ahead with their careers, many of our friends whom we'd known to be ambitious in college decided, for a range of reasons, that the top job didn't look all that attractive. They didn't want work to consume their lives, they began to prioritize family or volunteer work or simply spending time outside having fun—they liked the freedom that came with *not* being the queen of the mountain. But we also noticed that some of our friends decided to step away from bigger jobs for reasons that didn't feel entirely in sync with the ambitious people we knew them to be: It could be the difficulty, day after day, of putting yourself out there, clawing your way to the big job when it can feel like the world doesn't really want you there, or even the niggling sense that perhaps your spouse doesn't entirely want you to fight for that next high-level position, but you aren't precisely sure of all the why-nots. This isn't to say you should rail against your spouse or beat your head against a wall trying to move up in a company that is never going to promote you for reasons having nothing to do with your abilities, but rather that you shouldn't let these circumstances eat away at your ambition. Because, as we'll see later, ambition can't really be contained. It can be rechanneled for a while—you can convince yourself that you're perfectly happy with the life you have, that it works best for everyone, yourself included—but like water in a rainstorm, ambition will eventually find another way to run. So if you've recently asked yourself if maybe you're not as ambitious as you thought you were, that perhaps playing it safe and sticking with what you have is best for now, think again. It's possible that your ambition has changed. But it's also possible that it's just gotten more difficult to pursue what you really want.

▶ **Having children may radically alter your ambition, or do nothing to change it at all.**

Rachel, the health care nonprofit director, told us that "when I had a kid, everything changed for me." She and her female partner used a donor to get pregnant, and then split up once they discovered their parenting styles—and a lot of other elements of their relationship—were no longer compatible. Suddenly our friend was the single parent of a two-year-old and "couldn't be in a job that was eight a.m. to eight p.m. I needed to be able to leave at three o'clock if he was sick and pick him up." Her son is fourteen now, and she is repartnered and the stepparent to a nine-year-old as well. She's thought about moving up in her organization, getting more responsibility, more professional recognition, a bigger title, more money, but at this point, she's not willing to compromise time with her family for any of those things. Another project manager, this one for an infectious disease program, said that her "priorities have changed. Twenty-three years ago, I didn't have kids." Her contract was up recently, and she told us that even now that her children are in elementary school, she won't consider a job that doesn't have some work-from-home or part-time option. It's just not worth it to her.

Many of our friends underscored the point—something that seems to be a common understanding these days—that once women have children, they have an innate need to be present with and for them, which by definition means they can't be as hard-driving in their careers. On the other hand, we also saw many women whose ambitions stayed the course after children.

▶ **If you choose to downshift your career ambition, know that it may affect your career trajectory, so consider the long-term implications.**

The women we interviewed who scaled back their careers after having children or opted not to go for promotions that would have moved them ahead have redirected their ambition in often satisfying ways—but they have also made decisions that have limited what they achieved in their careers. For some of our friends, this was a fair trade-off. They love being able to meet the school bus, or being available for school volunteer work, or having the freedom to spend their time in ways that are deeply meaningful to them. Women shouldn't get discouraged if they feel they can't go for the big promotion exactly when they want it. Life is long and, as we'll discuss more in chapter 6, plenty of our friends—after feeling like they didn't want to put in long hours or devote such a large percentage of their mental space to work—are embracing precisely that challenge as their children grow up.

CHAPTER 3

MARRIAGE

Everyone loves a good power couple: They're magnetic, influential, wealthy, beautiful, and well dressed, and they seem to have everything together. The first documented use of the term *power couple*, according to the *Oxford English Dictionary*, was in a 1983 issue of *Newsweek*, in reference to Bob and Elizabeth Dole. At the time, he was one of the most powerful members of the Senate, on his way to becoming majority leader. She was secretary of transportation under Ronald Reagan, on her way to becoming the president of the Red Cross and later a senator from North Carolina. Somehow these two managed to be married and represent states halfway across the country from each other, which says a lot about what it takes to be a power couple.

Perhaps because of the power couple's prevalence in the media, perhaps because we both live in New York City, where simply paying a mortgage can require two hefty salaries and equally hefty careers to justify those salaries, we anticipated finding many of our High Achiever friends paired off with high-achieving men. We were ready for some good power couple stories—two partners with big careers, both suiting up in the morning, shoving laptops into compact roller bags and jetting off to various meetings around the country. Given that our classmates had been ambitious and aiming for prominent careers, it stood to reason that they would meet and marry spouses on the same career trajectory.

There has been an increase in assortative mating in recent years—spouses are more likely to have similar levels of education today than they used to—which lent credence to our expectation.[1] Logically it would seem that similar levels of education should lead to similar levels of career success—that is, when two MBAs get married, both are poised to become business executives and produce lots of little MBA-procuring children.

But of the thirty-nine women we interviewed who are either married or partnered, only 20 percent fit the classic power couple description: a chief marketing officer at a bank married to a corporate real estate vice president; a sought-after screenwriter married to a music executive; two corporate attorneys married to each other; two Wikipedia-page-worthy actors married to each other; a prominent doctor married to the general counsel at a brokerage firm. As we dug deeper into the numbers, we noticed that many of these power couples didn't have children, some because they weren't interested in being parents, others because they met their partners later in life. One woman had a medical issue that would have made childbearing risky. Once we factored in children, the number of power couples dipped, and we saw an unexpected pattern begin to emerge: High Achievers most often partnered with Opt Outers, and Flex Lifers paired mostly with other Flex Lifers (though a few married High Achievers).

And it wasn't always the women who opted out of or scaled back their careers. While our friends who were Opt Outers were nearly all partnered with high-achieving men (which afforded them the ability to opt out), many of our friends who were High Achievers in their own right did not end up partnered with other High Achievers. Rather, they were nearly always married to men who had chosen to opt out of their careers, or to stay in flexible jobs long-term rather than pursue promotions, in favor of being the primary caregiver. Some couples consisted of a high-achieving woman married to a man who had chosen to stay at home with the children, and sometimes it was the reverse. Sometimes both members of the couple had decided to scale back their careers in order to be more available to their children or to pursue other passions like volunteering or hiking. The three women in this group in same-sex relationships, it's worth noting, all ended up Flex Lifers, and the ambition in their marriages, as well as the distribution of domestic duties, broke down in different ways due to a number of specific and outlying circumstances, gender not among them.

Our friends did hew to the assortative mating theory, picking partners with similar educational backgrounds, but that track didn't always lead to two-CEO households. Among our interviewees, lawyers and doctors and PhD students met and married each other. A significant number of our friends partnered with spouses they met in college or graduate school. (This led to some funny conversations when we discovered that one friend had ended up marrying that baseball-cap-clad guy who was a fixture in our sorority house common room, or that another friend's formal date who answered to a frat house nickname throughout college had become her husband of nineteen years.) The majority of our friends with advanced degrees ended up with spouses who also had advanced degrees, yet once they became parents, only one person in these couples ended up with a classically successful career. It was almost as though, in families where one partner had a big job, all the career ambition had been allocated to that one person. So why do these couples behave as if there is an ambition cap on their marriages?

In part, we believe this dynamic is related to the expanding nature of today's working world. Since our peer group graduated from college, what professional life looks like has transformed. In 1993, there was barely an Internet. Email was something you had to go to the campus library to check, and as a result you'd often run into the person you'd emailed before you got their response. For us and our friends, first jobs included things like fax machines, navigating WordPerfect, making Xeroxes, and frequently checking voice mail. They also included lunch breaks away from one's desk, and a kind of peace that descended when you left your office for the day knowing you wouldn't have to think about work again until you went in the next morning. But for most of us in white-collar professional jobs, work is now a 24/7 endeavor.

The average workweek now encompasses seven more hours than it used to, and one study found that one in four respondents reported working more than fifty hours a week.[2] Of those additional hours, most are consumed by high earners,[3] who make up the bulk of our High Achiever group. Though anyone who has a smartphone and a job knows that work doesn't end just because the sun has set or it's the weekend. Professionals are connected to work via phone or computer for *at least* 13.5 hours a day, which, when you factor in sleep, leaves only 3 hours a day to do things like eat, shower, and figure out whether your kids should take karate or piano next month.[4] More than half of workers are checking their work messages over the weekend and while they're out sick.[5] And as a nation, Americans seem loath to pack a bathing suit and sunscreen, unplug, and relax, with four out of ten workers letting their vacation time go unused.[6] When people do take vacations, they're often still connected to work anyway, regardless of what their overly optimistic out-of-office email auto-reply might say.[7] As a result, it's not surprising that many of our friends and their spouses thought about what their lives would look like if both partners decided to pursue equally ambitious careers—two parents up until midnight returning emails, or dashing out the door at the crack of dawn for breakfast meetings—and simply said no thank you.

The construct of the work world has long depended upon an invisible, silent partner to buy the chicken for dinner, pick up the dry cleaning, collect the children, and, depending on which era we're discussing, prepare the minute-you-walk-in-the-door martinis. As one of our friends, a stay-at-home mother, put it, "We have a magically refilling refrigerator." When one partner can stay at work without needing to worry about the running of a household, it's often a boon to that person's career—their salary is likely to rise more quickly, and they're more likely to earn promotions than someone in a two-career household.[8] Many of our friends who are primary wage earners noted how important it was for them to be able to make early-morning meetings or fly off to Baltimore for a last-minute strategy session with the CEO. More than important, actually. It was this flexibility, the ability to instantly materialize at work when they were needed most, to say yes to everything, to embrace every opportunity, that allowed them to attain, and then retain, their C-suite jobs.

And conversely, our friends who stayed at home, filling their refrigerators with a regular supply of fresh food, turning that food into healthy family dinners, meeting their young children's steady stream of emotional and physical needs, often commented that their spouse's career success was contingent on their support. One friend, a former financial adviser for a major investment bank turned stay-at-home mother of three, said her husband, who works on Wall Street, watched as his friend's wife returned to her job after a multiyear hiatus and was a little shaken by the degree to which his friend's life changed. "His friend had to give up a lot in his career, like, stay home to get the kids on the bus and get into work later, which in [her husband's] industry would be like coming in at a half day. It would be laughable." Because our friend is home with the kids, managing their schedules and everything else on the home front, her husband is "able to just do what needs to be done as if he didn't have kids. That wouldn't happen if I was also working."

Everything You Know About Choosing a Partner Is Wrong

The idea that one spouse's career success is contingent upon the other spouse's career runs counter to the way society often tells women to think about finding a partner. Examples abound in the popular media of women who are searching for their equal—movies like *How to Lose a Guy in 10 Days*, *Bridget Jones's Diary*, and *Broadcast News* all feature strong women pursuing men who are as ambitious as they are, if not more. In *Sex and the City*, Big is presented as the only man whose career success can equal Carrie's, and therefore the logical person for her to end up with, even if he comes with a lot of baggage. And Sheryl Sandberg famously wrote in *Lean In* that the most important decision a woman makes about her career is whom to marry. She highlighted that point with examples from her own power couple marriage—two billionaires who lived in different cities for the first part of their marriage in order to sustain their glittering careers—which might not have resonated with a lot of women struggling in middle management, but at least it gave them an archetype to shoot for. As any ambitious woman who has ever been set up on a blind date by well-meaning friends can probably attest, your friends tend not to try to pair you with someone who is unemployed or living in their parents' basement. Instead, you're often matched up with someone your friend sees as your equal—an Ivy League grad, a partner-track lawyer, someone who has as much career ambition and general awesomeness as you do. (Hana still remembers a blind date with a man who worked in finance, where she struggled to find a single topic to talk about. She'd mostly dated moody creative types, so after the date she called up the friend who had arranged the date and said, "What were you thinking? He works for a hedge fund!" Her friend replied, "I know! He's smart and ambitious and makes a lot of money—that's why I set you up with him!")

But while high-achieving women might fantasize about pairing off with equally high-achieving men, our friends' trajectories indicate that one of the keys to achieving and sustaining a superstar career is to partner with someone who has *less* career ambition than they do, someone who is happy to either be a primary caregiver or content with a job that might not lead to being a master of the universe. The women in our group most likely to become High Achievers were those who partnered with spouses interested in supporting their careers not just with encouraging phrases like "You go get 'em, honey," but with the most valuable kind of support that exists in our emailing-at-two-a.m., breakfast-meetings-at-seven-a.m., conference-calls-on-Saturday work culture: more time.

Over a decade ago, Linda Hirshman, writing in *The American Prospect*, argued that career-focused women should find pretty much any marital configuration *other* than marrying someone equally ambitious.[9] She suggested marrying someone younger, marrying someone much older who is ready to ease up on his career, or "marrying down."

"Don't think of this as brutally strategic," Hirshman wrote. "If you are devoted to your career goals and would like a man who will support that, you're just doing what men throughout the ages have done: placing a safe bet."

Out of Hirshman's advice sprung a hundred Hydra-headed articles mocking her, including one in the *New York Times* by David Brooks, who called her essay "a full-bore, unapologetic blast of 1975 time-warp feminism."[10] But the truth is that, for our friends, there was no more surefire route to career success than marrying a spouse who prioritized our friend's career above their own. For some of our friends, this was a conscious decision made by two partners looking for a way to have it all: a successful career, a happy family, a well-run household. Other friends happened into the arrangement—a husband whose career didn't seem to take off quite as quickly as his wife's, a job lost in a recession and never quite replaced, decisions born out of economic need, or a wife who saw a career opportunity and, with her husband's support, went for it. Still others followed another piece of Hirshman's advice: to marry someone with "an ideological commitment to gender equality." In 2005, when Hirshman wrote her essay, this type of partner may have seemed like something conjured up in an early feminist porn fantasia, along with men who vacuum, make soufflés, and know when the kids need new socks. But for some of our friends, this was exactly the kind of man they partnered with, though in reality these men come across less as people who have read a lot of feminist theory and more as spouses who understand, unblinkingly, that they are in a partnership in which earning a living, raising children, and running a household are all tasks to be divided up according to interest, ability, and joy, rather than gender.

Some of our friends had explicit conversations early in their marriages about who would stay home with the kids and who would work. They understood that they did not want to live in a household fueling two high-powered careers, they valued having a parent home to raise the children, and they thought carefully and logically about which partner should own the career ambition. Before our friend Sarabeth and her husband became parents, they knew they wanted one person to stay at home, but weren't sure which one of them it would be. They met in law school, but neither decided to become a lawyer. Instead, she began a teaching career while her husband worked at a restaurant and figured out his next move. "Whoever had the best benefits and health insurance at work was going to stay at work. So if I had gotten a job first, I would have worked and he would have stayed home."

But by the time their first child was born, things had shifted. Kyle had been admitted into the foreign service, and Sarabeth was working part-time at the consulate. The original plan had been for Sarabeth to teach in each country the family was placed, but she quickly discovered she didn't have the right credentials to do so—and with young children to care for, finding time to pursue those credentials proved elusive. So she stayed at home, playing a vital role by hosting dinners and organizing charity events as her husband ascended through the foreign service.

In our friend Amy's case, she and her husband had several conversations about which spouse would own the career ambition in their marriage after the couple's children were born. In the end, they realized it would be best for everyone if the ambition went to her. We don't know explicitly that either Amy or Sarabeth are married to men who have "an ideological commitment to gender equality." Their husbands may simply have a commitment to rational decisions. Both couples weighed everyone's potential career trajectories evenly, and made choices that seemed to make the most sense for everyone in the family. And both couples were open to changes down the road, inherently aware that one or both partners might choose to do something different later, that the High Achiever in the relationship might want to step back ten years down the road, or that the Opt Outer might want to return to work, or that both of them might want to chuck it all and open a hydroponic tomato farm in New Hampshire. They acknowledged that people change, ambitions change, while at the same time recognizing that one person's career path is inherently intertwined with the other's.

High Achievers and Opt Outers

Amy grew up in a working-class suburb of Detroit and always knew she wanted to have a fancy job and wear power suits, though she wasn't quite sure what kind of career that would involve. She and her mother watched a lot of soap operas together in high school, and she took mental notes as she watched Alexis Carrington clomp her way through the hallways in impossibly high heels on *Dynasty*. Amy excelled at Northwestern—she majored in economics and was president of a prominent campus student group, and as graduation neared, she interviewed with a number of companies making the rounds on campus. With the nation in the throes of a recession, coveted jobs in banking and finance were scarce, and she ended up at an insurance firm in downtown Chicago.

"Insurance people always say no one really chooses to go into insurance," Amy told us. "You fall into it, and that's what happened to me as well. But once you're in it, it opens up all of these doors, and you realize there's a lot of opportunities in the insurance industry that probably a lot more people could add their value to if they knew about them."

After a few years at the company, Amy moved over to the in-house insurance practice at one of the big management consulting firms, where she met her future husband. She liked the work at the consulting firm, but the lifestyle was a killer. Amy was on the road four or five days a week, and when she looked around for female role models—women who could show her how to balance the grueling travel and long hours with a family—she didn't see any.

"The few women that I knew had these horrible, horrible lives where they never saw their families at all and they literally outsourced everything. They outsourced the child-rearing. Even the birthday parties for their kids were outsourced. I would look at people and think, 'There's nothing about that I want at all.'"

In the meantime, the consulting firm had gone public, their business model had changed, and Amy had started to find the work less interesting. With the new business model, the financial carrot at the end of the stick— making partner and earning a partner-level salary—disappeared. Amy's husband was the first to leave the company and took a job with a smaller consultancy in Atlanta. Since Amy traveled constantly for work, she made the move with him, but decided to stick it out awhile longer at her firm. And then an unanticipated shift began to happen. Her salary started to grow faster than his. It was a small shift, so small that it wasn't even worth noting at the time, but it would factor into the couple's decisions later.

By that point Amy had been with her firm for nine years, and she and her husband were ready to start a family. Shortly after she got pregnant, an opportunity came up for her to take a bigger job with an insurance company and move the family back to Chicago. The couple looked at their finances, and at the fact that Amy's career and salary were moving ahead at a brisker pace than her husband's, and decided that she would be the primary breadwinner and her husband would leave his job to stay at home with their child. "It was a practical decision," Amy explained. "It wasn't a path that either of us thought of when we first got married. We never thought about it until the opportunity presented itself, and it just made sense."

By the time their son was born, the family had relocated to Chicago and Amy had started her new job. It took some time for them to adjust to this new family dynamic—not only being parents, but being a single-income family with a somewhat untraditional division of labor. "It was a total shift for him because he had never envisioned that being his role, ever. He is a Korean first-born son, so in his background and culture that is not the norm, to say the least. It was very radical for him, so it took him years to work through being okay with it. Now he's embraced it, and it's wonderful."

Amy's husband's family was less than thrilled with his decision and her own family thought it was pretty weird, and as a result, the two were on the receiving end of a lot of pressure for him to go back to work. "It was just interesting, with his family and my family asking all the questions like, 'Of course this is temporary, of course this isn't going to last, and of course this isn't how this is really going to be, right? You guys are going to go back to normal and maybe, Amy, you would stay at home and he'll go back to work.' But I thought, 'This actually makes more sense doing it like this. I really like what I do. I'm having a lot of fun. I love my job and he's doing great at home.'"

Eventually, though, Amy's husband decided to try returning to work to see what that would be like for their family. They had two kids by then, and Amy's work provided subsidized day care right near her office, so the time seemed right. Plus, her husband was able to land a freelance consulting gig at Amy's company. The family of four commuted to work together, forty-five minutes each way from their rural exurb to the suburb where the two worked and then back again at the end of the day. But both Amy and her husband found being in a two-career family stressful. The kids hated day care and were frequently sick. And when they arrived home at the end of a long day, things didn't improve. "Ken would say, 'Oh my gosh. I need to decompress,' and he would sit on the couch and I'm like, 'What? *You* need to decompress? Are you kidding me?' The stress level for both of us was bad."

So they reevaluated, and decided that they preferred a lifestyle where one parent stayed home. They never considered a nanny—to them the logical choice was to have one breadwinner and one stay-at-home parent. They knew they'd have less income, but the trade-off was well worth it.

"When we moved back to Chicago, we made decisions financially that it would be one salary and that's how it would be. Sure, we could have extra stuff if both of us worked, but we don't need any extra stuff. It's nice to have, but we don't need it."

With the parenting duties solidly accounted for, Amy has been able to put in long hours at work when she needs to, or to travel at the last minute, all of which has helped her career flourish. She's happy that she hasn't had to "outsource" the child-raising, that it can all be done by a hands-on parent, and credits some of her career success to the psychological comfort of knowing things are taken care of at home.

"Not having to worry about things because my husband is taking care of everything has made me feel so much more at ease, so that I can say yes to work opportunities as they come up without even having to check."

Amy has excelled at her company—she's a member of the senior leadership team—and radiates confidence when she speaks. And she's thrilled with how her husband handles the family's home, laughing as she tells us that he maintains spreadsheets of the kids' academics and athletic activities. Amy does admit, though, that she's not completely absolved from household and parenting responsibilities the way some of her male coworkers seem to be.

"Sometimes I feel like I also need a stay-at-home wife in addition to a stay-at-home husband. He does a lot, but when I hear my coworkers who are men talk about their stay-at-home wives, they seem to do a lot more than my stay-at-home husband."

Recently, though, her husband's mother volunteered to help with the household chores. A few years ago, her mother-in-law moved a mile down the road and now takes on some of what Amy calls "the wife things." For Amy, this has its pros and cons; Amy was initially opposed to it but has come to see the help as a positive.

"Ken's mother said, 'You need to fire your cleaning lady because I'm going to clean your house.' I said, 'I'm very uncomfortable with you cleaning my house. You're not a cleaning lady.' She said, 'Well, I'm going to clean it anyway so you better get rid of the cleaning lady.' Ken's like, 'You better fire the cleaning lady because this is going to get bad.' So I fired the cleaning lady. She enjoys coming over and helping us around the house, which at first made me feel like, 'Why is she coming and helping us?' I felt bad. But she feels like that's her way of giving back. She enjoys doing laundry, for example. If she wants to come and do laundry, I'm fine with that now. But it took me a while to get there."

Laundry aside, Amy is unequivocal when it comes to the way the ambition is currently divided in her household. She works at a job she loves, she's achieved the kind of career she'd always dreamt about, and she feels secure in the knowledge that her children are well cared for and that her husband is cheering her on. But while Amy and her husband *explicitly* decided that all career ambition would be channeled in her direction and both thrived as a result, she is unusual in this regard. For most of our High Achiever friends married to Opt Outers or Flex Lifers, their careers thrived by necessity, as their partners' careers meandered or fizzled altogether.

For Jess, a C-suite banking executive, the decision that she support the family seemed to creep in, foglike, as though both spouses were unaware of reality until they'd been living it for nearly a decade. Both were working when they met in London; he's a British citizen and she'd been transferred to her bank's UK office. When they decided to move to San Francisco to be closer to her ailing father, he struggled to find work. He lost his job shortly before their daughter was born, and ultimately became a stay-at-home father, taking on occasional freelance gigs that he works on while their daughter is in school. The two never talked about what the division of labor between them would look like, but Jess continued to move ahead in her career. Though she wanted to be close to her father, as the primary breadwinner she also did what was necessary to advance at the bank, relocating the family to North Carolina and Vancouver before eventually returning to San Francisco. And today, eight years after becoming parents, the couple has never explicitly discussed who is the primary caregiver, who pays the bills, or anything in between. "We talked about all the things like, 'Do you want kids?' But not how we would raise them and who would stay home. My mom reminds me that he used to always joke that he would stay home and I'd be like, 'Ha ha, right,' and now he does."

Like Amy, Jess credits the fact that her husband is at home with some of her career success. She has a partner who was willing to make multiple cross-country moves so she could climb her way up at the bank. She's able to arrive at work early and stay late and still feel like her daughter is in good hands, being cared for by a parent. Jess said she would have pursued this kind of career regardless of her spouse's professional trajectory, but it's impossible to know for sure since she has always had the security of a partner handling things on the home front.

"James would say he's been my rock. That he's been my sole contributor and sponsor, but I probably would have [had this career] anyway. The people we went to school with were a bunch of alphas, a lot of very self-motivated people, and we were at Northwestern to go out and do great things, right? There was never any question that people were going to go on and do a lot after school. Because of that, I think I would say I'd have done it anyway, but, absolutely, knowing James was home or there to pick up Charlotte, and having that flexibility to stay late when I have to stay late has been important."

Perhaps in part because the couple never sat down and discussed that Jess would support them and James would stay at home, or because they seem to have fallen into this family structure rather than purposefully organizing it as Amy and her husband did, Jess still holds out hope that things will change, that their situation is only temporary.

When we asked Jess what would make her life easier, she sighed and said, "I would love my husband to step aside and go back to work and let me get a maid, a nanny, someone that I could tell what to do, because my husband doesn't listen to me."

But what she might not realize is that if her husband did go back to work, the family would likely need to rethink how ambition gets divided up between spouses. Jess owns all the career ambition; she's never known any other way. And while she credits much of her success to her own drive to succeed (and we can confirm that we've always known her to be sharp and efficient, with a no-bullshit style—exactly the type of person who can navigate a multinational bank and make her way to the C-suite), it's possible that she's succeeded in part because she had no other choice. The family relies on her for financial support, so scaling back her career was never an option—and she receives immense professional reward from her work, so the incentive to stay on that track is strong. Even as a new mother, at a time when many of our friends struggled to leave their newborns at home and return to work, Jess didn't flinch. "For me it was a no-brainer," she told us. "I just got on with it. It was like, okay, I have to do this, so I'll do it."

Our High Achiever C-suite friends who have partnered with opt-out husbands are part of a larger trend, but one that surfaces only if you look carefully across the map of the United States, finding little dots here and there representing spouses who have quietly slipped out of the workforce to support their high-achieving wives. According to a *Bloomberg Businessweek* article, nearly half the women who are currently CEOs of Fortune 500 companies are married to a spouse who opted to stay home or dial back his career to support his wife's ascent.[11] Jennifer Granholm, who served as the governor of Michigan for seven years, relied on her stay-at-home husband to do the bulk of the child-raising for the couple's three children. But many couples with this type of arrangement seem reluctant to speak publicly about it, which may be why discovering a successful woman paired with a scaled-back or stay-at-home spouse feels a bit like spotting a giant squid. A reporter working on a story that probed into the career of Mark Rometty, who is married to Ginni Rometty, the first female (and current) CEO of IBM, hit a brick wall when asking the couple about Mr. Rometty's work.[12] "He was emphatic that this was a subject he didn't want to discuss," the article noted. Our friends were also often reluctant to fully disclose their own arrangements, lest we think badly of them or their spouses. Each one thought she was probably the only one in our class who was the primary wage earner. When we first reached out to interview Amy, she wrote back, "I have a fairly unique situation." We guessed what that situation was before we met with her, and let her know she wasn't the only one.

While the media likes to fuel the fantasy of power couples, the reality for our friends turned that assumption on its ear: What we found was that, just as men credit their supportive spouses with their career success, the high-achieving women we knew also needed someone at home doing the laundry and scheduling playdates in order to reach career heights. Whether they started out as an ambitious duo and downsized, as Amy did, or fell into the arrangement, as Jess did, they quickly discovered that allocating all the career ambition to one person made life a hell of a lot easier for the family. We just wish the house husband wasn't such a big secret, something to be whispered about, as though one's spouse has failed, instead of being credited as someone who has made the phenomenally brave decision, in today's society, to cast aside gender-biased expectations and follow what works best for the entire family unit.

An article in *New York Magazine* on high-powered career women married to men who have opted out or chosen to scale back referred to the men as "freeloaders," introduced readers to a woman who explained away her higher salary as "an accounting error" so her husband wouldn't feel bad, and described a man who leaves IOU notes in his breadwinner wife's wallet, before concluding that most of these couples should probably head to counseling en route to their inevitable nasty divorce, during which the "freeloading" husband will surely seek alimony.[13] The media tends to reinforce this image of the loser stay-at-home husband who can't get his shit together paired with a woman whose sole desire is that her husband earn a living. What articles like this fail to acknowledge is that these roles might be temporary; the picture of the stay-at-home husband married to a high-achieving wife may merely be a snapshot of a moment in time. As we saw our friends move along the paths of their adult lives, we would hear about the zigzags of their partners' paths as well. Ten years earlier, a current stay-at-home dad might have supported the family at a demanding job while his wife worked part-time or attended school. Ten years from now, when the children are older, he might discover a work opportunity he just can't turn down and she might want to ease up on her career and spend more time rock climbing or volunteering or brewing her own beer.

Our friends' reality starkly countered the cynical, sexist visual of the freeloader husband chasing alimony after a failed marriage. The rate of divorce in our friend group was quite low (10 percent, compared to a national rate of approximately 42 percent[14]), and none of the divorced couples included a high-achieving woman married to a stay-at-home husband. Needless to say, most of our friends don't consider their stay-at-home spouses "losers." While Jess wished her husband would get a job so she could hire a cleaning lady who would keep the house tidier than her husband does, she also readily acknowledged that his role as primary caregiver contributed to her own success (not to mention giving their daughter an invaluable "present" parent at home). And Amy doesn't want her husband to work at all, at least not now. She's loved their arrangement from the minute she went back to work after her first maternity leave.

"I felt so secure in my husband's parenting that that made me feel safe and good about going back. Once I got past the first week, I was back into things and getting so much value from my career that *that* made me feel good. So I was feeling good about my career, and I was feeling good when I was with my kids, and that was making me happy."

A my and Jess both benefited, career-wise, from having opt-out partners who supported them on the home front and who cheered them on at work. Both were married to men who had careers but, once children arrived, ended up the primary caregiver. All the career ambition went to Amy and Jess. But for some of our friends, the state of career ambition wasn't a constant, inhabiting only a single person in the relationship for the duration. Ambition is fluid, moving across partners and coalescing in different ways over a lifetime.

The Ambition Switchers

Ellen grew up in Westchester, New York, and studied music at Juilliard in high school. She was disappointed when she didn't earn a slot in the music school at Northwestern, but quickly discovered a whole host of other interests she could pursue. She became a history major, took creative writing classes, joined the marching band, and earned a women's studies certificate. One of the women Ellen bonded with during sorority rush would serve as a lifelong role model: Both women were studying Hebrew in college, and the older woman was teaching Hebrew at the local synagogue and encouraged Ellen to teach, too. So when the older woman applied to rabbinical school Ellen's junior year, Ellen was surprised to find herself pondering that option as well.

"I had never, ever considered that," Ellen told us, in part because she couldn't identify with any of the female rabbis she had met. "The only women I'd ever seen who were rabbis were really socially awkward, they wore pastel suits and didn't feel fun or interesting. Now I realize that they were pioneers and they were two or three in a class of thirty men, but it wasn't a really attractive model to me." Her friend showed her a new model. "She did it and it made me think, 'If she's interested, maybe that would be good for me, too.'"

Upon graduation from Northwestern, Ellen spent ten months doing an intensive study course in Israel called an *ulpan*. When she returned home to New York, she applied to rabbinical school. She spent the first year of the program back in Israel, then the remaining four years in New York City, studying and teaching at a synagogue in New Jersey. "If you had asked me in high school, and even in college, if I would've thought I'd be a rabbi, I probably would have just laughed. I did take Hebrew and do all these Jewish studies classes that were interesting, but I don't feel like my Jewish identity was particularly strong in college. It was a time in my life that I got to explore all the other parts of who I was, and then came back to the importance of Judaism on my own terms."

Ellen spent her twenties in New York City as a single rabbinical student—a status her parents worried about. "No one's going to want to marry a rabbi," they told her. "What kind of man wants to be with a woman who is in charge in that kind of way in public?" For anyone who has ever met Ellen, the idea that someone would be put off by her having a large-and-in-charge career is pretty funny, given that she's the kind of person who lets you know, five minutes into meeting her, that she's filled with opinions and insights and ideas. Being a rabbi wasn't going to make her any more or less the person she already was. And Ellen wasn't worried. She quickly discovered that her unusual career choice helped sift out potential mates more efficiently. "In some ways, it was a litmus test. If someone was like, 'Oh, that's weird,' I figured, 'Okay, you're not for me.' But plenty of men were interested enough without just discounting me out of hand for having that kind of job."

Ellen met her future husband through her graduate school community. He was a fellow student at the seminary, but at the Los Angeles campus, studying nonprofit management. They met in Miami at a mutual friend's wedding, where they were placed together at the singles table. They hit it off and began exchanging emails, which led to visits back and forth for nine months, until he moved to New York City to pursue the relationship more seriously. He got a job in fund-raising for a Jewish organization in New York, and shortly after Ellen was ordained as a rabbi, they married. She took a job as the junior rabbi at a synagogue in New Jersey and her husband continued to work in fund-raising in Manhattan; they moved to the suburbs and eventually had three children.

Ellen loved her job, the congregation, the community. Her work was satisfying, and as the junior rabbi, her hours and responsibilities were less demanding than the senior rabbi's. After more than a decade in the job, she had been at it so long that the work was like muscle memory—still meaningful and satisfying, but not particularly taxing, which left her with enough physical and emotional hours to enjoy her time with her small children at home. "Even though I might not have been super challenged at work anymore, it's a balance. I was more or less perfectly challenged in just keeping my own family moving." The trade-off worked for her at the time.

Ellen's husband, meanwhile, had risen in his career as a development director for a national nonprofit. Ellen was proud of her husband's work as a "do-gooder" and was happy to strategize with him about what his next moves might be. "For a long time, we talked about his career being the one"—the one to be fostered and prioritized. "What he needed to do, or the choices he was going to make really took the front. I was secure and comfortable in my position because we had little kids, and I didn't feel ready to do more than I was already doing."

But as her youngest child grew into toddlerhood and beyond, Ellen felt her professional ambition tugging at her. As jobs do, hers continued growing and shifting, but not in the directions she really wanted. The job's structure offered Ellen time at home, which she welcomed, but also more administrative responsibility. "I was becoming increasingly dissatisfied with my job. I found myself running the institution and not getting to do the more creative, fun pieces, whether it was teaching or leading worship or using my music. I just was in my office, organizing people and making things happen. And I realized I wanted to be making things happen for me, not just making things happen for other people." Plus, raising three children in a New Jersey suburb doesn't come cheap—she and her husband knew they wanted to be able to afford vacations as a family of five, and to be able to send their kids to sleepaway camp someday. Camp was something Ellen and her husband had bonded over. It was important to both of their identities, but it came with a big price tag, and she wasn't ever going to get a significant salary increase at her current job.

Meanwhile, Ellen's husband continued working in fund-raising, where he had moved into development for Jewish camps. He enjoyed the work, but, with a career in nonprofit fund-raising, his salary wasn't expected to skyrocket anytime soon, either. He and Ellen had conversations about the direction of both their careers, and it became clear over time that he was content where he was. She was the one with career ambition.

"As it became more apparent to both of us that he didn't have a very specific driving passion about where he was going, we both realized that I was going to be the one to move on to a higher position. We came to an agreement that I was willing to do it and interested in doing it." Reflecting on their economic future, their ambitions as a couple, and her longer-term career goals, Ellen came to a decision: She wanted to be a senior rabbi.

At first Ellen just dabbled in a job search. The first year, she applied to one position and made it to the final round of interviews, but didn't get the job. The next year, she applied for more openings, made it a few rounds, but again wasn't the final pick. After that a more senior colleague who had been through the rabbinical job search before broke down the reality for her: "If you want to achieve a senior rabbi position, you've got to commit."

The following year, Ellen took her colleague's advice, and committed. She applied to seven different synagogues, a process that she says was like taking on a second full-time job in addition to her existing work and parental obligations. She put together a vision statement and traveled the country for interviews. And that year, she got an offer to be the senior rabbi for a congregation of nearly one thousand families in Cleveland. Two years ago, after close to two decades at her previous synagogue, Ellen accepted the position and moved her family to Ohio. Ellen's husband found a job as a development director at another Jewish camp, a job that gives him greater flexibility to be the primary caregiver at home, as Ellen's schedule demands that she often work nights and weekends.

Ellen and her husband have always both worked full-time, but their roles at home have shifted since their move. "I was the one who would leave to take the kids to the dentist or schedule my calendar so I could take the kids to the doctor. If the babysitter was sick, I would work from home and he would go into the city. Now we really have to flip that role." The couple clearly defined that shift, and while it hasn't always been seamless, it's working for them. "We said, 'If we're going to do this, you're going to have to be the one to pick up the slack at home,'" Ellen told us. "We knew straight out—it was articulated. It was not a surprise."

The flip in roles was not without some marital strife. At first, Ellen couldn't grasp why her husband didn't run the household the way she did. "I'd come home and be like, 'I don't understand. The dishes haven't been done. The laundry isn't sorted. I don't want to come home at eight at night and start putting the house back together.' He's like, 'I'm working. I got the kids where they needed to be. They got dinner. They're bathed, whatever. Cut me some slack.'"

Ellen worked to shift her expectations and embrace what a household run by someone other than herself could look like, and she and her husband also agreed that they needed more outside support. They decided to pay for more hours of babysitting, and hired someone to help clean the house and grocery shop regularly. "If he needs to be at work until six or seven, then the sitter is just going to be on her own. If he doesn't, then he's around and she's helping the kids with homework while he's getting dinner ready or vice versa." Or, to echo what others have said on the topic, they hired a part-time wife.

Ellen and her husband began their careers working in fields that they valued spiritually, morally, and intellectually. When they started a family, they seemed to share the same ambition level. Like Amy and her husband, they deliberately discussed their careers, their earning potential, and their individual and shared ambitions. When Ellen's husband, whose career had taken prominence in the first decades of their life together, was willing—in fact, happy—to have his career recede a bit, Ellen was empowered to front-burner hers. Ellen and her husband saw their ambition naturally shifting in their marriage, and then, after active conversations, Ellen made her career the driver. She's now the primary earner, and her job takes up a lot more time than her husband's. As her days and nights are more demanding, his are more forgiving—and it's a balance that works for them. "I have a husband who maybe can't buy me diamonds from Cartier, but he is incredibly supportive in terms of sharing the parental responsibilities and the house responsibility."

E arly on in her marriage, Ellen decided to allocate most of the career ambition to her husband so she could spend more time with her children and be the primary caregiver. It was only after they'd both been working for over a decade, after her children had aged out of diapers and she had room to think about her own career ambitions and whether she was satisfied with her job, that Ellen could even begin to conceptualize a life where she, not her husband, was the partner with a big career. Ellen is not a wilting wallflower of a person. She pursued a career that positioned her at the heart of a community, the leader of a congregation. She found a trajectory that worked for her intellectually and spiritually, yet she slipped into the traditional gender role of supporting her husband's career over her own. Up until the point where she realized that maybe it was better for everyone if the roles were reversed.

We have other friends who swapped roles in their marriages, too, but in the opposite direction. That is, they were the primary wage earners until they reached a point where they sat down with their spouse and said, "I don't want to do this anymore." These couples then worked together to figure out how to manipulate their lives to make sure both partners had what they needed. Our friend Sarah, the VP-level corporate training executive who left her job after realizing on her Outer Banks vacation that she needed to spend her days engaged in more creative endeavors, was one-half of these couples. The other half, her husband, Keith, was open to taking on different roles in the family at different times. He stayed home with their son when the two agreed that Sarah should be the primary wage earner, and when she wanted to leave the company, he took on the job of supporting the family financially. Sarah and Keith have always seen their careers, ambition, and happiness as intertwined, one person's desires adjusting as needed to support the other's, even if it means a lifestyle change, a move, or a complete reconfiguring of their lives. "If I had said, 'Keith, I need to quit and go train people in peaceful resistance for ten cents an hour,' he would've been like, 'All right. Let me sit down with the finances and figure out how we're going to do that.'"

Ellen's career also benefited from the fact that her husband was open to conversations around shifting ambition and household roles, though we don't think his openness was happenstance. Ellen told us that one of the qualities she's always loved about her husband is that he is "a kind, social justice–y person who loves working with teens and is fun to be around."

While Ellen found his kindness and desire to help others appealing personality traits, she was probably not aware that these same traits are related to a characteristic that supports career success in a marriage: A spouse's level of "conscientiousness" is a strong indicator of future job satisfaction, raises, and promotions.[15] Why? Because more conscientious partners, whether male or female, are more likely to take on household tasks and give their spouse the hands-on support they need to succeed at work. In short: a conscientious spouse = more time = a greater chance at career success.

It stands to reason, then, that an indifferent, disengaged spouse leaves you with less time. Though it's decades old, Nora Ephron wrote in *Heartburn* about exactly this type of spouse: the spouse who asks, "Where's the butter?"[16]

> We all know where the butter is, don't we?
>   (A little smile)
>   The butter is in the refrigerator.
>   (Beat)
>   The butter is in the refrigerator in the little compartment in the door marked "Butter."
>   (Beat)
>   But [he] doesn't mean "Where's the butter?" He means "Get me the butter." He's too clever to say "Get me" so he says "Where's."

If you want to succeed in your career, marry someone who gets his own damn butter.

Reclaiming Ambition
Without the Support of Your Spouse

Our friends who don't have this type of support at home are sometimes able to scale their way into rock-star careers anyway, but the imbalance at home makes things harder for them. When the effort is one-sided—in the case of our friend Julie, who decided to launch herself back into a high-powered career after years of staying at home, without much initial championing from her husband—the transition is anything but smooth.

The Household Divide Is Still Not 50/50

Julie arrived at Northwestern from Miami and spent her four college years playing on the soccer team and completing a major in economics. As a deft team player with strong business sense, she imagined going into sales or a client-facing business early on. "I had some sales experience in high school, and I always knew I wanted to be working with people. I was driven in the sense that I liked to work toward something. Here's the goal, you accomplish it, and you make money as a result—that really is what made me tick."

After graduation Julie entered a three-year training program for financial advising for a major investment bank. The program was "pretty intense," and a perfect match for her competitive streak. "I had to obtain a certain number of clients, do lots of training in New York. I ended up falling in love with the business." She also ended up falling in love with a colleague she met on the first day of the program, and the two married in their mid-twenties.

Julie's husband entered into the management track and was offered a big job in Miami—at that point, the couple decided to prioritize his career over hers, though Julie stayed with the bank and transferred her clients to Miami. The couple also began discussing their plans to start a family—they agreed they wanted to have children early and both jump back onto the career track. But, like many of our friends, they didn't quite have a picture of what that would look like.

"He met me in a very intense, career-driven moment," Julie explained. "He knew that piece of me so he certainly wasn't expecting me to be a stay-at-home mom, but we did talk about our long-term plan, and we both knew he was on this management trajectory." Both of their careers were thriving, they loved living in Miami, and Julie thought they would be there for a while, raise children where she had been raised, maybe. Then Julie's husband was offered another job, in Dallas. And like Ellen, Julie didn't think twice about prioritizing her husband's career ambition over her own. After all, the move made sense.

"We wanted to start a family, and living in Miami is expensive. We thought, 'Maybe it's time that I do something different so he can launch his career.'"

The couple moved to Dallas. Julie left the bank for a private financial-advising firm, working with high-net-worth clients, which turned out to suit her perfectly. "It was much less stressful because I didn't have to develop my own clients. It was a nine-to-five job and, in hindsight, really a dream job, sitting in the corner office having people just walk in." Julie coasted in the corner office, making good money, with civilized hours, for nearly two years. Then she got pregnant with their first child and gave birth on September 11, 2001.

Delivering her daughter on that day was a "really, really crazy experience. My whole plan was to go back to work and do this job that was not that difficult, but where I was making lots of money, but [having a child on 9/11] changed me. I thought I was going to go back after three months, but my manager said I needed another month." After four and a half months of maternity leave, Julie found herself still emotionally raw, fearful of leaving her daughter in day care.

"I was having a hard time with the fact that I wasn't going to see her all day, and that was really confusing to me because I didn't think I'd have those emotions. I think I was just dragging out the decision because it was a hard one, but I really didn't have any interest in going back to work at that point. For some reason, I wasn't that concerned about giving it up in the moment. In hindsight, it seems crazy, but given where my emotions were at the time, it made sense." Financially, Julie and her husband could make it work on his salary, so she quit her job, a decision that "shocked everyone who knew me."

When their baby was a year old, and Julie was pregnant with their second child, the family moved again for her husband's job, this time to Minneapolis. At home with two small children, away from her family, in a place where she knew no one, in a role she never thought she'd inhabit, Julie found herself becoming depressed. And yet she stuck it out for the sake of her kids and her husband.

"I continued to stay home, supporting my husband, supporting the family, getting the house set up. I didn't feel that I had a great social network because I'd lost all my work friends. Not having any family [nearby], any connections, being stuck in the house with the kids because of the weather was really, really challenging for me." Two years later the family, now with three small children, moved to Atlanta. In a new locale, Julie decided to do everything she could to get out of the house and meet people in the community, thinking that if she were more engaged, she'd feel more satisfied. Her attempts to forge friendships with other stay-at-home mothers didn't go very far, so she thought that broadening her network might help.

"I joined Junior League and a few other organizations, did a lot of volunteering with children and giving back. I was feeling . . . not depressed . . . but just like I didn't have a purpose. I wasn't feeling connected with the stay-at-home-mom community. Going to Gymboree every day and shopping and lunching was not satisfying at all." But Julie also knew that if she returned to work, she would have to make it worthwhile financially, since the couple now had three children. Day care would be expensive, not to mention the logistical burden it would place on a family that was used to having her on hand 24/7.

"My idea was, 'I've got to go big financially so I can afford the help. Otherwise I'm really going to be drowning, because I'm not only going to be tied to this eight-to-five job, I am literally going to be doing everything [at home] because we're not going to be able to afford help.'"

There were other family members besides her husband weighing in on her decision process. Julie's mother, who she describes as a free-spirited artist but also "very women's lib," had registered her surprise when Julie decided to stay home all those years. "'Are you sure?' she asked me."

Julie's mother-in-law, on the other hand, had raised five children as a stay-at-home mother, and Julie felt pressure from her not to go back to work. "You guys don't need it financially," her mother-in-law told her. "You really should sacrifice. The career's not that important." And even though Julie had been clear about her career ambitions when she met her husband, she knew that he had enjoyed having a mother who stayed at home, and that he had benefited from Julie's decision to leave her job. "He grew up in a home that was always put together, dinner was on the table, supporting the family was really what you do."

But Julie had her eye on what would make her happy, and she knew innately that one of those things was feeling productive at a job outside the home. Once they were settled in Atlanta, Julie started examining her options. At a professional seminar, she met a CPA who encouraged her to enter the field. It was flexible, entrepreneurial, and potentially lucrative. She began pursuing a master's degree in accounting as her first transition back into the workforce after six-plus years out. Her courses took about eighteen months, "a necessary transition because it got my mind thinking again. I was feeling engaged, I was on this campus with young people. I felt alive again." But she also realized that a career in accounting didn't feel dynamic enough for her.

And then the financial crisis hit. Though her husband had thrived thus far in finance, he and Julie watched as, all around them, people they knew were laid off. Julie panicked. Her husband was suddenly in danger of losing his job, they had three kids and a mortgage, and Julie felt helpless.

"That's what really triggered me to say, 'I'm going to contribute.'" Julie dropped the accounting program, updated her résumé with some of her volunteer work, and walked into the local office of a national private bank. She'd been applying online to a position there, but had received a series of form rejections because her adviser's license had expired. She knew that if she could just get past the gatekeeper, she'd have a shot at landing the job. What happened next reads like the script of a screwball work-life comedy starring Reese Witherspoon: "I snuck into the building. I met the head receptionist and built a relationship with her and I said, 'Give the hiring manager my résumé, he'd be crazy not to hire me.' I got a call two days later. They flew me to Chicago, and they said, 'For some reason we think you can do this,' and I had a job."

Eight years later, Julie sparkles when she talks about her job, buoyant that she's grown her team into a full-service financial investment boutique—she is the only woman at her rank in her region, and leads the bank's statewide women's initiative. Julie made the jump back into a thriving career beautifully. But the transition at home, after eight years as a stay-at-home mom and supporter of her husband's career, has been a little rockier.

"My husband had gotten used to having, essentially, a personal assistant to enable him to grow and develop. The minute that was taken away—because I now had a job and I couldn't cater to everything the family needed—it was a shock to him. The kids were fine, but this rocked his world. Even though I was bringing in money and it was helping the family, he just could not get his arms around the fact that he didn't have someone picking up dry cleaning and making dinner. I did it all. He really didn't have to do anything, and that helped him grow significantly in his career. He has a huge job and he didn't have any of those responsibilities."

Julie also found herself feeling guilty about going back to work, because once the financial crisis passed, the family didn't need her income. If she wasn't working to provide financial support, then what was she doing? "I almost felt that the job was selfish, like, 'Well, I want to do this for me.'"

The adjustment period went on for a while, as Julie and her family tried to navigate the complexities of a two-career family. "I was just trying to keep status quo in the family, but I was drowning the first two years, adjusting to the job because it was a huge position, and adjusting to the kids not having me home, then adjusting to [her husband] just being frustrated." Rather than sound resentful, though, Julie seemed to feel bad that she had abandoned her husband domestically—but at the same time, she simply couldn't give up the job she had so boldly earned and now dearly loved. She worked to make the transition less abrupt.

"His world was turned upside down, and I felt like he needed more time. I was just trying to slowly get him adjusted and give him concrete tasks, not all of a sudden it's fifty-fifty." The stress occasionally had Julie questioning her decision, especially when her husband would ask, "I don't know if this is working. How are we going to do this?" But even though it made his life more complex, Julie's husband saw how much happier she was to be back at work. "I think he knew, 'There's no way I'm taking this away from her. I'm not even going to suggest it.' He's been my biggest fan, for sure. He's my biggest promoter. It's wonderful. Inside the home we have our frustrations, but he knows this is what makes me tick. He remembers those years when I was at home and just not myself."

Over the years, the domestic divide has evolved, thanks to a lot of conversations initiated by Julie. "He understands that we have two careers and the only way it's going to work is if he helps out. He doesn't want to lose what we've built, and financially it's been tremendous, so he also doesn't want that to go away." But even so, Julie admits, the bulk of the child-raising and household tasks—and all of the emotional labor—still fall to her.

"He knows I'm going to handle things, and if I need his help, he knows how to help, but he doesn't drive it. In one conversation I said, 'I need you to own more things. Not help.' Maybe it's owning all the dry cleaning, or owning the homework, or owning going to parent-teacher conferences. Right now, it's more me managing the family and then he fills in." But

Julie is proud of the progress she and her husband have made over the years, and determined—did we mention she is determined?—to keep working on evening out the divide.

E ven though Julie is thrilled with her career, and relished telling us the story of how she managed to make it happen, there's no doubt that things are harder on her than they are on our friends who have spouses who do more than just "help" at home, who prioritize their wives' careers as equal to or above their own, and who have open, ongoing conversations about where the bulk of the career ambition should reside. It's not a coincidence that many of our friends who have opted out list all the things that happened to Julie as reasons they can't imagine going back to work. They support their husbands' careers, their husbands wouldn't be as successful as they are without a wife at home, the house is put together, the kids don't run out of clean underwear, dinners appear on the table like clockwork, school trips are chaperoned, vacations are planned, tuba lessons are scheduled. As one friend who has been at home with her kids for ten years told us, as she considers returning to an office, "I don't know how I would do it. [Her husband] works a lot of long hours and he travels, so most of the running the home and the kids is on me. Even the shoveling in snowstorms and stuff like that, it's me, it's not him. It has definitely allowed him to focus on his career."

The answer is, making it work depends on who you're married to.

Making Joint Decisions About Career

Some couples in our interview group worked out their careers together, as though they had recognized the symbiotic relationship between their career tracks from the beginning. We don't believe they did this consciously—when they met and fell in love, they didn't then sit down and draw out a map of who would do what when, who would earn how much money, and who would leave work early to pick up future children. But now partnered and with children, and well into their careers, these couples do seem to have ongoing conversations in which both careers are considered equally important. They check in with each other often on whether each person is working enough or too much, or spending the right amount of time with the kids, and they both seem to have a say in the other's career choices. For these couples, one career could not exist without the other, from both a financial standpoint and in terms of work-life balance. These couples are in agreement on how much they want (or don't want) their careers to dominate their lives, how much time they want to share with their children, and, for many, how to balance a livable salary with the need to do meaningful work. For these couples, the ambition seems to be spread evenly across two careers. Neither member of the couple is shooting for the stars right now—they're happy to be working in jobs they enjoy, being able to pay the bills, and making it through the daily parenting grind—but they're also open to the possibility that at some point down the road, one person's career might take off.

The Two Flex Lifers

If you'd asked us back in college what we thought Melissa might be doing twenty-five years later, we would probably have said she'd be a lawyer working on behalf of women's rights. Which is exactly what she's doing. "College was the first time that I saw any house on fire. The house that was on fire for me was all the women getting sexually assaulted and raped on campus." Melissa felt driven to get involved in countering violence against women. She took two forty-hour training programs, one with a local rape crisis center and another on campus sponsored by the university, to become certified as a sexual assault crisis counselor, and then began volunteering with both organizations. "Sexual violence had become my preoccupation by my junior year of college," she explained. For the off-campus organization, she began doing court liaison work with sexual assault victims, and decided she wanted to prosecute sex crimes.

After graduation Melissa enrolled in law school, and while she quickly discovered litigation wasn't for her, she found a robust subcommunity of like-minded students interested in social justice work. After finishing law school, she made her way to Asheville, North Carolina, where she landed an associate job at a nonprofit. She was enjoying her work, but didn't know many people in town, and found herself spending her evenings and weekends watching and rewatching old movies. So when a friend offered to set her up with his old college friend Rich, she agreed.

The blind-date setup was a good one. Melissa and Rich hit it off. Like Melissa, Rich was conscientious about social issues, a nonconformist free spirit. "When I met Rich, he thought he wanted to go into forestry. He was driving a cab and smoking a bunch of dope. When we started falling in love, it got to the point where I was like, 'I love you but I'm probably not going to live in a forest.'" Rich was still trying to figure out a career direction when Melissa started her legal advocacy career. He knew he loved literature and had held jobs in independent bookstores and for small publishers, but his more permanent trajectory was uncertain. A couple of years after meeting, Melissa and Rich married. When Melissa was offered a bigger job at a legal nonprofit in Raleigh, a few hours away, she accepted, and the couple moved. Still loving literature and learning, but uncertain how to channel that into a career, Rich decided to pursue a master's degree in library and information sciences. Though her wages were nonprofit low, Melissa supported them both while Rich was in graduate school.

Once Rich graduated, he found a decided lack of library jobs out in the world. Melissa and Rich began strategizing "to figure out, what does somebody with a master's of library and information sciences do?" Melissa was ready to stop being the sole wage earner, so she encouraged him to broaden his search to the corporate world. Also driving that was Melissa's mother, who "put pressure on [Rich] to conform to more of his . . .

gendered role in society and in the family," aka to get a job that could support his family. Soon after, Rich took a job at a large publishing company as an information architect, a field that was growing, and that paid well enough. Between their two salaries, they felt financially secure.

Melissa's and Rich's individual financial contributions to the household were on a more even playing field now, and a few years later, their first child was born, and shortly thereafter, their second. When their children were babies, Rich briefly floated the concept of becoming a stay-at-home father, but Melissa nixed the idea. She had fought her entire life for gender parity in her relationships, had become a successful legal director at a nonprofit anchored in dismantling the poisonous tree of the patriarchy, but having sole financial responsibility for supporting her family was not the parity she had envisioned. "I was like, 'No way. That's not fair. I want to be able to hang out with my kids. I don't want to have to be the breadwinner all the time.'"

Melissa and Rich are both Flex Lifers. They have stayed at their jobs for more than a decade (Melissa for nearly two) because they value their time together as a family as much as, if not more than, their career advancement. They each considered channeling more of their ambition into their careers to take them to the next level, but neither of them has—that's a strategy that they consciously discussed—because they don't feel they can devote more time to work and still be the kind of parents they want to be. They haven't prioritized Rich's career over Melissa's purely because he's a man, and Melissa hasn't been the one to scale back further because she's the mother; they have kept their professional lives equally static and manageable to meet the communal needs of their family.

"I can't say that I picked the nonprofit sector because I wanted the work-life balance for raising kids. I picked it because I wanted to do social justice work. Likewise, he's working corporate because he feels pressure to make more money than you would working at a bookstore."

Melissa and Rich talk about what they envision for their future, when their children are older—they seem to actively discuss and shape their life as they see it. They assume they'll both have to work until traditional retirement age to meet their financial needs. Rich would like to get into consulting and gain more professional independence, and Melissa envisions becoming more intensely involved in her work once her children are older, in part to compensate her company and the world at large for the scaled-back lifestyle she has today. "I'm going to be putting in really, really long days. I think that's just what the universe has in store: me paying back the universe."

In the meantime, they divide their ambition equally between them, both working at careers that meet enough of their intellectual needs to keep them interested and financially stable, while also leaving time for Melissa to meet the school bus a few days a week and take long weekend trail runs, for Rich to bake whole-grain bread and homemade cake for the kids' lunches, and for the family to enjoy a home-cooked dinner together most nights.

Melissa and Rich were one of a handful of couples in which neither partner was interested in shooting the moon with their careers, which meant that both were available to take care of the children and run the household. This led to a more egalitarian split of household and child-raising duties for these couples. Another friend, Laurel, and her husband are both attorneys who chose to take themselves off the partner track in favor of less stressful, more flexible jobs. They, too, have a fairly even split, even though Laurel cited "luck" as a factor in her marital arrangement rather than the more likely cause—that she actively sought a partner who wanted a marriage with an equitable divide of responsibilities across spouses.

"I am very fortunate that my husband is a full equal partner. We both work. We aren't in a relationship where one spouse is the primary earner and one isn't. For us, we're both equal in our careers and equal at home. If I stayed at home, I would expect to do more, or if he stayed at home, he would expect to do more. It has to be a partnership, and it really is. He is very involved and probably cleans the house more than I do. He's neater than I am. He cooks more than I do. I'm really bad at that stuff. It's not my strong suit, but I'm okay with that."

As with Melissa and Rich, Laurel and her husband played active roles in shaping each other's careers, in saying, "You do X and then I'll do Y." They looked at their careers as a joint effort, along with child-raising and running a household, and saw those three elements as inextricably linked, ever-changing, and always open to negotiation and reconfiguration.

What we've learned from our friends' stories is that marriages are living, shifting organisms that require constant give and take around the concepts of ambition and work success. One person's career does not magically take off without the help of their partner. Our friends with big career ambitions and minimal support on the home front had a harder road than those married to spouses who were willing, or actively wanted, to scale back their careers.

For our friends, Sheryl Sandberg's advice is accurate: The most important career decision you make is whom to marry. Not because you need a pat on the back and someone to tell you that you did a good job at work today (although we welcome those gestures), but because a marriage can only sustain so much ambition. And how that ambition gets divided, and adjusted over time, is a conversation that depends entirely on who the spouses are in any given marriage.

The good news is that our friends who are in marriages that involve ongoing communication around the distribution of ambition, and especially those where career ambition and roles are considered equal and fluid, may be part of a growing trend. Today, only one-third of men and women want marriages in the traditional mold, with men as breadwinners and women as primary caregivers.[17] That number has dropped precipitously since the '70s, when 74 percent of men and 52 percent of women believed men should work and women should stay home. Perhaps more significantly, men's and women's attitudes have converged. Whereas many more '70s-era men were in favor of this arrangement than women, today men and women agree in equal numbers on what a marriage should look like. There are other subtle indicators that a shift is under way. Men notoriously overreport the amount of housework or childcare they do,[18] but as Stephanie Coontz points out in *Marriage, a History*, in the '50s, men used to underreport it or risk being seen as doing "women's work."[19] With all these changes afoot, it's possible, maybe even hopeful, that we'll see more and more couples for whom the norm is an even playing field where everything—work, housekeeping, childcare, and ambition—is on the table.

Here's What We Know About Marriage

▶ **If you're a High Achiever, marrying a Flex Lifer or Opt Outer could make your life easier.**

Certainly, power couples exist—possibly more so in places like New York City or the Bay Area, where the cost of living is high and most people arrive with outsize goals and the determination to achieve those goals—but for our friends with children, being part of a power couple wasn't the norm. Simply knowing that other configurations exist within marriages opens up a whole different way of thinking about partnership. If you're a High Achiever type, you may have always dreamed of meeting someone equally brilliant and ambitious— maybe even a smidge more brilliant or ambitious—but the reality is that life for our High Achievers who are not part of a power couple is a lot simpler and calmer than that of the rare high-achieving duo.

▶ **Ambition is something fluid that can be shared between spouses.**

Our friends who recognize the intertwined nature of their careers seem to have more ebb and flow, and possibly more balance, than our friends who behave as though their career functions on an entirely separate plane from their spouse's. The reality is that in a two-career family, career prioritization can be a daily conversation. Who gets to take the business trip and who stays home so the kids don't burn the house down/starve? Who cancels a meeting when the school calls to say your kid threw up all over the kindergarten classroom and needs to be picked up immediately? Who waits at home for the exterminator and who goes into the office? If all those responsibilities fall to the same person, has that been clearly articulated?

> ▶ **You will not magically marry a man with an ideological commitment to gender equality (and if you marry a woman, you'll likely start out in a better place on that front).**

Our friends Sarah, Ellen, Melissa, and others didn't just happen to meet men who were born thinking about feminism and angry about the failed passage of the Equal Rights Amendment. (In truth, since we haven't met most of their spouses, we can't say that with 100 percent certainty, but we feel it's a good guess.) Instead, what these women have in common is that, as they told us their stories, they presented their own career trajectories, and by extension their needs and wants, as important, serious, and valuable. When Melissa told her husband she wouldn't marry him if he continued pursuing his forestry degree, it was because she knew herself and what she needed to be happy. Similarly, Sarah and Ellen had conversations with their spouses where they laid out what they wanted and what they thought would make them happy. The women who were in equitable relationships didn't land there by accident. They explicitly told their spouses what they needed, and they pushed back when the plan their spouse had didn't work for them. Ultimately, *they* took their own career ambitions seriously and demanded their husbands did, too. Our friends in same-sex marriages benefited from starting with a blank slate when it came to deciding who would do what. Without traditional gender roles to fall back on, each spouse thought deeply about the tasks she wanted to take on and what she wanted her career to look like. These couples tended to struggle less with whose career would take priority, or how the childcare or housework would be taken care of, probably because they weren't overcoming any ingrained assumptions based strictly on gender. Instead, these women told us they adopted the tasks they liked, that they were good at, or that were simply more convenient or logistically smart for them than for their partner. For these women, career-marriage balance was something they worked out individually within their partnerships.

▶ **Shifting roles within a marriage isn't always easy, but it's not impossible.**

The way your household is divided today is not the way it has to be until the end of time. Even if you've been married for more than a decade, and even if your spouse hasn't been an equal partner at home, change is possible. But you will probably have to demand it. Our friends Audrey (the government lawyer) and Julie told their spouses they needed more than just assistance at home. They needed their husbands to own specific domestic and child-rearing responsibilities. They didn't want someone who would "help" with the kids—they wanted a co-parent. Even if the balance didn't become 50/50 right away, or ever, for these two women, the burden did shift significantly—and the conversation around who was responsible for what became a regular, ongoing one.

▶ **A super-egalitarian husband is likely to help your career, but he probably isn't going to do domestic chores or child-related tasks the way you think they should be done. Learn to be okay with that.**

Several of our High Achievers are married to husbands who either stay at home or who had less career ambition and so naturally became the partner who could be home more. Despite traditional expectations, our friends were comfortable being more ambitious, sometimes absent from family events, and the higher wage earner. They all credited their husbands' support at home among the factors that allowed their careers to soar. But they also all griped a little about the way their spouse washed pots, or oversaw homework, or prepared or served meals. Everyone we interviewed seemed to be certain that domestic work should be done a particular way. But instead of micromanaging their spouse, they all actively worked on accepting their spouse's way of doing things. Letting go of that urge to control all the domestic duties freed up time for them to focus on their careers. There are many ways to set up work, life, and marriage. There are also many ways to load the dishwasher, pack lunches, and help with science fair projects. Being open to the varying ways different human beings can accomplish the same jobs is essential to setting yourself up for career success.

CHAPTER 4

PARENTING

For this group of women, the contrast between the parents we are and the way we were parented back in the '70s (when *parenting* was not yet a verb, but simply the thing one did to keep one's children alive through age eighteen) is the stuff of Internet memes. Our '70s and '80s childhoods were filled with hours spent unattended, often alone, after school (instead of at planned, paid-for, chaperoned, STEM-friendly activities), interrupted by seatbelt-free car rides in the back of the station wagon, recess on playgrounds made of asphalt dotted with scorching-hot metal slides, lunches consisting of processed meats on white bread and Capri Sun. Children went places on their own (one of us used to hike over a mile through the woods after school to get to the library; the other was a latchkey kid on and off from the age of nine). Our own kids' childhoods seem more like performance art, the phenomena of childhood and growing up now fetishized and curated by families of a certain socioeconomic class.

All the places where parenting has evolved into a hyperstrategized act—from what goes into a school lunchbox to which of the ridiculous number of extracurricular activities a kid is signed up for—require an increment of time that used to be devoted to something else now consumed by parenting. It is no longer enough to register one's child for the local day camp. Today's parents must choose between science camp, wilderness resilience camp, coding camp, girl-power-magazine-making camp, put-on-a-full-scale-musical-in-two-weeks camp, Harry Potter camp (not to be confused with Percy Jackson camp), and on and on. After-school activities are no longer "Go outside and don't come back until dinner." Instead kids are on traveling sports teams starting at eight years old, with long practices and weekends eclipsed by games; they are scheduled not just to play board games but to develop their own games and learn game design. Between the two of us, our children's activities *last year alone* included ice skating, chess, skateboarding, soccer, gymnastics, tae kwon do, hip-hop, cooking, two rock bands, lacrosse, and saxophone. Here's what we ourselves did for after-school activities over the course of *all* of elementary school: swim team, one year of softball, gymnastics, a few months of piano, one season of ballet, and three weeks of calligraphy class.

To further complicate matters, children are no longer assumed to be able to get themselves from place to place alone. As a result of highly publicized abductions starting in the '70s and up through the present day, many parents are loath to allow their children to walk even a few blocks to school. Parents who breach social norms and allow their kids to travel unescorted risk not just sneering looks from other parents, but legal intervention. In 2014, a mother who let her nine-year-old play in a park alone near the mother's work was arrested for child endangerment.[1] A "free-range" parenting couple who let their ten- and six-year-olds walk alone in their neighborhood had their children picked up by the police and taken to Child Protective Services.[2] And when free-range-parenting blogger Lenore Skenazy wrote about why she allowed her nine-year-old son to ride the subway by himself in Manhattan (armed with a subway map, quarters, a MetroCard, $20, and instructions on how to travel all of two stops before switching to a crosstown bus), she was called "America's worst mom" on national television.[3] We've cultivated a landscape where parents are expected not only to spend time planning activities during which their offspring will be hovered over by multiple adults in a culturally appropriate setting, but also to figure out ways to get them to these activities that don't include sending them down the block unescorted.

This shift in what parenting means predates our generation's entry into motherhood—we've been caught up in a parenting frenzy that has been building since at least 1996, when sociologist Sharon Hays coined the phrase "intensive mothering" to describe what she saw women around her doing when they enrolled their kids in one class after another.[4] Since then, much has been written about the causes behind this shift. In *Perfect Madness*, Judith Warner traces the rise of anxiety as a dominant parenting force.[5] Starting in the mid-'80s, the media seemed to relish running one terrifying story after another aimed at making working mothers feel bad for not being home with their kids. Highly publicized day care abuse scandals and expert opinions on the dangers of group care ran constantly in newspapers and TV reports.[6] Hollywood was more than happy to indulge in mommy-horror with films like *The Hand That Rocks the Cradle*, which came out the year before we graduated from college and left the distinct impression that mothers who handed their children off to caregivers got what they deserved. This rise in hysteria around caregiving ran parallel to women entering the workforce in growing numbers. Women started heading to work in the '50s, in large part to meet the needs of a growing economy. As the decades wore on, more and more women (and, thus, more mothers) went to work—a social change that happened faster than society could process it. In other words, society freaked out about who was watching the kids. Would they be okay without their mothers? This anxiety solidified into a new way of thinking about motherhood. Warner explains, "The result was that by the 1990s, when 73 percent of mothers with children over age one were working . . . certain beliefs— that mothers' work was bad, that separation was agony, and that children needed full-time mother care—no longer sounded like mere worries or opinions. They were articles of faith."[7]

In the decade since *Perfect Madness* was published, this rising tide of anxiety has become more like a tsunami. In Jennifer Senior's 2014 book, *All Joy and No Fun*, she describes how parents engage in "concerted cultivation," a term coined by sociologist Annette Lareau, in order to develop their offspring into not just functional but excelling members of society.

Hyperparenting, Senior says, "reflects a new sense of confusion and anxiety about the future." Attempting to make their children as perfect as possible, middle-class parents are simply doing their best to arm them for the uncertainties that lie ahead.[8] But that drive toward perfection requires a significant number of human hours—and to what end? Is this cultivation actually making our children happier or more successful—and what defines success for an eight-year-old, anyway? Or are these efforts more a totemic display of our children as our own best accomplishments?

That competitive, helicopter parenting has become the norm among middle-class families, that we are out-parenting each other year after year with academic achievements, leisure activities, and even meals, explains the degree to which our friends simply accept this paradigm as what it is to be a parent today. They rolled their eyes one minute at how over-the-top parenting has become, while telling us in the next that they make their child's lunches with homemade bread. "It's an interesting time to be a mother," observed one friend. "You feel an intense amount of pressure on how you parent, and it's really hard not to buy into that. It's like we're getting trophies for being parents, and it's just obnoxious."

Melissa, our nonprofit lawyer friend, deconstructed the time-consuming steps it takes to get her two kids through a single school day in a lengthy monologue that was one step away from a *Portlandia* sketch:

"My husband and I roll out of bed probably around five thirty to start rote tasks: take the dogs out, empty the dishwasher, start on the kids' school lunches. Lunches, lunches, lunches, lunches, all the time. You also have to make sure they have snacks because they have late lunches. Then you go back through the stuff you laid out. Is it library day or do they need their bike helmet? You make sure that you initialed where you needed to initial in their folders because the night before you were so tired that you don't trust the way you did it before you went to bed. You have to redo it when you're feeling sharper and you've had a cup of coffee. Then you've got the vitamins and glasses of juice waiting for them on the kitchen table when they wake up. I get in about forty-five minutes of work before I go pull their lazy, lazy selves out of bed. Then I talk to them constantly for the next forty-five minutes. I say, 'Get clothes on, I need socks on and shoes on. Have you had your breakfast? Did you drink your juice? Did you take your vitamins? Did you do this? Did you do that?' I'm getting dressed. Maybe I'm going to take a shower that morning, but maybe not. Then I take them out to the bus stop and put them on the bus, rush back for the last couple things I have to do before I leave the house, and make sure that I've shoved some food in a bag for me. Then I go to work, where I can rest."

Melissa fast-forwarded through her workday, on to four p.m., when her kids get off the bus from school: "Two days a week we have after-school care. Three days a week we don't, and they have karate and violin and guitar and blah, blah, blah. You get to dinnertime, where ideally you have made enough food over the weekend to supply you through the week. Often you're trying to scramble something together. God forbid, because it's not our demographic, we don't let ourselves do takeout or premade food. We're eating by seven o'clock. Then we're both yelling at them to get their pajamas on or finish up their homework or practice their musical instrument. By nine o'clock you are guiltily turning off the light because they're going to bed too late again. Then I usually end up going to sleep by ten o'clock and promise myself that I'll wake up by four thirty the next morning to do those things that I didn't do before I went to bed because I got sleepy. Sound familiar?"

Her refrain did sound familiar, and by the time she finished, we were exhausted, too. The most common sentiment we heard about parenting from our interviews with nearly forty mothers, mostly of young children, is that getting through each day is laborious—a labor of love, but a labor nonetheless. Our daily marathon to win at parenting, to be as present as we possibly can, consumes our time physically and emotionally. The myriad reasons that drive us all to participate in this maniacal marathon, sometimes as if on autopilot, aren't our primary focus here; rather, we are interested in how choosing to do so affected our friends' and our own overall work and life trajectories.

The Struggle for 50/50 Parenting

This expansion of parental duties would be less noteworthy if it were shared evenly between parents. But what we learned from our friends is that many mothers still bear the burden of what sociologist Arlie Russell Hochschild termed "the second shift." In her 1989 book of the same name (a mainstay of a popular sociology class at Northwestern), Hochschild chronicled her study of marriages in the '80s in which women worked a "second shift" of childcare and domestic work after their paid workday ended, totaling an entire extra month of work hours every year.[9]

Many of our friends describe being happily married and, in the early years of their relationships, appeared to be in what Hochschild labeled "egalitarian marriages," where both partners engaged in equal spheres of work and home life, and shared an equal power in the marriage. Once children arrived, though, the second shift reared its head—and vaulted the balance toward women doing the lion's share of the parenting work. The second shift is alive and well for our friends, thirty years after Hochschild's study. What has changed, though, is that many of our friends acknowledged not only that the second shift exists for them, but told us that they have *chosen* to take it on. And they provided what, on the surface, sound like perfectly logical explanations why.

Natalie, the TV reporter, described the breakdown of household and parenting duties in her two-career family: "I pretty much take care of all domestic things, whether it's figuring out what camp the kids go to, figuring out what they're going to have for lunch or dinner, figuring out who the babysitter is going to be if our nanny's off or if it's going to be me. Part of that is because I'm a planner and a control freak, and part of it is because my husband is really disorganized and doesn't always have the best judgment when it comes to domestic things. Also, I have the flexibility at work, and he just doesn't."

Like Natalie, many of our friends actively took on more of the parental responsibilities, rationalizing their decisions with thoroughly structured arguments: They like being present with their kids, they have more flexible jobs that allow them to shuttle kids to school or activities, they enjoy doing arts and crafts from scratch, and, most of all, they are "type A" and "control freaks"—they need parenting done their way, the right way, and can't relinquish any duties to their partner without risking that something will not be accomplished competently. Some women admitted that they'd allocated work to their spouses only to find it was done at a B level (or worse). The result was so unacceptable, the women took those tasks back into their own hands.

Our friend Audrey, the government lawyer, asked her husband to take their daughter to an ENT specialist for a consultation on taking her tonsils out. "It was one of those times where, 'I have done every appointment, you're taking her to this one.' What I learned from him through that appointment was so unsatisfying that I had to go get a second opinion elsewhere." She wasn't the only unforgiving taskmaster. For as long as our nonprofit lawyer friend Melissa has overseen her family's budget, she and her husband have been discussing having him take over the financial management. It still hasn't happened. For one thing, she explains, he wouldn't be "stellar" at it because he was an English major (though somehow she manages to do it despite her own degree in English), and, in order to retain her fifteen years' worth of institutional knowledge on their finances, she said, "We'd have to do a half-day continuing education course just to transition that job over." A third friend, a stay-at-home mother, is also unwilling to let her husband handle the finances or do home repairs, because she needs the control. "I am so type A, I don't know that I could let him pay the bills because I don't know that they would actually get done. He has his fortes, but that's not it. So I'm the one who ends up doing all those things."

In a widely shared essay published in the *New York Times* in 2015, Judith Shulevitz wrote about how mothers across all socioeconomic strata end up taking on the greater share of psychological parenting.[10] Shulevitz cites a number of studies showing that while men might take on an activity like coaching a sports team (a common occurrence among our friends' spouses), women do the bulk of the scheduling that makes the family run. They're the ones who find and book the after-school activities, figure out which academic enrichment classes a child needs and how to make those classes fit into an already overbooked schedule, are aware that their kids need socks, and know this year's shoe size and which winter coat to buy. In what became a running funny/not funny joke between the two of us, we asked every parent friend we interviewed which partner makes the pediatrician appointments. One hundred percent of the time, the friend smiled at us and said, "I do," regardless of whether she was a C-suite professional married to a stay-at-home dad, a Flex Lifer married to another Flex Lifer, or a stay-at-home mom. In the several two-mom families in our interview group, that task broke down along other lines, but in the heterosexual marriages, it didn't veer from this pattern even once.

If this phenomenon sounds familiar, it's because it is now called *emotional labor*, a term that women across the world have claimed to explain why they feel so drained all the time, why their brains never stop churning, and why they feel "fed up" with all the unpaid labor they are contributing to their marriages and families.[11] Being the emotional workhorse, the primary psychological parent, and the primary doer—even if you excel at it, even if you have chosen it—can be exhausting. This sometimes self-imposed role left a number of our friends feeling resentful, in a major crunch for time, and, yes, fed up. Yet many of them chose not to change a thing.

Part-Time Pediatrician, Full-Time Carpooler

Jill was a biology major at Northwestern and had always dreamed of becoming a doctor. "From the time I was a little kid, I loved my pediatrician and thought, 'This is what I'm going to do.'" She was accepted into a top medical school in the South and enrolled. Her college boyfriend became her long-distance boyfriend when he got a job in a different city. He moved to live with her for her last two years of medical school, they married when she graduated, and he applied to business school as she was being matched for her residency. They did the dance of trying to end up in business school and residency in the same city, which proved challenging, so he deferred business school for a year and got a job in the North Carolina city where she was assigned for residency. "He never really minded the fact that he had to change jobs in order to follow me around initially," Jill said. Early on in their relationship, Jill's husband seemed to prioritize her ambition at least as highly as his own. The following year he was admitted to a competitive business school in the same city, and when they finished residency and business school at the same time, they had the luxury of being able to choose their next city together.

While Jill and her husband wanted to have children on the earlier side, she wasn't ready while she was still in residency. "I was working eighty- to one-hundred-hour weeks. You're on call every third night, staying in the hospital, and in my mind it was just, no way." Even before they got serious about having kids, Jill had an idea of the kind of mom she hoped to be: "I wanted to be available and there for my kids." But she also knew she wanted to enjoy life unencumbered for a few years. "I didn't really feel the biological clock ticking. I wanted to work, I wanted to have fun, I wanted to travel and take vacations and not worry about having little ones in tow at that point." Right after she finished her residency, Jill got placed on a rotation in Africa. Her husband came with her and lived there— again relocating his life for her career—off the map, away from friends and family, for three months. When the rotation was completed, they both applied for jobs in a city in the Pacific Northwest. "We wanted to be in the mountains, preferably not too far from an ocean. Someplace where we could do a lot of hiking and camping and skiing." They were "blessed" to both get hired for the jobs they wanted, and they moved together to the city where they have lived for the past fifteen years.

When they first settled in the Pacific Northwest, started their jobs, and found a house, they felt "pretty ready to have kids," though Jill doesn't recall having a lot of conversations with her husband about how the division of labor would line up. She had their first son at thirty-two, hired a nanny, and went straight back to work full-time. "I had always thought, 'I worked so hard to get to this point in my life to become a doctor.' I didn't want to give that up." She continued at her pediatric clinic full-time for the next year and a half.

Jill loved seeing patients and the community of other physicians she became a part of, but managing the rest of life was a drain. "It was pretty crazy, because you'd have your weekends off and you'd be cleaning the house and doing the laundry and going grocery shopping . . . all those chores that you have to do, plus taking care of a really needy baby who didn't want to be put down, and we had a puppy at the time. It felt like we didn't have any time to do anything fun because we were doing all of our chores on the weekends." But then, as if the work-life balance deities had heard her SOS, she learned about a possible solution. One of her partners at work was about to have a baby. Their clinic offers job shares, in which two physicians split a full-time workload, with each doctor working two and a half days a week. The pregnant colleague presented the idea to Jill, and Jill grabbed it. "At that point, I was so overwhelmed with the work-family balance. It's probably the best decision I ever made, because it's the best of both worlds." She's enjoyed that hybrid of worlds for the past fourteen years. In that time, Jill and her husband had two more children. Her husband has also worked in various positions at the same large tech company for the past fifteen years. He briefly pondered scaling back his career, as Jill did. "When the kids were really little, he talked about wanting to work part-time and be home with the kids part of the time so that we didn't have to worry about childcare." But that path didn't seem as efficient for him, Jill explained, since he's in management. "He's got big teams of people that work under him. It's hard to advance in a career like that, to be a supervisor when you're not there all the time. It wasn't really realistic for him." Plus, Jill, who has always identified as the more primary parent, admits "he would have been miserable at home with the kids, especially when they were little. He's great with the kids now that they're older, but he had a harder time with them as babies and toddlers."

Their children are fourteen, eleven, and nine now, and life looks about like what one might expect for a working mom with three kids. On the days she doesn't work in the clinic, she'll "get up and get all the kids to school, take the dog for some exercise. Maybe go to the grocery store, maybe have a dentist or an eye doctor appointment. It just always seems like there's tons of stupid little errands to do. Maybe I have to run to the pet shop, or Target, or one of the kids needs something for a project for school, or some piece of furniture broke that I'm needing to get repaired, or I'm working on planning some kind of vacation. There's always this huge list. Then I pick the kids up from school, get them to activities, then come home and try to get some dinner, and then sometimes there's activities at night. Every day's a little bit different."

Jill's husband now works from home, so he arguably could have some flexibility in his schedule, but she still feels that the burden of child-rearing and life logistics falls on her. "He'll do specific things if I ask him, when he's available to do them, but it's up to me to organize everything and make everything happen. If one of the kids needs to be somewhere and neither of us can go, he's not going to find a ride. If the nanny cancels, he's not going to figure out who's watching the kids. All of those little details fall on me."

When Jill's son was accepted into a magnet middle school that required a half-hour commute, she and her husband discussed how they'd handle getting him to and from school. The two agreed that the school was a great fit for their son, and they'd both do what it took to make it work. But Jill says that "over the past two and a half years, he's driven that carpool twice, and I do it four times a week." She concedes that's partly because he's working during most of the carpool hours, but also that she doesn't demand he participate more in the school-commuter hell that is the reality of many parents today. Her husband goes up to his home office around eight a.m. and finishes work around four p.m. most days, she says. While the carpool has been difficult to fit into his schedule, Jill notes that her husband does find time to go to the gym regularly, something she'd love to do herself.

Jill told us that of the five primary priorities she feels a person needs to balance—work, spouse/family/friends, health, finances, and giving back—she was only doing two, three at best, at any given time. One of the biggest sacrifices has been her own personal physical fitness. "I was super athletic in college, and even afterwards for most of my adult life, but since having kids, it's been really hit or miss. There might be six months that I'm back in the pool and I'm swimming two or three times a week, or for a while I took up jogging. That worked really well because at the time we had a dog who needed a lot of exercise and I would go running with the dog, and two kids in a double stroller, but I made it work." But most of the time, Jill finds that there aren't enough hours in the day to accomplish everything that needs to happen to keep both her work and her family running, so exercise gets the ax. While all the other members of her family—including the dog—are able to work exercise or sports into their days, Jill is so busy making sure everyone else gets physical activity that she's left with no time for her own.

What Makes a Mother a Mother

We heard from so many of our friends about being overwhelmed, about something always getting the short shrift, about the vast stores of time and energy that emotional labor vacuums up, that we couldn't help but wonder why these women didn't do more to even the parenting burden and give themselves more time in their days. Was it really possible that so many of our friends were type A control freaks married to disorganized spouses who seemed unable to navigate their way out of a shoebox, despite the fact that these men seemed to be perfectly capable, organized, and functional at work? To what degree was this about men not doing enough or not doing things "the right way" versus women being unwilling to cede control?

While part of the parenting imbalance is surely related to the fact that some women resist asking their spouses to participate more, or that their spouses require asking in the first place, we also heard from women who need to be the primary doer at home even though their spouses are very involved in childcare and domestic duties. What we eventually came to understand was that these women *wanted* to be the one to sort out the intricacies of how their children's lives work. They wanted to take on the primary responsibility for their children's health and social engagements and emotional well-being. They wanted to own the emotional labor, be the hub of the family wheel. We heard this sentiment especially from mothers who work: They enjoy being involved in the minutiae of their children's lives, even if it made things more complicated in their lives overall.

Melissa, the nonprofit lawyer, acknowledged that she not only likes being in control, but also gains deep pleasure from making sure everything is just right for her children. As a working mother, the more control she has, the more she feels she is a hands-on parent despite her guilt over not being present for every single moment of her children's lives. "I want to be that involved and invested in my kids' lives. I like getting them on the bus every day. You feel that pull between, 'I really should be the one being in the office twice a week at least at seven a.m.,' but on the other hand, I love knowing that they've got everything they need to have in their backpacks. I love being able to see them in the morning and kiss them and tell them to have a good day and 'make sure you keep your hands to yourself and don't whistle during class.'" It's as if, by inhabiting the archetype of the perfect, present, nurturing mother during the hours she is home with her children, Melissa can assuage some of the ambivalence she feels about working full-time, even though she unequivocally enjoys her job and is gratified by the meaningful work she does.

"[As part of] that two-working-parent guilt, you find yourself over-compensating. My kids have homemade cake in their lunch and my husband makes bread. Their sandwiches are on homemade bread!" As many working parents struggle to feed even one or two healthy meals a day to their families, Melissa was going full Well+Good-meets-*Pioneer Woman* with breakfast, lunch, and dinner. "It's got to be a homemade dinner." She laughed, simultaneously mocking and doubling-down on her internal barometer of parenting perfection—while also clocking in every day to smash the patriarchy.

Ellen, the senior rabbi, also told us about bending over backward to prioritize her children as much as humanly possible while holding down a demanding job. Even though she's married to a man with a more flexible job than her own, and even though they have an explicit agreement that he will do more of the hands-on caregiving than she will, she is also willing to sacrifice her health and time to be there for her children. "There have been times that I've worked all day, gone to [a child's] concert at six p.m., and then my husband's taking the kids home and I've gotten back in my car and gone back to the synagogue for a meeting. If I can do it for them, I will. If it's an extra strain on me physically, so what? In ten or fifteen years, they're just not going to be around, or they're not going to care that much if I'm there or not. I think about it all the time, and I make decisions that aren't necessarily healthy for me as a person, but that are healthy for me as a mom and for my family."

In fact, the occasions when she wasn't able to be there leave her feeling guilty years later. She told us about a time when she was on the phone with her eight-year-old son while at Target buying Valentine's Day cards to distribute to his class. The store was lean on options because it was getting close to the holiday, she told him, so he announced he wanted to go with homemade cards instead. She quickly pivoted away from the card section and toward the arts and crafts section, making a mental list of the additional items needed for the project. "I bought some fluorescent poster board and we had glitter and metallic Sharpies, because of course we have metallic Sharpies at home, so we're set." What Ellen didn't have was the time to execute this project, so she delegated it to her babysitter, with clear art direction and project management. "My sitter is really artsy-craftsy, so I called her and said, 'This is what I'm thinking,' and they did them. It was great, but I felt such sadness that I hadn't done it with him. I like to do crafts, but I just can't, so at least he's getting to do it, even if it's not with me."

Jess, the C-suite banking executive whose husband is a stay-at-home dad, told us that, despite her hectic schedule, she is the one who tucks her eight-year-old daughter into bed each night. It's a parenting task she would never want to hand over to her husband, in part because she sees it as the time in her day when she administers to her daughter's emotional well-being. "We talk about school and what happened that day and she confides in me even a little bit more than my husband, who's the stay-at-home dad. So I'll go back and say to him, 'Did you know this? She just told me this is happening,' and he's like, 'What? I had no idea.'"

And Amy, the insurance company executive also married to a stay-at-home dad, has taken note of the things that her children need her to do personally, like cooking dinner, and she makes time to ensure those things happen. "There are certain things that my kids really enjoy that I do, that once I learned how much joy they get out of them, then I said, 'Fine, I'll continue to do those.' They love when I cook them dinner. What I told them though is, you can't expect to eat early like these other families in the suburbs. If you like that I make dinner, then this is what you're going to get. We don't eat dinner until seven thirty at night. They're like okay, that's good. If I leave the cooking to my husband, it would be all completely unhealthy fast food or pots of chili every night. That's not acceptable to me or the kids."

Some of this need to exert control likely comes from our friends' need to be perfect, "present" parents even when they're at work, to reach beyond their desks and conference rooms and into their children's hourly lives even when someone else might be doing the hands-on caregiving. But we also found that for nearly every mother we interviewed, there was some essential element of managing their children's lives that defined motherhood for them, something that, if they didn't do it, if they let someone else do it or they let it slip, would make them feel as if they were not being a mother at all. The elements our friends found most meaningful about motherhood—the very things that made them feel most essentially a mom—were as varied as the women themselves. Melissa couldn't imagine not knowing what was in her children's backpacks, while other mothers might be perfectly content delegating that task to someone else. Whether it was making Valentines, meeting the school bus, packing lunches, or scheduling the after-school activities, every woman had a series of items that were deal breakers for them. Without owning this specific task, whatever it may be, they would have felt they were failing at motherhood.

When a Child's Health Outranks Career

One area where our friends appear to be nearly united is in caring for their children's health (there's a reason they all make the pediatrician appointments). This was especially apparent for our friends whose children had medical needs that went beyond yearly well visits to the doctor. Sixteen percent of our friends have a child with an ongoing medical condition. For many of these friends, managing their children's health consumes so much of their time and energy that they have none left over to devote to work, especially if they are unwilling to cede household and parenting responsibilities to a spouse.

Our friend Katie seems to have tried every configuration possible to balance being the parent she wants to be with the career she'd also like to maintain. She has hopped between a demanding full-time job, a full-time job working from home, a job share, and a part-time job working from home; when we last spoke with her, she'd left work entirely to be a stay-at-home mom. Regardless of how many hours she was working,

Katie was the one to run her household and take care of her two children the vast majority of the time. Katie admitted that she chose to take on most of the child-raising and housekeeping, while also confessing that the stress of cramming everything she needed to do into one day left her a little on the verge. As the parent of a child with a life-threatening medical condition, she felt she needed to be the one to take charge of managing her daughter's health. We heard this from a number of our friends whose children live with medical conditions—there was no possibility that they wouldn't be the parent primarily responsible for the extra hours, appointments, therapies, and research that goes into having a child with ongoing medical needs. They shouldered the extra burden with little consideration that the other parent in the relationship might bear some responsibility for keeping their offspring healthy.

I'm the Fact-finder and He's the High-Fiver

Katie attended Northwestern on a swimming scholarship, bringing a welcome dose of West Coast attitude to our Midwestern campus from her home state of Washington. She did work-study jobs to help pay the bills during college, and got a general degree from the School of Speech, thinking she would be good at sales someday. Tall and athletic, Katie met her husband a few years after graduation when a group of former athletes from college decided to hike to the base of the Grand Canyon together. A football player friend of hers brought Katie's future husband along, and they've been together ever since. Before they married, Katie worked her way up through a number of different sales organizations, eventually landing as a sales rep for a health care company in California. She received accolades for her sales numbers, enjoyed the competitive nature of sales, and liked the feeling of accomplishment she got from hunkering down and working hard. Katie's husband also worked in sales, and the two assumed they would both continue working once they became parents.

The couple had two children. When Katie's oldest child hit preschool age, she began constantly getting sick, visiting the emergency room more times than seemed normal. Eventually, she was diagnosed with a serious, rare degenerative disease. The disease is treatable, but the treatment requires suppressing the child's immune system. Untreated, it could lead to organ failure and death.

Katie managed her daughter's illness well enough that her daughter was able to start school, but even then, she was "going to preschool part-time, just long enough to get sick, so the days we were home, she either had a fever, was coughing, or was vomiting. This cycle happened over and over again." This, plus a full-time schedule with California commute times ("we would leave the house at six thirty, it took an hour to get to work, and we would get home at five thirty in the evening") had Katie hanging on by a thread. When the option arose for her to downshift her full-time job into a job share, she quickly accepted. Her daughter's health wasn't improving, and with another small child to care for, even the job share didn't feel tenable for long. "I reached this point where I had two kids, my daughter has a chronic health issue, and I just said, 'You know what? I would rather go live off the land somewhere. I've got to get off this hamster wheel.'"

Katie quit her job and the family moved to a suburb outside Salt Lake City. Her husband was a sales manager for a company based in the northeast, so he could work from anywhere, though his job would continue to require regular travel. They could afford to lose her salary because the cost of living was so much lower in Utah than in California, and Katie agreed "to give it a try to get out of hell." Katie's daughter started kindergarten, and Katie enjoyed "two solid years with my little guy where he'd go to preschool in the morning, and the rest of the time, I had him. And it was one of the best decisions I've ever made in my life, to just take that time." Not one content to chill after Mommy and Me yoga classes, Katie says she overcompensated with volunteering. She did the school yearbook and was the PTO president.

Highly gregarious, funny, and eminently likeable, Katie impressed a lot of coworkers over the decades she worked for the health care company. And those coworkers remembered her work ethic and her performance. When we first spoke to Katie, she told us the company had called two years after she quit and asked her to return. "I decided to dip my toes back into working, and it's been hard." She had been back to work for a year at that point, and had arranged a pretty good gig for herself. "They asked me to come full-time, and I said, 'I won't work summers.' I can't get over that hurdle, mostly because of my daughter's health issues. And they said, 'We'll give you the entire summers off.'" She knew that was too good to pass up.

But even with flexible hours and summers off, Katie found that attempting to run a household, care for a sick child, and keep her work performance where she wanted it was exhausting.

She wakes up at four ten in the morning, goes to bed at ten at night, and hurtles along at full speed seven days a week. In addition to going back to her full-time job, Katie does a lot of fund-raising for a research organization for her daughter's disease. "I'm heavily involved in that, because I can't just shrug my shoulders and say, 'Well, this sucks.' In this world, with all the technology and all the advances, there's got to be something that makes this disease happen in people's bodies. And right now, they don't know a cause and they don't know a cure." Katie's gone above and beyond in her volunteer work for the research organization, creating teams for fund-raising runs every year, and this year raising the highest dollar amount by a single team in her region.

Ultimately, the energy Katie needs to put into managing her daughter's health trumps the energy she has for her career. "This illness has completely changed the way I am, the way I parent, how I see the world. It has rocked us to the core. You can't control something that your little girl has. She's doing great and she's going to have a wonderful life, but it's really affected me. The stomach flu was going around school, and I was just on eggshells. If she gets it, she relapses." When we caught up with Katie a year later, she had once again quit her job. "The ten months that I was working, my personal quality of life was so poor, in terms of the stress and the heaviness I felt and the lack of sleep, it ultimately just wasn't worth it anymore." Katie misses the work, and "finding solutions to things beyond 'Where is my right shoe?'" but she doesn't miss "feeling like I'm going to have a heart attack every day."

An undeniable factor in Katie's difficult juggle year after year, she acknowledges, was that no matter which job scenario she had, she tasked herself with all the primary caregiving, particularly managing her daughter's health, leaving her husband free to focus on his career. "I'm the fact-finder," Katie said, referring to the volumes of research she has conducted on her daughter's disease. "I don't know if it naturally progressed that way, because [her husband] travels so much for work. But even when our daughter was a newborn, and he traveled, I just started to assume all of the daily tasks. I'm the one who monitors the medicine. I make sure that we test her daily to make sure her blood and protein levels aren't off. He'll ask, 'How's she doing? How many more weeks on medicine does she have?' And I'll say, 'She's got three weeks. We're tapering now.' He'll answer, 'That's great!' It's like I'm updating someone walking down the street. I'm the parent, and I hate to say this, but he's the high-fiver."

The parenting burden Katie shoulders extends beyond health management into basic child upkeep. For example, "I volunteered at the school game night, but neither of my kids wanted to go. So I said, 'Well, I've got to go, I committed myself.' So they stayed at home with their dad. And I came home from game night and asked, 'Has our son done his homework?' My husband said, 'I didn't know he needed to do his homework.'"

Katie understands full well that she allows this arrangement to continue, and because of a combination of factors—her established role as the primary parent, her unwillingness to relinquish the micro details of her daughter's treatment, her husband's physical absence due to work travel and his willingness to let his spouse handle everything—she, like Jill, is resigned to it. "I created this mess," she admits, "so I'll own it."

When we asked if Katie and her husband had ever discussed the possibility of his scaling back his job to take on more of the management of their daughter's illness or more of their domestic life, she balked. "It's not possible," she said resolutely. "We're very fortunate. He's been with the company almost twenty years now. It's a good company, it's stable. Since I've been in his life, his career advancement has been great. I don't know if I would ever ask him to leave that, because it has provided such a great opportunity for him." Katie was one of several women we interviewed who said they couldn't imagine asking their spouses to compromise on their careers in any way, wouldn't dare ask them to jeopardize their advancement—even though she had abandoned hers entirely. When we last spoke to her, the same company she had resigned from twice had offered her yet another job. She says she's not ready to reconsider working yet, but doesn't want to close any doors, either.

Type A Management
at Home Can Hinder Your Career

Katie prioritized her spouse's career over her own, but that wasn't the primary factor leading her to leave her job. Rather, an essential piece of motherhood—managing her child's health day to day—became a job that so consumed both her time and emotional energy that she was no longer able to maintain a career. Managing her daughter's rare disease and participating in disease-related fund-raising were more meaningful and necessary to her than her paying job. No sane or empathic person could fault Katie for that choice, but not every woman we interviewed who had a child with special health needs took this all-or-nothing approach.

Ellen, our rabbi friend, has a child on the autism spectrum. When she was researching preschools for him, she met another mom with a child on the spectrum. Ellen told us how this other mother marveled at how calm and collected Ellen seemed to be around the all-important preschool decision. "I told her, 'Because it's not my entire life.'" She is fully committed to getting her son the services he needs and the best education possible, but she concedes that "taking care of my children is part of who I am, but it doesn't fully define me. I feel a sense of loss and frustration and challenge that I have this child who needs this extra support, but it's one of the many pieces of my life. For me, having a job, one that I find really challenging and fulfilling, gives me more patience and space with my children."

Katie clearly gains fulfillment from motherhood and from her research and fund-raising work for her daughter's illness, but she also seems ambivalent about relinquishing her job. We couldn't help but wonder, if she had had more support on the second shift at home, would she have had to make that choice? Jill, Katie, and several other women we interviewed appeared to be in egalitarian marriages, in which both partners worked and valued their careers, but once they became mothers, it seemed a foregone conclusion that the women were the ones who would scale back, leave early, or quit altogether in order to handle the parenting.

In this regard, our friends are part of a larger trend. The 2014 study of Harvard Business School graduates that we referenced earlier found that while male and female graduates had similar hopes for their levels of career success early on, 77 percent "believe that 'prioritizing family over work' is the number one barrier to women's career advancement." One alumna noted that "a key factor is still deep-rooted attitudes that a woman should be the primary caregiver, so it is 'understood' that her career may have to take a backseat for a while as similar male colleagues move ahead at a more rapid pace.'"[12]

Even among High Achievers, like Harvard MBA alumnae and our friends Katie and Jill, there remains an ingrained assumption that women are better at handling the childcare and domestic details. Men's stable, good jobs can't withstand disruption for any domestic needs, but women's jobs can. That assumption leaves us with a range of emotions, including frustration, bafflement, and simmering resentment. What is keeping these women from asking for more support—demanding it—from their husbands? As products of Second Wave feminism and earners of women's studies certificates, we believe objectively that men are just as capable of childcare and housework as women are. Plus, when fathers are actively engaged in their young children's lives and feel confident in their parenting, their children do better—they're less likely to have behavioral problems as they grow up,[13] and they do better on cognitive tests.[14] In *All Joy and No Fun*, Jennifer Senior suggests that the perfectionist mothers she interviewed, who we imagine have some things in common with our type A supermom friends, could, in fact, take a lesson from some of the very good modern fathers (in most cases, her subjects' own husbands) she interviewed on how to be an imperfect yet still loving and present parent, and thus maintain some sanity and sense of self in the process.[15] Or as our friend Ellen's husband reminds her when she comes home after a long workday and not everything at home has been executed the exact way she would have done it, could she please cut him some slack? As much as we identify with the desire to protest, "But they aren't wearing the pajamas I laid out for them!" we couldn't help but agree that she—and we—could benefit greatly from some slack-cutting.

We understand viscerally the drive to be the primary doer, the VP of Emotional Labor. For many of our friends, though, and for ourselves, the combination of needing to exert control, needing certain jobs to be performed perfectly, and having some tasks that could under no circumstances be handled by someone else, is slowly curtailing our careers. For every task we refuse to delegate because we won't stand for anything less than an A+ job, a chunk of time is divested from our career trajectories— ten minutes, an hour, a day, several years. It is tempting to proclaim, by way of correction, *"Ambitious women friends! Stop insisting that you own everything!"* And in some of our interview postmortems, that's precisely what we told each other the solution was.

As with many issues we discuss here, though, it took us a bit longer to fully unpack this dilemma, to grasp that transferring one's ambition directly from hands-on parenting into a career isn't necessarily a linear move. Instead, for some of us, these mundane, often seemingly inessential tasks are some of the most essential for our hearts and souls. We find joy in making a grilled cheese sandwich, cutting it into two triangles, and placing it squarely inside a paper towel–lined neon-plastic geometric bento box. Imagining our children opening the box later in the day and being nourished by that simple sandwich is a fundamental expression of our affection and nurturing. Preparing homemade challah and teaching her children to braid the dough for a holiday meal is an act one friend not only enjoys, but one she needs, to remind herself of the simple pleasures parenting can bring amid a noisy mess of necessary, often soul-sucking daily tasks. So suggesting that women stop making homemade this or that, or to let the handcrafting go, when what we really want and need most is to see our child proudly munching bread they helped make or drawing love notes to friends with glitter Sharpies is not realistic. What's more productive is to consciously articulate the tasks that bring you joy and make you feel closer to your children, and also those you find less vital, and try to delegate or split those with a partner (you might be surprised to find your partner has different ideas about what tasks bring him or her joy). If you love a bake sale and school fund-raising, by all means, keep on keeping on with that homemade banana bread—but recognize the ways you choose to allocate your time, and what other commitments (paid work, sleep, exercise, friendship) you sacrifice by doing so. Balancing the division of labor in parenting and childcare within marriages is an essential step toward women prioritizing their own careers—and prioritizing time for themselves in general, as both Jill and Katie have struggled to do.

More Equitable Parenting,
One Conversation at a Time

In contrast to our friends who didn't feel things were evenly divided on the domestic labor front, several of our subjects prided themselves on being in marriages where both spouses tackled parenting and domestic work equally.

For some, this seemed to happen organically, like corporate attorney Laurel, whose husband is a "full equal partner" both professionally and domestically. For most of our friends, creating an egalitarian division of labor was the result of a constant, ongoing conversation with their spouses, with duties divided up and redivided based on which partner needed what at any given time. For many women, these conversations are part of an endless battle against an ever-encroaching tide, with responsibilities slipping back into their corner over time. Melissa pointed out to her husband one day that she spent more mornings getting the kids off to school than he did, days he was able to go into his office and jump-start his workday. Her husband's response? "Let's switch that up," so that she could go into work early a couple of days a week while he readied the kids for school.

Audrey, the government lawyer, felt the balance of labor in her marriage go awry after she had her second child—but she refused to sit by idly and accept it. She found herself struggling to be the hands-on parent she had envisioned being while maintaining a demanding career. She had scaled back her law career to make family life more manageable, but when that wasn't enough, she tweaked the setup on the home front, too. Just as Audrey demanded her rightful promotion earlier in her career, she also demanded equity from her husband in parenting, noting that without an equal partner, her life won't function the way she needs it to.

All the Bullshit Things I Do That He Would Not Even Think to Do

Audrey met her husband at a cute rooftop bar in Washington, DC. At the time, she thought it might just be a summer fling—he was seven years younger than she was, and she doubted he was taking the relationship seriously. But at the same time, she was in her early thirties, knew she wanted to have kids, and didn't want to waste time.

Over happy-hour rosés, "I said, 'Look, I get that you're young, and I'm not trying to pressure you, but I'm thirty-three years old. My biological clock is ticking, so I am definitely not just dating for fun anymore.' If he was dating someone his age, they could date for years and then get married five years later and still have plenty of time for a family. I just very bluntly said to him, 'I can't do that. I'm on a much shorter time frame.'" Her future husband, then still in his mid-twenties, was expecting more years of sexy careless coupledom. "I said, 'I can't wait for that, so if that's what you want, I understand completely, but we should probably break up, and I'll give you your freedom because I'm just not on that time scale.'" He was shocked, but considered her argument and got on board; they were engaged shortly thereafter.

The consummate lawyer, Audrey was used to laying out the ground rules, her needs, what she wanted, and opening up the discussion for negotiation. So not only did she need her then boyfriend to commit quickly to marriage, but she also told him she wanted to have kids soon after they got married. She'd been reading a slew of articles on fertility ("They scared the crap out of me") and she wasn't interested in waiting to become a parent.

"I think we negotiated a year, but I ended up moving it up six months, which he agreed to reluctantly. I would have liked to have waited until he felt more comfortable with his career, but I just couldn't."

Audrey ended up getting pregnant relatively quickly after they married, and she made partner at her law firm a week into her maternity leave. Audrey's husband was just starting his own business in commercial real estate, and Audrey remained the primary financial provider. During her maternity leave, she started to question how her roles—partner in a corporate law firm, new mother, and possibly primary caregiver—could coexist without a total sacrifice of her sanity. To make matters more complicated, Audrey and her husband had bought a house during her maternity leave. It was a fixer-upper, something they could afford and that her husband, embarking on his startup business, could put sweat equity into and feel good about. "He was just starting out, so it was very important to him since he wasn't bringing in money for us to buy a house that we needed to fix up and for him to be in charge of that." But during Audrey's maternity leave, her husband's dogged commitment to the fixing-up wore on her. "He was working on the house six days a week, trying to get it ready for us to move into. Here I am, sole breadwinner and taking care of the kid by myself six days a week, so that was definitely rough."

Audrey knew early on that she needed to clearly articulate to her spouse her expectations around work and parenting if her career were going to continue to function. Her husband had grown up in an Eastern European enclave in Staten Island and was raised by immigrant parents who inhabited traditional roles—a mother who handled all the childcare and domestic duties, a father who was the sole breadwinner—so while he knew his relationship wouldn't be exactly like his parents' (he'd married a hard-charging corporate lawyer who had negotiated the terms of her childbearing, after all), neither he nor Audrey had a model of what their marriage and parenting should look like. Audrey very directly stated her expectations. "I said to him, 'When I go back to work, my job comes first. You're going to have to help a lot more.' And he did. He was an equal partner with our first child when she was a baby. We took turns on the pick-ups and the drop-offs so that I could work late when I needed to. We traded off on sick days and stuff like that."

The next year, Audrey and her husband began trying to conceive again. "I did the whole starting-before-I-was-ready because I was thirty-seven and thought it would take a long time. Then it happened almost immediately. I was like, 'We're not ready!'" She had wanted to have at least two children, though, and was grateful they hadn't struggled to conceive. Her husband's business was expanding, slowly. When she was eight months pregnant with her second child, he was offered a project that had a lot of growth potential for his business but little income, and would require a lot of hours.

"He was going to be gone six days a week, eighteen hours a day. We had already decided to drop our nanny share, because that's when the financial crisis hit its peak. I said, 'We'll all just be on maternity leave together since you're not working, and then we'll get our own nanny for two kids once I go back to work, but we'll take a four-month break of no nanny to save money.'"

Her husband decided to take the project, and Audrey became apoplectic. "I was like, 'Wait a minute. I still get a full salary while I'm on maternity leave, so I'm going to be the sole breadwinner *and* I'm going to be taking care of two kids fourteen hours a day, six days a week.' My oldest daughter had some issues and was a very difficult toddler. I just could not believe I was in this situation. It had become unacceptable to me."

She loved her husband dearly, but this was a breaking point. "I said, 'If you take this job and put me in a situation of being alone with the kids all day, every day, when I had to give up the nanny and I've had to give up all this stuff, and I'm the sole breadwinner *and* the sole caretaker, that just doesn't work for me.'" Audrey identified her resentment and spoke up about it before it became a destructive force in her marriage—she views speaking up as integral to shaping an equitable domestic and parenting partnership with her husband. "I think he didn't realize how bad things had gotten. He was shocked. He immediately said, 'I won't take the job.'"

Her husband had to make some difficult decisions during that maternity leave. He closed his business. "That was a rock bottom. I said, 'You have to be more involved. It is not fair to put all this financial pressure on me to be the sole breadwinner when my law firm's imploding and I'm the primary caretaker of the kids. I'm doing everything.'" Her husband understood, and agreed to make sacrifices in his career to even the scales. "It was a constant tension for a while, as with every couple, but he ended up getting a great job during my maternity leave, so he did work, but much more reasonable hours." They hired a full-time nanny once Audrey returned to work. Following that rock-bottom ultimatum, Audrey continued to assert her needs to her husband. "He has been a very involved father. We're both home by six now. He does pull out the laptop to work in the evenings, but that's fine. He does a lot of the eight-to-eleven-p.m. work, but he's home. He does the cooking most of the time. We take turns at drop-off and pick-up. I still do most of the field trips."

Even with what she calls a very involved spouse and co-parent, Audrey acknowledges that the parenting roles aren't always equal. "He thinks he does so much. So one time I gave him a list of all the bullshit things I do that he would not even think to do: cutting nails, buying their clothes and shoes, organizing the summer camps and the after-school activities, the doctor appointments. All those little things that are important to their lives, he just does not even think about. It doesn't even enter his head."

Audrey's trying to tweak this pattern (even though she can't give up making the doctor's appointments) one task at a time. One thing she knows is that continuing to openly discuss their domestic and parenting roles is key to their partnership's health. "The pendulum is shifting," Audrey noted. "That's healthy in a marriage."

A udrey was one of the few women we interviewed who identified a marital-parenting breakdown that she felt wasn't fair, and addressed it directly with her spouse. Rather than quietly bubble with resentment, she faced it head-on, even though it was a difficult and painful conversation to initiate. When it comes to emotional labor, as well as all other kinds, Audrey is a workaholic. Even though she struggled with her husband's different style of executing domestic tasks, she knew it would be better for both of them, for their whole family, to share the workload. When it came to establishing a paradigm that she believed would define her role as a mother, a wife, and a professional for many years to come, Audrey could not be passive, or even passive-aggressive—and her straightforward conversation with her spouse triggered positive change in her marriage and parenting.

Setting Limits

While many of our friends struggled to meet their own internal parenting demands and others figured out ways to divide responsibilities more evenly with their spouses, another group rallied against the ever-expanding state of modern parenting by explicitly stating things they simply would not do and setting clearly defined limits. While these boundaries didn't magically create an extra ten hours in the day, they did provide a sense of control for our friends, as they imposed order on an otherwise chaotic corner of their lives. Amy, a high-ranking insurance executive, told her children at the beginning of the school year to pick one school event each for her to attend. Just one, for the entire year, thereby attempting to eliminate guilt over all the events she would have to decline. As we'll discuss below, one of our friends allows her kids to host one sleepover a year. "One and done," she told us. And one of us declared a moratorium on attending her children's elementary school field days and curriculum nights. Among the litany of weekly requests she was getting to show up at her kids' classrooms as a "learning partner" or volunteer, those were two she could dismiss with the least amount of regret. These women took a look at how their lives worked, knew they wanted to be successful at work and at parenting, logically assessed their time commitments, and came up with clear plans that helped them determine, realistically, what they could and could not give their children.

The One-Sleepover-a-Year Mom

Laurel, a corporate lawyer at a midsize Atlanta firm, had a strong desire to become a parent—and a specific idea of what parenthood might look like for her. She was adopted at birth and grew up in Massachusetts. When her mother, whom she calls her "best friend," was diagnosed with pancreatic cancer when Laurel was in college, she transferred out of Northwestern to a college closer to home to spend more time with her mom. Her mother succumbed to the disease when Laurel was twenty-two, and it shook Laurel to her core. It also confirmed that she wanted to have a close relationship with her kids, like her mother had had with her. Even closer, maybe, because Laurel's mother had worked, and Laurel wanted to be around more for her kids.

She modeled her work-parenting plan in contrast to her mother's. "Our plan was, I was going to work until my kids were in the third grade and then I was going to quit or do something else," Laurel explained. "That was important to me, because when I was young—and I do not begrudge my parents this at all, but—my mom went back to work." As a result, Laurel missed out on having a parent around a lot during her elementary school years. "There were certain things I couldn't do. She wasn't home to take me to gymnastics," for example. "My husband and I made the decision that it was better for us to both be working during the baby years and to be home during the elementary school years to be able to do those things. I didn't want my kids to miss out on those things because I had been a working mom."

As time went on, though, Laurel discovered that she was valuable enough to her company that they would give her flexible hours and allow her to work from home two days a week. Her family was accustomed to living on two salaries, and Laurel was now hesitant to give up some of the luxuries they enjoyed—extracurricular activities, nice vacations, a very comfortable house in the suburbs. When she returned to work after each of her kid's births, she kept waiting for the pull to leave her job and stay at home, but that pull didn't come. She liked working, it turned out, and had no desire to quit. So she didn't.

Even with the flexible hours, though, Laurel can't be everywhere all the time. To reconcile her desire to give her kids all the after-school activities she missed out on while still maintaining her career, she relies on a nanny to shuttle her now preteen and teen kids to sports practices and other activities. And sometimes the workday bleeds into the weekend, like those conference calls that happen at the same time as her daughter's Saturday morning volleyball tournament.

Laurel has observed some of the highly competitive parenting going on around her, and has come to the conclusion that she's never going to "win" at that kind of parenting—doesn't even need to play the game, in fact. "My daughter went to a volleyball meet, and another mother, on a whim, said, 'Hey, I'm going to have all the girls sleep over on Friday night.' No sweaty palms, no sweaty pits, just, 'I'm going to have all the girls sleep over.' Then I pick my daughter up the day after, and not only did she host a sleepover, they did a craft! And not like some crummy craft. I mean, she went out and got each girl a picture frame with her initial on it, and filled them with photos from volleyball."

Laurel recounted this story with awe, as though it existed on the border between gossip and urban legend: the mom who could just whip up a full-blown, perfectly executed sleepover on a moment's notice. When she came to the part about the crafting, she rolled her eyes and the three of us burst out laughing, because we'd all been there, on the receiving end of a parenting grand slam that momentarily reduces our own parenting efforts to rubble. "My coworker and I have a line: 'I'm just not that mom.' And it's true. I'm just not that mom. There's a part of me that wishes I was, but let's be honest, I've never been laid-back. I'm not wired that way." We've all met that mom, or at least we're all familiar with her—the one who outdoes you at every turn, who has a well-kept home, buys presents for her children's friends' birthday parties months in advance, and brings beautifully architected homemade treats to every school function. But Laurel is candid about what she can give. She sets realistic limits on the amount of super-hands-on parenting she does. Take sleepovers, for example: Laurel is the friend who allows her daughter and son to host one sleepover a year at their home. Her kids beg for greater frequency, and Laurel feels guilty that she won't give in, especially when other alpha moms seem to have a greater bandwidth for hosting, but it's one tiny way she can maintain her sanity in the face of being pulled between "present" parenting and demanding work.

We heard about occasionally breaking the rules in favor of sanity, too. Ellen, the rabbi, takes the keep-calm-by-any-means-necessary strategy with her three children—starting with weekday mornings when her husband leaves early for work. "I'm up at six doing the early morning routine: I empty the dishwasher, put on the coffee, get lunches made, pack the kids' bags, give them breakfast. Anything I can do to make that a peaceful experience, even if it's breaking a lot of our rules, that's fine. If my daughter is watching *Sofia the First* on the iPad and the boys become interested in watching that, and they're all sitting at the table eating, not getting up, not annoying each other . . . Maybe that breaks my rule of no screens in the morning, but I actually got what I wanted: a calm and lovely time where we are all just hanging out, and five minutes to sit down with my cup of coffee."

Solid boundaries around parenting or not, a number of our friends copped to regularly comparing themselves to other moms, an unavoidable if futile exercise in self-flagellation. Laurel shared her fantasy of stay-at-home moms as patient, hyperinvolved superwomen. "I have this vision: They never lose their tempers. They never yell. They never need to hide in the shower and pretend nobody's around, [like] I do. To me, they're like my mom on that pedestal, even though she worked. There's a part of me that feels like all the things that I think I do wrong as a parent, I suspect they're doing right. I think everybody is judging themselves or judging others in terms of how they parent, or 'I wish I did that better,' or 'I wish I could be more like that.'"

With the support of other full-time working moms, Laurel is trying not to buy into it, trying to be kinder about her own parenting, confident that she is parenting in the way that works best for her—even if that means doing it in fits and starts. "I'm trying to be more like that seventies mom where they would just tell them to get out of the house and go have fun. I'm not really good at it because I'm still watching out the window trying to make sure that they're not going into the road or doing whatever. I'm working on it."

Here's What We Know About Parenting

▶ **Some elements of parenting are likely to be nonnegotiable for you.**

As our friends defined, over the years, what kind of parents they wanted to be and what the essential elements of "present" parenthood were, different tasks emerged as important to them. Our nonprofit lawyer friend Melissa needs to pack her children's backpacks and usher them out the door to the bus each day, while Jess the C-suite banking exec needs to tuck her daughter in each night, and our health care sales rep friend Katie needs to manage her daughter's illness and also raise research funding, because, for her, doing any less would be unacceptable. Each of these items, small or monumental, was not negotiable to our friends; they were a defining element in their role as a mother.

No one can tell you which specific pieces of parenting will be the ones to make you feel like your heart will burst if you're not the one doing them. Between the two of us, friends with a twenty-five-year history, the things we're willing to delegate and the things that we'll stop the world to make happen for our kids are as diverse as rocks on a beach. One of us would rather send her kids to school naked than allow them to eat the school lunch, while the other hates making lunches and has crossed it off her list of parenting tasks, allowing her kids to make their own lunches or get school lunch. (Lunches are a big deal, and a topic that came up consistently in our interviews. Women are oppressed by lunch.) That said, all our friends felt this way about their children's health. So if you have kids, there is a strong likelihood that you'll be the one making the pediatrician appointments.

▶   **Once you know what you *must* do yourself, you can figure**
out which things it's okay to offload to someone else or to do a
less-than-perfect job on.

After our friends determined which items in the never-ending list
of parenting tasks were nonnegotiable for them, they were able to define which items they could delegate or forgo altogether—freeing up
new pockets of time to foster their careers or other elements of life
that were important to them, like exercise, time with friends, or volunteer work. Most of our friends who had developed a work-parenting
balance strategy conceded that they had to drop some ball, somewhere; identifying those spheres was a concrete way for them to
manage their time. Our friend Heather, who is chief marketing officer
at a bank, prioritized being the math team coach at her kids' school,
but knew she couldn't attend most of her children's after-school activities. Our friend Amy, the insurance exec, made herself available for
one school appearance a year, but had breakfast with her middle
school–aged son most mornings. And Celina, a teacher who takes on
the primary parenting responsibility, also draws a line at certain
housekeeping tasks. "I'm not going to clean the pool," she told us.
"It's not going to happen. What's something else I'm not going to do?
I'm not going to put up the Christmas decorations. I'm not going to do
it, so just go ahead and know that that's not going to happen. But also,
I don't see him in the laundry room all that much, so those kind of
things have been established over the years. We would have no clean
clothes, so that's how I know that. This [pointing to the shirt she's
wearing] is the only clean thing I have, as a matter of fact."

▶ **Things that feel nonnegotiable to you today may be elements of life you're willing to delegate down the road, so regularly revisit who owns what.**

For some of our friends, the items that were negotiable and non-negotiable shifted over the years. Many of them wanted jobs that allowed them to be home to meet the school bus, but once their kids got older, they found this felt much less important. Liz, one year (the year she stopped working in an office full-time), prioritized being involved in her kids' school—she started a lice check program and a farm-food delivery service, served on the auction committee, and joined the school leadership team—while also being at pick-up every day at 2:40 p.m. Three years later, she dialed down her involvement to just one PTA meeting over an entire year, choosing instead to divert that time into growing her career. Being a "present" parent for her still means picking up her children from school most days and overseeing their homework and teacher communications, but she has set some internal boundaries around school involvement in order to funnel more hours into editing, writing, and other paid work. You may have parenting roles or philosophies about which you feel intransigent one year, and a year or a few later, you may wonder why you were so insistent on being the one who took your kids to karate, or why it felt so urgent that they take Mandarin lessons after school. On the other hand, you may find new things cropping up—a tween who really needs you to spend one Saturday a month at an all-day chess tournament with him, a teenager whose rock climbing competitions are the way you now spend your Thursday nights, or maybe just being the parent who always brings the oranges to soccer practice. Being open to these shifts, and knowing that the way things are today isn't the way they'll always be, will help you manage the balance between parenthood, work, and marriage.

▶ **Talk to your spouse about the division of labor.**

Natalie, the broadcast journalist, said she and her husband "had no plan, no conversation" about having kids—it just sort of happened. Many of our friends echoed this, and the ensuing logical next step: They didn't have conversations about how having children might affect their careers, or what things would look like once those children arrived. Audrey said, "Like every other woman, I just thought I'd have kids and it would all work out. And then you get to the other side and are like, 'How did I think *that* was going to work?'" Parenting probably will not just "work itself out," and what happens to a woman's career post-kids will not magically just work itself out, either. Our friends who have ongoing, open discussions with their spouses about who will do what, who revisit that conversation frequently, and who are willing to speak up when they feel the burden is unfair or derailing their careers or health, end up with more egalitarian household divides, and with time left to devote to building their careers. The women we interviewed who shy away from these conversations with their spouses end up doing the majority of childcare and domestic labor, and often find their careers or mental health suffering as a result.

CHAPTER 5

ECONOMICS

Women don't talk about money. We might happily share the details of the inner workings of our uterus over coffee with a friend, or go into great detail on how something our spouse said made us feel, but we don't discuss our finances with friends or family, and we feel uncomfortable when someone brings up the subject.[1] The same women who were told they could grow up to be astronauts or the secretary of the treasury were also most likely taught that it is not polite for women to discuss money.[2] (Liz's mother fiercely adhered to the adage that you don't publicly discuss voting habits, religion, or money, and refused to reveal her salary even to her own daughter for many years.) Making decisions about investing and saving, society tells us, is men's work. And overwhelmingly, women have listened, ceding longer-term financial decisions to their spouses while they manage the day-to-day budget.[3]

In our interviews we heard from quite a few friends whose husbands manage the money for their household with little to no input from them. Our friend Claire, a middle school teacher in Dallas, relies on her husband to tell her when the family should be spending less money. "There are times when we go on what we call 'shutdown,' when we're not buying things just because we feel like it. He tells me when those times are, because it really doesn't interest me." She's tried to be involved in financial conversations, but told us it's challenging to hang on to the details due to her lack of interest. Plus, her husband is on it. "I trust him and I know he's got things under control."

And Audrey, the government lawyer who married in her mid-thirties, told us that one of the things she'd looked forward to about being married was turning the finances over to her spouse.

"That was the one traditional aspect of marriage that, when I was single, I really coveted, because I hate doing the finances. When I would talk to my married friends, they would be like, 'Oh, my husband does it.' I thought, 'When I get married I'm going to make sure my husband does it.'"

But it turned out that even though she hated managing the family's money, Audrey was better at it than her husband was, so she reluctantly took that task back.

"When we were engaged, he acted like, 'Oh yeah, I'm really good at this,' and I believed him. Then I learned the hard way, he's just not very good at budgeting at all. So I do it. Not well, but I do it."

The fact that Audrey, who was open to a non-gender-based breakdown of responsibility in nearly every other aspect of her life (she was the primary breadwinner for a period of time and now brings in half the financial contribution to the household, wrote out a list of tasks that needed to be divided up between her and her spouse, and routinely speaks up when the divide feels unbalanced) fell so naturally into the thought that her future husband would manage her finances points to just how societally ingrained this idea is.

The prohibition against money talk doesn't start and end at the threshold to our homes. Women are also notoriously silent when it comes to asking for raises. In *Women Don't Ask*, Linda Babcock reports that only 7 percent of the women she interviewed tried to negotiate their salaries after receiving a job offer, as opposed to 57 percent of men.[4]

Jane Pratt, former editor of XO Jane (and, as founding editor of *Jane* magazine, a driven, in-charge heroine from our early work days), has said that from the employer perspective, while she wants to be sure people are being paid fairly for their work, women's inclination to try to defuse tense situations often means they don't get the money they deserve. "When people take the attitude of 'I'm fine! Don't worry about me! I'm okay the way I am!' they don't get as much," she told *Elle*.[5]

All of which perhaps explains why, as we first embarked on our interviews, we weren't planning to ask many questions about money, financial planning, raises, how our friends divided up their household income, or even what they thought, broadly, about economics (supply-side: for or against?). We understood that underneath many of our interviews about dreams and plans, implicit in the choices and paths our friends had chosen lay the benefits of a private college education and a degree of economic privilege. But over the course of our interviews, we also began to notice lots of micro ways that economics influenced our friends' ambition trajectories. Some were driven by a desire for financial independence or financial success; others compromised economic comfort for greater freedom or to follow a less-than-lucrative passion. Some didn't return to work after having children simply because they crunched the numbers and the cost of childcare versus their salary didn't add up. All of them landed in their respective paths in part thanks to economics, and we saw that we couldn't tell a story about women's trajectories without discussing the topic. As we dug deeper, we discovered that not only was economics central to how our friends had shaped their lives, but that many of them were guided by very strong, visceral feelings about money.

The '70s and '80s were a stormy time to come of age, with divorce rates skyrocketing,[6] unemployment hitting double digits,[7] a recession, and the worst stock market crash in US history.[8] A number of our friends came from homes rattled by emotional instability and economic turbulence: mothers who settled for entry-level jobs after an abrupt divorce or who weren't sure how they'd pay the mortgage after their husband's sudden death, parents who vanished and reappeared sporadically, fathers who left families and took their paychecks with them, and, in some cases, mothers who were able to keep the family not only afloat but well-off because they'd fostered, and held on to, their careers. Our friends took note of the swirl of events around them in their childhoods and seemed to come to one of two decisions.

One set of women raised a fist and vowed, Scarlett O'Hara–style, that they would never depend on anyone else for an income. These women felt they absolutely must support themselves financially, regardless of what their spouse earned. They drew a straight, thick line between making their own money and stability.

The other group simply didn't feel this way. While they, too, pursued stability, or vowed that they would create the secure family they never had, they didn't necessarily see earning their own paycheck as a route to either. Instead, they tended to seek out partners who could shoulder the financial responsibility, which in turn allowed them to create the solid home and the quiet, calm existence they craved.

Earning Stability and Independence Through a Paycheck

For women who feel intensely that they must rely on their own earning power to support themselves, economics are front and center as they plan their careers. They might not talk openly about money, but they think about it a lot over the course of their careers, starting in college or even earlier. Our friends in this group majored in economics or math or political science and kept their sights on a career that would pay the bills; they made conscious choices to pursue professions that would allow them fiscal freedom. After graduation, they factored finances into career decisions, discarding career tracks that wouldn't lead to lucrative jobs and weighing their future salary prospects with every move: business school versus a management-track career; a year with a nonprofit or a job with a big tech firm. Ultimately, while they might not have ended up in jobs they adored, they achieved their dreams of being beholden to no one but themselves.

The Power to Support Myself

Growing up in Nebraska, Nicole knew one thing for certain: She wasn't going to let what happened to her mother happen to her. "When my dad had his midlife crisis, he dumped my mom. She had been faithful forever, and all of a sudden she was on her own, and the best thing she could find was a secretary job."

Nicole wasn't sure what she wanted to do with her life—she majored in economics at Northwestern because everyone else seemed to think it was a tough major, yet it came easily to her. Whatever she did, she knew she would be economically independent.

"I wasn't going to choose anything that I couldn't depend on for certain. I wanted absolutely to have the power to support myself just in case I got dumped," Nicole told us candidly.

But even with security as a driving force, she struggled to find the right fit for her interests and skills. After graduation, she spent time as a customer service rep for a health insurance company, and then thought she might become a veterinarian—she'd always been interested in health, and she liked animals, and that seemed like a solid, secure job—so she took a few classes at the University of Nebraska and worked at a hog confinement operation. (At this point in our interview transcript, there is a lot of back and forth where we ask "A *what* operation?" and Nicole says "hog" and we say "fog?" and she says "hog" and then finally she is forced to literally spell it out for us.) "It's not what most people from Northwestern end up doing," she admitted.

Nicole liked the work, how removed it felt from college, where she'd never quite felt like she fit in, and enjoyed feeding the pigs and working with her hands. To make ends meet, she began working part-time at an animal shelter, and later that year she sent in an application to veterinary school. While waiting to hear back, she began volunteering at a local vet's office where the doctors complained all day about the difficulties of the profession.

"They were like, 'Don't go into vet med. Don't do it. It's such hard work. There's no pay. It's long hours. It's as many calls at midnight as a physician on call, but you're not getting paid enough for it.'"

And at the same time, the work at the animal shelter was wearing on Nicole. She'd always loved animals, but working with dogs and cats for long hours left her nerves frayed. "They would just bark, bark, bark, and then the cats would pee all over the place. They had way too many cats. It really started to make me question my choice."

Meanwhile, her father offered her a part-time job at his dental clinic. He was, she learned, passionate about his job. "He's like, 'It's art, it's science, I love dentistry.'" Nicole withdrew her application to veterinary school and applied to dental school instead. The money was good, it was a solid career that she could take with her anywhere, and she hoped she'd develop a zeal for it as her father had.

After graduating from dental school, Nicole began practicing in Nebraska. One day some patients of hers, a couple from her hometown, mentioned that their son was home from optometry school and needed his teeth cleaned. Nicole penciled him in, gave him a good cleaning, and a year and a half later the two were married. After the wedding, they quickly decided it was time to leave the Midwest—they were sick of the cold, and with jobs that could take them anywhere and no kids yet, they wanted to live somewhere fun. Nicole's husband bought an optometry practice near Hilton Head, South Carolina, and Nicole found a job working at a Marine Corps base nearby and supported them while her husband got his practice going. And then, after several years of trying to conceive, she became pregnant with their first child.

After six years in South Carolina, and now the parents of two children, Nicole and her husband were ready for somewhere new. As transplanted Midwesterners, they had never really felt like they meshed with Southern culture, and Nicole's in-laws were relocating to Orange County, California, so the family decided to move with them.

Over the years, Nicole has made her way through a variety of work configurations. She's owned her own practice, worked part-time at a small shop and longer hours at a larger one, and, when we last spoke to her, she was alternating days at two different practices. Her husband works full-time at an optometry clinic inside a Walmart. After nearly fifteen years practicing dentistry, Nicole admits that she doesn't love the work. At least not enough to have her own business anymore.

"I owned back in Nebraska, and realized you need to be really passionate about it, and put a lot more focus and time into it if you want to run the business. I realized in that little teeny practice in Lincoln that I'm just not that into it."

And while her parents are proud that she's a dentist, and it gives her something in common with her father, she doesn't adore her work the way he does.

"They're really proud that I have a career where I can put doctor in front of my name. Dad, especially, because it's his career path. But he's sad that I don't love it like he did. He loves being a dentist and he's sad that I don't have that."

But at the same time, Nicole has achieved the thing that is most important to her: economic independence. "I don't love my career," she told us, "but it pays pretty well for the amount of energy I put into it. I know I could support myself if I have to."

The economic independence part is so important to her that she and her husband keep their finances separate. They maintain two checking accounts, and pay for different things in the household depending on who is currently earning more money. A few years ago, the family took a vacation to Hawaii, a trip Nicole paid for. When her husband suggested they go again last year, she told him she didn't have the money for another Hawaii trip right then, but if he wanted to pay to take the family to Hawaii, he was welcome to do so. (They didn't go.) As Nicole's kids approach high school age and eventually college, she's realizing that someone needs to earn more money for the family, and that someone will probably be her.

Nicole wasn't the only one of our friends who admitted to not loving her job, but valuing the economic independence it afforded her. Laurel, the furniture company attorney in Atlanta, quickly brushed aside our questions about her career ambitions. She made it clear that for her, the point of working was to earn a paycheck, not reach intellectual nirvana.

"It's not a career I'm passionate about, but I don't need to find passion in my career," Laurel told us. "It's about dollars and cents, not saving people's lives. I like my job, and like all lawyers I disparage it when I talk about it, but it's a perfectly decent way to earn a living."

Unlike Nicole, Laurel's interest in being self-sufficient didn't come from having divorced parents or an economically turbulent background. She just always thought of herself as someone who would pay her own way. Even though she and her husband are both lawyers and could get by on one paycheck, she's not interested in depending on someone else's salary. She likes the control, and she's willing to sacrifice hands-on time with her kids to ensure that the family lives at a standard that is acceptable to her.

"I don't want to be perceived as choosing money *over* my two kids so much as choosing money *for* my kids. Could we live differently and do all that? Absolutely. But I choose to continue to work to secure my kids' future," she explained.

We also found that our friends who prioritized economic independence tend to be in more egalitarian marriages. Because the adage is true: Money talks. The women who bring home sizable paychecks have more say over what happens to that paycheck, and also more say over what happens in the household. Many have their own credit cards in addition to a joint credit card with their spouse. Some, like Nicole, maintain separate banking accounts. They don't ask if it's okay to buy a new fall jacket or feel guilty about spending money on themselves. And many of them choose to spend their income on hiring outside help to take care of household tasks that otherwise would have fallen on their shoulders. In essence, they buy themselves time.

Ellen, the rabbi in Cleveland, told us that when more of the housekeeping became her husband's responsibility after she took a higher-paying job and started working longer hours, they went through a rough period where they argued about dirty dishes and the state of the house. She felt overwhelmed trying to balance doing the tasks she used to do— tidying up the house, preparing meals—with her new responsibilities at work. Around this time, she came across a study that pointed her toward hiring someone else to do these jobs. Even though money was already tight, the article made her realize that her hourly rate was higher than the rate she could pay someone to do the same job. And that peace of mind was worth the expenditure. "I want to come home and have my house clean. Not that I don't know how to do it. I *have* done it. I *can* do it. I do a pretty good job of it. But I don't want to spend my precious few hours at home cleaning my stove or washing my toilets."

For Ellen and other women like her, money brings them the independence they yearned for from an early age, but it also reinforces a cycle leading to financial independence. Because they are able to spend their money on outsourcing childcare or domestic work, they have more time to focus deeply on their careers. And that, in turn, bolsters their salaries as they win promotions and bigger jobs. The more money they make, the more money they are able to sock away for the future, or contribute to the household finances, or freely spend on support that will make their lives easier as they pursue new opportunities at work. For these women, money does equal independence.

Gaining Stability and Independence Through a Partner

While some of our friends grew up knowing they would support themselves, either due to a tumultuous childhood or simply a worldview that said they were responsible for their own financial soundness, others looked around at a world peppered with divorce and fraught with insecurity and saw a stable partner as the surest route to a fulfilling life. Just as the first group of women felt an instinctual drive to earn their own paycheck, this second group deeply desired a home and family that would run seamlessly—and were willing to relinquish the responsibility of earning to their partner. They have a strongly rooted need to give their children the emotional stability their own childhoods might have lacked, or in some cases to provide them with the same warm, loving environment, complete with a very "present" parent, that they enjoyed as kids, and found shelving their own earning power a tolerable trade-off. Which is not to say that waving good-bye to their own money came easily to all of them, or that they feel great about needing to ask their spouse for funds, but it was a leap they were willing to take.

Stability Was My Number One Ambition

Brooke was born to hippie parents who were unable to care for her, and she grew up being shuttled back and forth between family members. For a while she lived in her aunt's strict religious home. "I wasn't allowed to go to birthday parties on Sundays. Other than going to a hospital to pray for sick patients, we did not patronize businesses on Sunday, because that was the Lord's day," Brooke explained. When she was eleven, she lived with her paternal grandmother, whom she called Momma. Her grandmother had an entirely different style of parenting. The religious restrictions were out, and pageant competitions were in. Despite her erratic home life, Brooke was the star of her small southern Ohio town. Her singing voice was melodic and resonant, and she was certain it would take her far. "I thought my name was going to be in lights," Brooke told us. "I thought I was going to be singing at the Met."

In addition to moving between homes, Brooke's family fortunes changed midway through her childhood. Her stepgrandfather, who had been fairly affluent, sunk money into a furniture company that went bankrupt. Brooke went from never thinking about money to worrying about how she could possibly pay for college. Once she got into Northwestern, her grandmother encouraged her to "take every loan and scholarship" she could so that she'd be able to attend, even though it would have been easier, and cheaper with in-state tuition, for Brooke to attend Ohio State, where she'd also been admitted. "I had loans up the wazoo," Brooke told us. "And here I was a music major. How was I possibly going to make enough money to pay that back?"

For Brooke, as it was for many of our friends, arriving at Northwestern "was like a slap in the face. Everybody was talented, and I felt like most people were better than I was. But I still had it in my head what I wanted to do: be onstage and perform all the time." Brooke's singing voice was legendary in our sorority. Sororities (or at least our sorority) involve a lot of singing. Weekly sorority meetings began with a song. Weekend parties often included an interlude featuring one or two drinking songs. And on the final night of sorority rush, the women in our sorority would put on an all-musical performance, featuring Beatles songs, to entice prospective pledges. The highlight of pledge night, which most of our friends still remember twenty-five years later, was Brooke singing John Lennon's "Imagine." She's petite, maybe an inch or two over five feet, with a slightly old-fashioned way about her, which makes her larger-than-life singing voice all the more impressive. Lots of women in our sorority were known, *Breakfast Club*–style, for something specific—getting the best grades, heading organizations on campus, being the biggest partier, the political one, the stoner, the artist. Brooke was the singer.

After graduation Brooke headed directly to the New England Conservatory in Boston with a plan to launch her singing career. Once graduate school ended, Brooke went on audition after audition, and cobbled together a collection of day jobs to pay the bills. She waitressed for a catering company and worked as an administrative assistant at Fidelity Investments, but her focus was on landing acting or singing work. "I was going down to New York, doing lessons at Juilliard monthly, and doing every freaking audition I could possibly get to in New York and in the

Boston area. I still thought that maybe I could do it, but nothing was working out."

Brooke had been auditioning consistently for more than two years when Momma got sick and her career focus changed.

"I went home for the last time for Christmas, and I could tell something wasn't quite right. She had early-onset Alzheimer's. I don't know that that changed my view, but I started looking in another direction. I stopped doing lessons, I stopped doing coaching sessions, I stopped going on auditions. I started giving up on the 'I'm going to be a star' thing and just looking at regular jobs. I thought, 'Maybe I'll take this financial industry thing to something.'"

With her showbiz dreams scuttled, Brooke felt lost, but she channeled her energy into what was directly in front of her: financial services. She got licensed to do her own trading, left her work as an admin at Fidelity, and switched to another firm. When an opportunity came up to move to the firm's Chicago office, Brooke jumped at the chance to go back to the city she'd enjoyed exploring during college. "I was like, 'I'll go to Chicago! I love Chicago, let me go!'"

Brooke had spent so much time being a performer, it's hard to imagine that it wasn't tough letting it go, but she says that the decision felt like the obvious, rational thing to do. And when she stopped auditioning and singing, she didn't miss it.

"I didn't feel relief, or I don't even know that I missed it at all, either. I just looked at it like, 'Well, that didn't work out, I need to try something else.' Even though I wasn't remotely interested in the financial industry, I thought, 'Why don't I do it the best I can, get my licenses, and see how I progress?'"

Brooke hoped she'd find somewhere else to be a star. But financial services never really clicked for her. And on top of that, her personal life wasn't so hot, either. She'd been in a relationship with another musician back in Boston, but when Brooke looked at their life together—two musicians working multiple jobs to try to make ends meet—she didn't think that was the kind of life she wanted for herself. "Where are we ever going to get health insurance if we're both trying to go this direction?"

In fact, if Brooke was certain of anything, it was that the primary thing she desired was someone who would help her create the stable home life she'd never had. That didn't necessarily mean marrying someone who would make a lot of money, but she knew that ultimately, she wanted to end up with someone like the dad from *Leave It to Beaver*. Someone who was reliable, whom she could trust to stick with her and build a family.

"Because I came from a broken family, the driving force in my relationship-building was stability. The boyfriends that I was closest to were always from these perfect families. I wasn't just looking for love, I wasn't looking for financial stability, I was looking for family. I wanted my kids to have a mom and a dad who were going to be there forever. I wanted that more than I wanted to be a famous opera singer. I didn't know if I was going to go anywhere with the singing. That was just a dream. So marrying someone who made enough so that I didn't have to work, so that I could be home with the kids, that was a home run."

About a year after moving to Chicago, Brooke met Paul. He was an estate planning attorney whom Brooke describes as having "absolutely no creative bone in his body. He was an accounting major at Purdue." At a time of unnerving disequilibrium for Brooke, he was exactly what she was looking for. As soon as they got engaged, Paul took charge of the couple's finances and helped Brooke get out of debt.

"He said, 'All right, what kind of debt are we talking about on these student loans?' I pulled out the statements and he started writing checks from his checking account to pay off my student loans. I thought, 'Oh, that's how that goes.'"

Was it odd, we asked, to have someone eliminate all your loans with the stroke of a pen? "It was a weird feeling," Brooke admitted, and after the two married and became parents, it took a while for Brooke to adjust to the economic reality she now lived in. She left her job while pregnant with their first child and struggled with the uneasy fact that someone else's paycheck now paid her bills. Brooke and Paul maintained separate checking accounts (and continue to do so to this day), and when her funds started to run low she found herself having to ask her new husband to transfer money into her account. "I didn't like that feeling at all."

The fact that the money didn't really feel like hers made her question every purchase. "Whenever I was buying something that wasn't benefiting the whole family, I felt like I needed to tell him. So I'd say, 'I got these boots today.' And after a while he was like, 'Why are you telling me?'" But as time went on, Brooke found herself getting more comfortable with the arrangement. She basked in the feeling of being taken care of in a way she'd never experienced in childhood, and also saw that her contributions to the family, while not financial, played an instrumental role in creating the kind of home she'd always hungered for.

"I realized, I have this great person taking care of me. But I'm taking care of myself and the kids, and so after that I didn't look back. That feeling that I owed him an explanation of what was going on financially disappeared."

We heard this sentiment from a number of our friends across both groups, some who stay at home full-time and others who contribute financially to the household but aren't the primary wage earner. Though they may not be cashing a paycheck that pays all the bills, their homes and families, and in some cases their spouse's career, would not function without their contributions. As our friend Ashley, a part-time public health project director, put it, "I do a hell of a lot around here that is very valuable. I contribute in ways that aren't money makers but that keep everything going and moving forward. You can't really put a price on that. It's all contributing to the overall good of our household." These women are proud of the lives they've built, though some also acknowledge that outwardly, those lives might not look like the most thrilling existences.

"I'm a suburban mom," Brooke told us. "I drive a minivan, sliding doors and all. I'm not cool, I don't know what goes on in the city. Which sounds like I'm not happy with it. I'm totally fine with it, but it is like *Groundhog Day.*" She has three kids now, and her days are filled with the messy mundane elements that raising three kids in a Chicago suburb entail, but it's the life she always wanted, and she shines as she tells us about it. She has the family she dreamed about as a child. She works hard to make sure her kids are happy and healthy, and she's able to live her life free from the worries that plagued her own childhood.

As with many of our college friends, Brooke's ambition spills out into her suburban life. Without money as a driving force, she's explored other ways to channel that ambition into work that is psychically and physically gratifying. She's "been the president of everything I can be president of," including the PTA and the neighborhood newcomers association. When being in the same spot every morning for six a.m. power yoga no longer satisfied her, she earned a yoga teacher certification and began teaching the six a.m. class at a national yoga chain. She was such a popular teacher that the company eventually asked her to start running teacher training. She's also started teaching voice lessons a few times a week.

"I want to figure out a way to get the music back in my life somehow," she told us. "And I'm excited about being a fitness person, and a person who guides people. Where that will go, I'm not sure."

What Causes Women to Feel So Differently About Money?

Some of our friends knew, without a doubt, that they would be economically independent, just as they knew the sun would rise in the east, and others felt equally driven to build home lives filled with warmth, calm, and ease. But why? How could these women have such strong yet nearly opposing viewpoints when it came to money?

At first we wondered if having a volatile childhood led women directly into one group or the other, but as both Nicole and Brooke illustrate, it's possible to come out of an emotionally or economically unstable home with fairly different feelings about money.

Some of our friends who had rocky childhoods emerged as Brooke did, searching for a man who would put on a tie each morning, grab his briefcase, and head out the door to his job in the city (we found it remarkable how many of the women who married for stability were paired with men who still wear ties to work, despite the fact that so much of the modern working world now finds jeans and a button-down to be acceptable office attire).

We use the word *man* here pointedly. None of our friends in same-sex relationships looked for someone else to be the economic support in the relationship. All of them were driven from their early years to be financially independent. Some make more money than others—one woman is a high school teacher who lives modestly and chose not to have children, while another is a director at a large nonprofit who helps support a son and a stepson—but none of them thought for a minute that they wouldn't pay their own way. Some of these women told us that from early on they didn't plan on partnering with a man, weren't sure what their lives would look like, and knew they'd better figure out how to support themselves, echoing theories put forth by a number of economists.[9] On the whole, lesbians do better than straight women when it comes to supporting themselves. They earn more than straight women,[10] are more likely to be in a two-income household,[11] and are less likely to work part-time or quit work entirely to care for children.[12]

Other friends, like Nicole, lived through volatile childhoods and decided they would never rely on anyone other than themselves.

"I think the biggest lesson I learned from my childhood is, you cannot depend on someone else to take care of you and that you need to take care of yourself," Audrey, the government lawyer, told us. She'd watched her father abandon the family, then her mother's consequent attempts to cobble together a career, and nearly had to drop out of college when her father abruptly stopped sending the few hundred dollars a month he contributed to help make her tuition payments.

Marly, the real estate agent in St. Louis, also saw, growing up, how hard it was for her family to make ends meet. "I was interested in [money] because I saw my dad working really hard, but it seemed like the family was always stretching to pay the bills. When I wanted a new shirt or a new pair of shorts, that was a stretch. I knew I had to earn the money to get that pair of shorts. So early on, I saw earning and investing money as my route to acquiring the things I needed in life." And after her father died suddenly, she watched her mother claw her way up through a series of entry-level jobs, and decided then and there that she would always be able to pay her own way.

But others simply shrugged when asked where they got the idea that they should be responsible for their own economic security. "I've just always been like that," many said. The drive to be self-reliant came easily to them, second nature.

"I'm not really sure where I get my balls," mused Meredith, the owner of a PR firm who married in her mid-forties and has always supported herself, by both choice and necessity. "I have two older brothers who didn't treat me any differently than they treated their buddies. I wasn't littler, I wasn't younger, I wasn't stupider. Anything they could do, I could do. They treated me like a dude, and I just grew up around that."

When it came to our friends who grew up in families as enviable and stable as one on a TV sitcom, we couldn't identify any grand unifying theory as to why some of them were driven to be economically independent while others didn't give it much thought. The clearest conclusion we can draw is this: The women who took it upon themselves to gain financial independence, who held themselves solely responsible for their own economic situation, who wanted to be able to pay the bills and make their own decisions about whether to spring for a manicure or save for a vacation, succeeded at that goal. Today, if they are partnered, they are equal or the bigger wage earners in their relationships. If they are single, they are able to shoulder mortgages in some of the toughest real estate markets in the country, make car payments, and take Instagram-worthy trips several times a year. Married or single, parent or not, the women who wanted to be economically independent made it happen. Which leads us to believe that the single most important factor in determining which of these women would support themselves financially is whether they possessed a deeply rooted desire to do so.

How Passion Fits In

In considering the divergent trajectories Nicole and Brooke followed, we thought a lot about the different ways the two women planned their careers paths. Nicole pursued a career that she'd hoped would spark passion the way it had for her father, while Brooke worked to follow her dream of singing onstage at the Met Opera. Both started out hoping to earn a living doing something they felt passionate about, but, in part because they held different perspectives when it came to the importance of money and financial independence, they ended up in different places. Neither one ended up with their dream job, but they both fulfilled other, perhaps more important goals in their lives—economic independence for Nicole, a stable home life for Brooke. And yet, as we spoke with them, we noticed a tiny sense of loss hanging in the air as they talked about their early post-college lives, back when it had felt, for a moment, that they might find work they felt truly inspired by. We also knew that these women were not alone in feeling they had to choose between passion and money. So we wondered about the relationship between following your heart and finding a job that is financially rewarding but possibly not the most ardor-inducing way to spend your time. How had our other friends managed to balance the two? And how do these choices play out for women who seek financial independence?

After our interviews were complete, we polled our friends on whether they'd prioritized passion or economic independence. More than half our friends told us they'd opted to follow their passion and hoped that the money would work itself out, but hidden in that number was an interesting story. For our friends who didn't see earning money as a do-or-die prospect, when the thing they were passionate about didn't lead to a lucrative career (or, in some cases, any career at all), they gave up working altogether. "I think if I was doing something that I loved, I would've been insistent and said, 'No, I still need this in my life,'" Brooke told us about her decision to quit working when she was pregnant with her first child. "But I was ready to get rid of the job."

Our friend Wendy had similar feelings about her job, even though it was in an area she'd originally loved. Wendy was a journalism major, and before she got married, she'd had a job in PR in downtown Chicago handling big clients, working in a sleek office building and feeling "like I'd made it." But when her husband took a new job in Knoxville, Tennessee, she begrudgingly joined a small, local PR firm with industrial clients. "I went from working with fun spokespeople for Quaker Oats to working with the CEO of a trucking company. It was just not as interesting for me." And when, a few years later, her first child arrived, it wasn't that big of a leap to leave a job she wasn't thrilled with anyway. "I wanted to be with my daughter more than I wanted to be going to that office every day," Wendy told us.

We heard this sentiment from many of our Opt Out friends. If they'd loved what they were doing, they would have found a way to make it work, but they didn't love it, so it made sense to give it up and stay home. These were also women who had the economic freedom to stay home. Their spouses earned enough that they could give up their jobs without dramatically changing their lifestyles. And, most significant, they were women who did not equate money with independence. They were comfortable relying on someone other than themselves to pay the bills and contributing to home life in other ways.

Other friends, when confronted with the choice between a job that was good enough and staying at home, opted for the job, propelled by a desire to support themselves, to not have to ask anyone whether it was okay to buy boots. These were the same women who were driven to be economically independent. While some of them struggled to infuse passion into their jobs, others found ways to feel stimulated by, if not passionate about, their work. And still others, like Laurel the attorney, saw work and passion as two entirely separate realms. Which made us wonder when it was, exactly, that passion became a thing that had anything to do with work. It's a luxury, no doubt, to feel that the same activity that pays your electric bill should also bring you pleasure, satisfaction, and deep fulfillment. So why did so many of our friends get hung up on the idea that if they didn't love their job, then it wasn't worth doing?

This idea that passion and work should fuse together into one blissful career seems to have evolved only in the past few generations. Our grandparents, we imagine, never gave a second thought to whether they loved what they did. They were drugstore workers, city employees, small business owners, police officers, men and women who showed up at work each morning out of economic need, not out of love for their jobs. In the past, hard work was considered virtuous and meaningful not because that work changed the world or brought people pleasure, but because it meant you could take care of yourself and your family, that you'd all have a place to sleep and food to eat and clothes to wear.[13] But over the past few decades, things have changed.[14]

"There's little doubt that 'do what you love' (DWYL) is now the unofficial work mantra for our time," Miya Tokumitsu wrote in an essay that outlines how this is mostly Steve Jobs's fault.[15] When Jobs strode across stages at Apple in his casual black turtlenecks, he was selling not just the latest Apple invention, but the idea that if you follow your passion, you can change the world, wear comfy clothes to work, and generally get rich and be happy. In 2005, Jobs gave a commencement speech at Stanford where he told the newly minted graduates that "the only way to do great work is to love what you do." The speech went viral—as of this writing it's been viewed more than 9 million times—and gave voice to an idea that had been brewing in our collective consciousness for a while.[16]

The idea that you should be passionate about your work predates Steve

Jobs—the 1970 book *What Color Is Your Parachute?* formally introduced the world to the idea that work should be connected to love, along with steps on how to get there—and it started to gain momentum right around the time we graduated from college. The phrase "follow your passion" began appearing in print with increasing frequency around the time *Parachute* was published, disappeared for a while, and then, in 1990, while we were in college (and right around the time the baby boomers were hitting forty and possibly starting to freak out about being middle-aged), the phrase again began to pepper books and articles.[17] In the past decade, the concept has seeped into every aspect of the way we talk about work, with magazine articles exhorting young women to "Get That Life" (wherein *that life* involves a super-cool job) and job listings for house cleaners specifying that prospective employees should be passionate while they mop the floors.[18] This idea has spread like a contagion, Tokumitsu argues, because "do what you love" is actually about class, not about love. Being a person who loves their work sends the message that you are approaching Steve Jobs–level success in society. You are not merely an automaton tightening screws in a factory, you are someone with ideas and fire and gusto, a person with control over your career and thus your destiny.

This explains why some of our friends seemed mildly embarrassed that they hadn't found their true calling, the thing they could fall in love with, as though their lack of all-engulfing passion somehow minimized their achievements. It also explains why so many of our friends felt they needed to be passionate about their work in order to keep doing it. Based on these conversations, we suspect that the idea that one should feel fervently about one's work disproportionately affects women, who may already feel that their job is a hardship for the family. For women who don't inherently see their role in the family as "economic provider," staying in a job that might not pay much and that they're not crazy about feels frivolous and selfish.

Further complicating matters is the murky overlap between being passionate about work and finding it meaningful. It is perhaps possible to do work that is meaningful and *not* be passionate about it (could you do administrative work for Doctors Without Borders and hate it?), but more commonly people find passion in things that feel meaningful to them. And women, much more than men, are driven by a need to find meaning in their work.[19] In fact, when male-dominated professions like computer science and mechanical engineering offer opportunities to work on projects that are societally meaningful—such as designing a low-cost solution for providing clean drinking water as opposed to, say, launching the next cryptocurrency startup—women sign on in droves.[20]

We don't want to deter anyone from following her dreams or working to build a better society, but it's worth stating the obvious: Passions often don't translate into lucrative careers. Our friends' passions included acting, singing, Chicago sports teams, and yoga, all activities those friends tried to monetize at one time or another, for very low pay. While intellectually most women know they won't earn much chasing a dream, the reality of trying to balance a low-paying job with raising a family and running a household, especially if your spouse way outearns you, is enough to make many women leave the workplace, particularly those women who don't feel they *must* be economically independent.

Many of our friends who followed their passion with no economic plan ended up out of the workforce for years. Ariel, an aspiring screenwriter (more on her in the next chapter) who left teaching and film school to stay at home with her children, said she'd never received any guidance beyond following her bliss. "One of the biggest things you need to realize as an artist is you have two lives you need to lead. One that can economically support you, and one where you're following your passion. My mother was a huge supporter of my passion. She is a true believer in following your dreams. But I needed someone who could say, 'This is what's going to be required of you for your art, and this is what's going to be required of you to live.'"

Following your passion doesn't always lead to happiness, either. Rather, being good at something can create passion for it. In one study of college administrators, those who had been working on the job the longest were more likely to see it as a calling. Those who were newer to the job viewed it as simply a job.[21] Which aligns with what we saw with our friends: Amy, the insurance company executive, didn't pick her field because she was wild about insurance. But when we talked to her, she exuded enthusiasm for her career. Over the years, she became good at it, and her expertise sparked passion. And our friend Heather told us that her banking job wasn't a passion—that hadn't been her guiding principle, anyway. She was interested in being able to support herself above all else. But we saw that her work was clearly something she cared about very deeply, a job that paid her back for her hard work, for being really good at something, by boosting her confidence and awarding her success.

Learning to Love the Thing You're Good At

If you put all our friends' families on a scale from *Leave It to Beaver* to *Breaking Bad*, Heather's family might be off-the-chart normal. When her friends meet her parents, she told us, "They say, 'Wow, it really is like that.'" Heather grew up in Grand Rapids, Michigan, where her father was a doctor and her mother was what Heather describes as "a professional volunteer."

"My mom didn't work, but she was never at home," said Heather. "She was president of Mobile Meals, delivering meals to people who can't get out. She was president of Keep Grand Rapids Beautiful for a while. She ran a children's concert society. She was always doing things for the community, which I really respected." And the whole family participated in her mother's efforts, delivering meals to the sick or needy. On the other end of the career spectrum was Heather's aunt Jackie, who served as another important role model. Jackie had gone to law school at the University of Michigan in the '60s, was one of the first women to make partner at a major law firm in Grand Rapids, and later became a judge.

When Heather arrived at Northwestern, she decided to follow what interested her, which was math. She was accepted into a competitive mathematics major, and when she graduated, she had a job offer from Lehman Brothers. A job there was prestigious, sounded interesting, and paid well, so she took it, figuring it would lead somewhere positive, though she had no idea where. "I can't say that I've ever had any kind of master plan in my life. I know some people are very diligent about that, but I'm not one of them."

Heather did well at Lehman and worked her way through the firm's various offices, doing a stint in New York and then London, where she was one of two women the firm had on the trading floor. After two years with the company, she left to attend business school at Wharton, and post-graduation moved to a large consulting firm in Boston to be closer to her boyfriend. The two were planning on getting married; he'd already landed a Boston-based job in financial services, and Heather easily found a job with a top firm in the city.

Heather spent a good portion of her career at the consulting firm, working her way up to partner while getting married and having two kids. When her kids were very young, she scaled back her work hours to part time, and later worked from home a few Fridays a month. But more important, Heather says, she took a significant piece of advice from senior women at her consultancy: get the help she needed at home to keep her career on track, even though at the time, that help took a large chunk out of her salary.

"They said, 'If it's hard to make ends meet at the very beginning, think about it as a long-term investment. Because over time, it pays back in multiples of the investment.' And that's really how we thought about it."

What that meant was that Heather and her husband hired nannies, some live-in and some live-out, as well as general household help, so that when they were at home, they could spend time with their kids rather than scrubbing kitchen counters, and when they were at work, they could focus entirely on their jobs, knowing that their kids were being cared for.

"The nice thing about consulting is, if you want to be home at ten o'clock on a Tuesday, you can make sure you're home at ten o'clock on a Tuesday. But if you have a CEO meeting that day, you can't, and you might not be home till seven or eight. So you have to have a nanny for that role, because the hours are uncertain."

When we first interviewed her, Heather was a couple of years into a new job at a midsize bank and had just been promoted to chief marketing officer. Throughout our interview, she spoke matter-of-factly about her career, about how sometimes the work was hard and the hours were long, about how once, early on in her career, she'd had to fly her father in from Michigan to babysit her kids when she and her husband both had business trips scheduled on the same day, and about how after a while, the work at the consulting firm felt like less of a good fit for her, so she'd jumped to a different kind of job in banking.

She used phrases like "fantastic experience" and "exciting" and "very fun." She told us how she got to ring the bell at the stock exchange when the bank went public. So when we asked her how she'd prioritized following her passion versus being economically independent, we were surprised when she shrugged her shoulders and told us, "I don't know what a passion would be for me more than what I do. If there was something that I was incredibly passionate about, then I think it would be an interesting trade-off. On the whole I enjoy what I do, but is it a passion I can't live without? No."

Heather likes her work. In fact, she seems to derive a deep satisfaction from excelling, moving up, being great at what she does, and being rewarded for it with bigger paychecks and bigger jobs. She's clearly proud of being a successful woman in business. And she has strived to make her job work for her. Her husband has an equally demanding and lucrative career, so if she weren't driven by a deep desire to work, to support and challenge herself, she could have quit long ago. Even though he is one half of a two-High-Achiever family, one of our power couples, Heather's husband has been nothing but supportive of her career. The couple view their careers with equal importance (though yes, Heather is the one who makes the pediatrician appointments), they both value their time at work, and they don't get caught up in the parenting guilt trap.

"We both know that there are times when you have to work really hard, there are times that it's slightly less hard, but there's no guilt. I don't believe there's a time when either one of us ever asked the other not to do what they were doing. We're both rooting for each other to succeed, which is critical."

Heather speaks so confidently and enthusiastically about her work that we had assumed she was driven by a burning dedication to numbers, finance, or business strategy. But more likely, what we mistook for passion was actually the satisfaction of a job well done, the pleasure of a life that has come together the way she envisioned it as a child, the enjoyment of being able to support her family not only emotionally but financially.

"There are hardships to both of us working so hard, but there are also freedoms over time if you manage your careers jointly," Heather explained. And what she means is, there is economic freedom. Heather told us that when her bank was contemplating either going public or being sold to another entity, the men in her office hung on every nuance of the impending sale, while she felt that either way, things would work themselves out, because she wasn't the sole earner for her family. "I got to say, because I have a husband who is still working, we're not going to starve in any shape or form. The men I work with, they said, 'I've never been able to think about my life that way.'"

Economic freedom also means that now, as she moves toward the later part of her forties, Heather has the room to contemplate switching jobs entirely. Some days she thinks about retiring to teach math to middle schoolers. She coached her children's elementary school math team for five years, meeting kids at the school at seven fifteen one morning a week to work on math problems before heading into the office. The team won their local championship three years in a row thanks in part to her coaching, and since then, she's wondered if teaching math could be a good second career for her. Other days she thinks she wants to go for the next big job and stay with her current employer for another decade or so.

On the whole, our friends who had big jobs in finance or for large cor-
porations or consultancies seemed content with their jobs, willing to put
in long hours or work hard when needed, happy to get up in the morning
and go to work, interested in what they were doing—but didn't view
themselves as people who had followed a passion. In other words, they
viewed their jobs as, well, jobs. Jobs they enjoyed, but jobs nonetheless. It
paid the bills, gave them economic independence and security, supported
their families, but it wasn't their everything. If they wanted to give back to
their communities or do meaningful work, they did that outside of office
hours, by volunteering at animal shelters or in national parks or organizing community events or, sometimes, by writing checks. If they wanted to
do things they were passionate about, they made time for ski vacations or
book clubs or long runs or sharing things they loved with their kids. They
didn't waste a whole lot of time asking themselves if their jobs were worth
the hours they put into them in a cosmic sense, as though the universe was
keeping track of how everyone on the planet spends their time and weighing their worth on that basis. They didn't ask if the value of their jobs was
worth the sacrifice of being away from their kids. They wanted to support
themselves and their families, and they found enjoyable and intellectually
fulfilling ways to do that.

While some of our friends followed Heather's path and found pleasure
in careers that might not have been born of passion, others figured out
how to balance their need for passion with their drive to be economically
independent. Leona, another performance major in our class, also had an
aspiring opera career that didn't pan out, but she found other ways to earn
money singing. "I started singing at weddings and funerals so I could
make some money, and subbing in and cantoring at different churches.
Then I realized how much I enjoyed doing that. I enjoyed doing that more
and more, and I enjoyed auditioning less. Especially because if you're a
lovely soprano, you're a dime a dozen." She now works as a choir director
in her church, and while her husband earns more than she does, the family relies on her paycheck to make ends meet.

And our friend Ashley, who was interested in using her writing skills in public service, prioritized passion at some points in her life and finances at others, a sine curve with "meaningful work" on one side and "income" on the other, ebbing and flowing as her own needs and the needs of her family shifted over the years.

Shaping Passion into a Career That Pays the Bills

Ashley grew up in a small city in Pennsylvania and knew she wanted to get into politics from a young age. At Northwestern, she enrolled in the journalism school, but from the start she had no aspirations of becoming a journalist. "I thought I was going to be the press secretary at the White House, that I'd be heading to Washington, DC, after graduation," she told us. "I met part of that goal." After graduation, she packed her bags and moved into a cheap house share in DC with college friends. She'd landed an internship for the congressman from her home district, which she figured was a good way to get her foot in the door. After a few months of interning she was offered a full-time job there. It was prestigious, but paid $18,000 a year. At that point, Ashley wasn't worried about money. "I was so excited. I was like, 'I'm working on the Hill, here we go!'"

Looking back, Ashley says she had never really included economics in her career planning. "I was fairly clueless," she told us. "I tried to find something I could do related to what I'd studied, but I had no sense of what things cost relative to my salary level and desired lifestyle. Turns out that my skills and interests don't fall in high-paying areas. Bummer!" But at the same time, she knew she wanted a paycheck and the ability to support herself at an income level that would allow her to live a comfortable middle-class existence.

After five years as a legislative aide on the Hill, Ashley was ready for a change. She'd been eyeing grad school as a possible avenue, but needed to earn more money to pay her tuition bills, so she began looking to make a move. Even though she was searching for a higher-paying gig, she also wanted to stay with a job that kept her fired up and felt meaningful.

Ashley ended up working for a large PR firm with health care clients. She had some private sector clients, but her work with the CDC and National Institutes of Health helped feed her need to do socially meaningful work.

In scouting around for a place to land, Ashley knew she wanted to stay on the communications and policy side of things, but wasn't quite sure how to channel those skills. At first she thought about business school, but then realized, "I'm not a numbers person, who am I kidding?" Nonprofit management seemed attractive, too, but after spending a lot of time reflecting on the types of things she liked reading and learning about, and figuring out what would keep her motivated to get to work every day, Ashley settled on health policy.

"I realized that health was something that always intrigued me. Public health is such a broad field that you can really stick your feet in anywhere and feel like you're making a positive difference. I thought, 'If I'm going to invest time and money, that's the background and specialty area that I want to invest in.'"

Ashley ended up enrolling in a master's degree program in public health. Midway through the program, a former colleague contacted her about some freelance work. It was mostly writing and editing, fairly simple and straightforward, but the project intrigued her. It was an HIV prevention study with a prominent medical center, something she'd be able to work on part-time from home while she finished her graduate studies. The project was a good fit while she pursued her degree, and when she graduated, the medical center offered her a job and she took it. Eleven years, a marriage, and two kids later, Ashley became the project director of the study.

When we first spoke with her, she marveled at how what had seemed like a little decision back in grad school ended up affecting her career trajectory for more than a decade. Without even knowing what her criteria would be for a good job later in life, she managed to end up with a career that allowed her to work from home, meet her kids at the school bus, engage in work she felt was important, and also receive a solid paycheck. Ashley's husband is a family medicine doctor, and while he earns more than she does, she says she'd be more than capable of supporting herself on her own if she needed to.

A year after we first interviewed Ashley, the project she was running ended and she switched jobs. She's now with a professional association for scientists. She enjoys the work, though it doesn't give her the thrill that working in public health did. For now, she's prioritizing other things on top of passion. The job provides health benefits for the whole family, and also gives her flexible hours so she can be home with her kids in the afternoons. Her husband often comes home after dinner, so she likes being there when her kids get home from school, spending time with them on their homework or kicking a soccer ball around with them in the backyard.

Once her kids are older, Ashley envisions herself stepping back into public health, once again prioritizing passion over economics. Ashley was one of a number of our friends who started out with an interest that might not be traditionally viewed as a road to riches (writing and journalism) but who, with some back and forth, has managed to feed both her passion and her income over the course of her career.

It's well and good to want to incorporate passion into your career. As writers, we are hardly in a position to tell anyone not to study art, make art, or try to eke out a living selling your art. But ultimately our friends who didn't conflate passion with paychecks, who wanted to be able to support themselves doing something they liked but didn't feel they needed their job to be their everything—who didn't need to be saving the world and stoking their creative side and also getting paid well for it—were the ones who earned financial independence. Some of them earned it ten times over, becoming High Achievers, outearning their spouses, and ensuring they could support themselves through their working lives and beyond. Others vacillated between years where passion drove their choices and years when money did. The two of us both fall squarely into the latter group—we've always been insistent upon providing for ourselves financially. We both knew from a very early age that we would earn enough money to walk out any door that needed walking out of. We equated money not only with stability but with power, and we didn't want anyone else to have that power.

But we also both wanted to be writers. Given that we weren't living in nineteenth-century England, we knew we weren't likely to find benefactors who would fund our art while we strolled around through the countryside thinking about sentences we wanted to write. And so we both—separately, with no discussion that we were doing so—worked out ways to feed our competing desires to produce art and also earn a living. We have both taken on jobs that were purely pay-the-bills gigs at times when our lives demanded we do so. We have spent years working in places that were good enough, jobs that might allow us enough flexibility to write on the side, or where writing *was* the job, just not the kind of writing we'd be doing in a perfect world, or bringing the same skills we'd honed in writing to other, more lucrative careers. Early in our careers we both surveyed the writing landscape and opted for money or growth potential, with Hana working in corporate communications for a large consulting firm, then following the lure of the burgeoning Internet away from writing and toward tech, and Liz taking jobs at glossy fashion magazines, not her dream niche in publishing (she would have preferred staying in the LGBT or political press) but a then probable route to an enviable résumé in the New York writers' world. We knew that these early jobs would pay the bills (or get us to the next jobs, and those would pay the bills), even if they might not have been our dream jobs. We prioritized money and stability and figured the passion part would work itself out. And, as we write these words, it has.

Here's What We Know About Economics

▶ **Figure out what stability and independence mean for you.**

Our friends fell into two groups when it came to their feelings about stability, independence, and money. Where do you fall? Do you see earning money as the path to a stable life, or are there other elements that feel more important than financial stability? Are you comfortable relying on someone else to pay the bills while you build a life for your family at home, or does the thought make you break out in hives? Are you okay with being supported for a short period of time, for example, while you pursue an advanced degree and your spouse works a corporate job, or is even that unacceptable to you? Understanding how you feel about money is crucial because, unlike nearly everything else we've covered in this book, it's not likely to change. While the women we interviewed who relied on their spouse's income sometimes needed to overcome some initial discomfort with spending money that didn't feel like theirs, they were also women who were able to step away from a paycheck. Some women can do this and others would rather be poked continuously by tiny needles. The way you feel about money and its connection to stability and independence will be a driving force in your career, so identifying these feelings early on and articulating them will help you make decisions later. Women who take financial independence as a given, who behave as though this is the only and obvious way to live life, end up able to support themselves. So don't fear—if this is what you want more than anything else, you'll achieve it. But not everyone wants or needs financial independence to feel secure and stable. Know what's important to you. Own your stability.

▶ **Society tells us that women shouldn't think about money. Don't listen.**

In college, men and women begin self-segregating into majors with very different economic outcomes.[22] One study found that men monopolize majors that lead to high-paying tech and engineering jobs, like civil engineering, computer science, and mechanical engineering. Of the ten highest-paying majors, nine are populated primarily by men (at levels that are insane—mechanical engineering is 89 percent male), while women dominate six of the ten lowest-paying majors, including social work and anthropology.[23] The reasons behind this segregation are varied and complex, but the outcome is clear: Men are more likely than women to graduate from college with majors that will lead them to financial independence. Our friends who prioritized earning money did so starting in college. They considered which kinds of jobs would meld their skills with a paycheck large enough to support themselves and, down the road, a family. They did this even though no one told them to, motivated either by past experiences or a clear vision of what they wanted their lives to look like and how they would get there. They did this even though the social pressure against them could be great. They were often one of only a handful of women in the room, showing up in places where men told them they weren't needed or questioned why they wanted to be there, working their way through male-dominated fields like finance, utilities, and technology.

By contrast, many of our friends who ended up opting out did so because their salaries didn't cover the cost of childcare. Economically it just didn't make sense for them to continue working, and many of them seemed surprised by this realization, possibly because they hadn't thought about the financial implications of their choices until it was too late. So even though you may not have been raised to do so, let this serve as a wake-up call: Think about money. Think about how much of it you want to earn compared to your partner, and realistically how you will go about doing that, given your skills and your interests. Think about how that money will pay for children, if you want them. Do not shut your eyes and hope it will all work out. Reclaim conversations about finances and long-term investments and raises. This is not men's work. It's your work.

▶ **Don't conflate passion with work.**

For some of our friends, like Nicole and Laurel, the desire to be financially independent was so all-encompassing that they set aside any concerns about chasing their passion. For them, work and passion were two entirely separate imperatives. They both have things in their life that they care deeply about or feel excited by (travel, book clubs, going to concerts, testing new recipes). Those things just don't happen to be work. And they've both achieved the financial independence that was paramount for them.

You can have a successful career, achieve a lot, and feel rewarded in many areas. Feeling that you must also be deeply, madly in love with your job puts a lot of unnecessary pressure on what is ultimately a way to feed yourself and pay bills. Work can be meaningful in a lot of ways, so consider what makes work meaningful for you. Not everyone needs to be saving the world in order to justify time spent away from kids or hours spent in an office. Women can derive meaning from supporting their families, gaining recognition in their field, showing other, younger women in the office what it looks like to be a successful woman, or simply getting better at a skill. And a few of our friends who reached C-level positions were able to start initiatives within their companies that were meaningful to them, around work-life balance and gender equality. Figure out creative ways to do something you care about and are good at. Don't limit yourself by precluding work that might not immediately inspire love poems.

▶ **If you must be an artist, and you also must support yourself, understand that these are competing desires.**

The two of us have suffered over the course of our careers from competing goals. We both wanted to be financially independent, we wanted to be mothers, and we wanted to be writers. Early on, we realized that it was not possible to do all three of these things exactly the way we wanted to at all times. If you're an artist at heart, and also want to earn a steady paycheck, know that you're likely to be moving between these two goals continuously over the course of your life. And know that adding motherhood into the mix makes things more expensive—therefore more complex—unless you become a super-famous and wealthy artist, which we hope you do.

▶ **Follow the thing you're good at, and you will be rewarded.**

You may never wake up in the morning feeling ecstatic that you get to think about supply-chain management all day long (or wherever the thing you're good at leads you), but if you excel at it, you'll find yourself earning promotions, climbing up the ranks, earning more money and power and recognition, and stoking your ambitious side. We are not suggesting anyone should stay in a job they loath, but rather that there are ways to take a job that might not sound like your dream gig and turn it into a career that makes you proud of yourself and the life you've achieved.

CHAPTER 6

CHANGE

One morning early on in this project, we were sitting in Liz's kitchen trying to process what we'd learned from our interviews. Hana grabbed a folded-up piece of scrap paper with a kid's homework assignment on the back, and together we began sketching out our friends' trajectories. Beginning directly after graduation we drew a straight line shooting upward over time, representing how our friends had all seemed to move together as a cohesive unit in those early years, undertaking first jobs, starting graduate school, some meandering for a while and then landing on a career path. At the point where our friends started to have kids, we drew their paths diverging as some chose to stay home, others continued on an upward career trajectory, and still others settled into flex-life jobs: our three trajectories.

Some years have passed since we began our interviews, and in that time our college friends' lives—and our own—have continued to shape and reshape themselves. Looking back at that piece of scrap paper, we saw that those lines don't simply end where our interviews started. We found ourselves wanting to add in curves and circles and curlicues and U-turns. As our friends have rounded forty-five, the majority of them are experiencing significant life transitions, whether heading back into the workforce after time at home with their children, divorcing or marrying for the first time, or flipping ambition levels with their partner. Just as having children splintered our original straight line into three different trajectories, our friends' mid-forties represent another fragmentation point, another opportunity to shift trajectories, reinvent, do something completely different.

When we asked our friends about their dreams back in college, they dutifully recounted the things they had fantasized about doing and the people they'd envisioned becoming with all the knowledge and wisdom of a recent college grad. Which is to say, back in college, they possessed dreams, but didn't give one second's thought to how those dreams would evolve once they hit middle age. As college students, forty was so far away, it wasn't even worth contemplating. But now that these women are actually *in* their forties, they have all come to the collective realization that turning forty doesn't mean life is over or that the ambitions they had in their twenties and thirties were the only ambitions they could ever have. Instead, their ambition remained elastic over the twenty-five years, ballooning some years, compressing others, always playing a part in how they defined themselves and their lives.

It's not breaking news that people hit forty and enter a midlife crisis; in fact, it's so commonplace as to be surprising if you don't have some kind of middle-aged freak-out. But that clichéd crisis has always been male: a middle-aged balding white man trades in his longtime loyal wife and his responsibilities for a red Ferrari and Pamela Anderson. According to popular media, middle-aged women don't have the luxury of these same abandonment fantasies. After all, we've known since 1986, when *Newsweek* featured a study that said single women over forty were less likely to get married than to be killed by a terrorist, that the most terrifying thing that could happen to a forty-year-old woman was to remain single.[1] (Key side note: This study was later debunked.) When we entered college, even if we didn't know exactly what we wanted to be doing by forty, we knew we needed to have everything figured out by then, as Sally Albright articulated in *When Harry Met Sally . . .* : "[Forty] is just sitting there, like some big dead end!" No one seemed to have much to say about what happened to women beyond forty, as though society collectively wished women would simply fade into oblivion once they stopped being young and cute. Therefore, no one gave much thought to what midlife crises might look like for women.

But the way women over forty are thought of, discussed, and represented in the media has shifted radically since we graduated from college. Many in our mothers' generation believed that women over forty shouldn't wear miniskirts or have long hair (seriously, this is a thing one of our mothers told us: that long hair on a woman over forty looks ridiculous), but now more than ever, women over forty are expected to deliver substantial badassery. Yes, ageism and misogyny remain systemic obstacles for women in the workplace and beyond, but now that we, the women of Gen X, have reached our forties, older women are deep in a renaissance. We're celebrated for our wisdom and professional experience,[2] our longevity (Jane Fonda and Lily Tomlin, '80s feminist film heroines, are still ruling the screen with gusto, and Elizabeth Warren and Ruth Bader Ginsburg have become their own memes among millennials), and our strength and beauty, headlining fashion advertising campaigns.[3] We are also now acknowledged, for better or worse, for our sexual viability—in the '80s and '90s it was understood that no one but Mrs. Robinson (played by a then thirty-five-year-old Anne Bancroft, just to make sure audiences found her attractive) could be sexy over forty. By 1999 Stifler's mom from *American Pie* had introduced the world to the term *MILF*.[4] The term quickly entered the common parlance, joined shortly by *cougar*. It was as though the world had collectively discovered—who knew!—that women do not crumple into a wrinkled heap of dust on their fortieth birthdays. We could keep our hair long, slide into leather pants, and date a hot twenty-three-year-old if we felt like it. Oh, and sit on the Supreme Court and, eventually, run for president.

Now that Gen-X women are several years past that "big dead end" of forty, we've discovered that the other side isn't actually an infinite abyss of pain, loneliness, and gray hair—quite the contrary. We definitely heard stories in our interviews about our friends' struggles with economics,

212 The Ambition Decisions

careers, identity, and being part of the "sandwich generation"—taking care of both children and aging parents—but the more marked impression we got from our friends was that while some of them had undergone midlife-crisis-esque moments in their forties, the crossroads had led to positive, often exciting changes. What resonated more for this group of women was a feeling of IDGAF liberation,[5] the ability to care less about others' opinions, to zero in on their true desires. For our college friends, forty was an opportunity to start down a different path, to evaluate what they wanted to do with their next span of time, to consider how they wanted to break their days down differently, what they wanted to achieve or do or have happen next.

When You've Spent the First Part of Your Life Following Everybody Else's Plan

For some of our Opt Outer friends, their mid-forties—with fewer child-care demands and more hours to themselves in a day—presented an opportunity, and in many cases, the financial necessity, to assess what they wanted the next part of their lives to look like. Several of these women acknowledge that they spent the first part of their lives doing things other people wanted them to do. Some had also gotten what they wanted out of those decades: They'd looked forward to being stay-at-home mothers, and they'd enjoyed their time at home with their kids. But for varying reasons—older kids who didn't need as much hands-on parenting, a divorce or a spouse's lost job that meant a change in financial fortunes, the long-awaited opportunity to pursue a degree—these women were ready to move on to paying jobs that fed their intellectual and financial needs. For one friend whose impassioned first Skype interview stuck with us for years, a relatively simple but long-held dream—to be a teacher—proved elusive, until she reached middle age and found a way to get her career going.

I Was Pretty Entangled in My Mother's Dream

Sarabeth was raised in Charleston, South Carolina, by a strong-willed, divorced mother with big plans for her daughter. When we asked Sarabeth the same first question we asked all of our friends—"When you got to Northwestern, what was your plan?"—her answer spoke volumes: "My plan, or my mother's plan, was to go to law school. I was pretty entangled in my mother's dream." Sarabeth's mother, after a nasty divorce from Sarabeth's father, became a single mom in a community where there weren't many single moms, and "she was determined that her two daughters were going to be financially independent." Sarabeth would be a lawyer, and her sister would be a doctor, end of story. It mattered little to her mother how Sarabeth pictured her future career. "I wanted to be a teacher. She was vehemently opposed to that, because when she was my age, she was told that she could only be a teacher or a nurse, and she wanted to be a diplomat. Being a teacher was the bottom of the barrel. It was so gender-oriented toward women, she thought it was the worst job ever."

Sarabeth had a complicated relationship with her mother, but, like most children, still yearned to earn her approval and make her proud—something she had already done at least once by being accepted to a prestigious private college, even though financially it was a stretch for the family. To make her tuition payments, Sarabeth participated in a university work-study program; even then, the quarterly tuition bills were a source of stress.

Sarabeth majored in communications studies—she relished her classes in public speaking and performance—and also took classes in education, dreaming of one day opening a charter school. But as she entered her senior year, her mother refused to let the law school plan drop. When Sarabeth told her she wanted to get an education degree instead, her mother wouldn't hear of it. And so, as if she'd been conscripted by the military, Sarabeth made a deal with her mother: she would go to law school and graduate, and after that she'd be free to do whatever she wanted. Her mother was certain that if she went to law school, she'd come around to the idea of being a lawyer.

After graduation, Sarabeth dutifully enrolled in a South Carolina law school. She was a good student and a diligent worker, and even if her heart wasn't in it, she stuck it out for three years. It wasn't all a laborious chore; during her second year of law school she did a semester abroad, where she began dating Kyle, a third-year law student from California. After he graduated, he moved to South Carolina to be with her during her last year of school.

When Sarabeth finished law school, she felt like she'd been set free. She was finally ready to pursue what she really wanted to do: earn her teaching credentials. "My mother said, 'You're not going to take the bar?' And I said, 'Oh no, we made a deal. I went through hell for the last three years of my life for you, and now I'm done.'"

Sarabeth enrolled in a master's program in education and found a job at a private school teaching children with disabilities. She and Kyle married, and he took an administrative position with the local government— he didn't want to be a lawyer, either. Between their two salaries, finances were tight, and Sarabeth now had law school loans to pay back, plus grad school tuition. And then her job ended abruptly. Her supervisor "came to me one day and said they couldn't give us our paychecks. We were living paycheck to paycheck at the time, so I decided to quit."

The couple knew they were at a transition point. Kyle's parents were in California and happened to need a house sitter for a few months. Kyle was entertaining the prospect of going into the restaurant business with a friend, and Sarabeth discovered she could get an emergency teaching credential for the California public school system. They were still paying off law school and college loans, but with no other ties and little to lose, the couple moved west. Sarabeth found a job teaching special education while simultaneously working toward her teaching certification. Kyle began his foray into restaurant entrepreneurship but quickly discovered the business wasn't for him. The two were in their mid-twenties and not quite ready to settle down in California. They both wanted to live abroad, and both wanted to serve their country in some way. So they decided to apply to the Peace Corps together. They filled out applications and slid them into envelopes. "Then we started doing the math, before I put the stamps on the applications, and we realized it was going to cost us money. The interest on our education loans was more than the stipend they gave Peace Corps volunteers. That kind of eliminated that idea." Sarabeth still has the applications in sealed envelopes filed away, just in case.

Then Sarabeth learned about the foreign service. "I thought it would be perfect for Kyle, and I thought, 'I can teach anywhere in the world.' I was going to kill two birds with one stone." Kyle was accepted and the couple immediately moved to Washington, DC, so they could begin learning Spanish in preparation for Kyle's first posting. Sarabeth left her job and her master's program, assuming she'd be able to finish it sometime after she moved abroad.

When we first interviewed Sarabeth, she'd been living abroad with Kyle and their two children for fifteen years, and had yet to complete her teaching degree. In every country, she'd attempted to maintain a teaching career, with limited success, usually teaching for very low pay or for free. She taught English at a university in Panama City and in small communities in Moldova and Slovakia, and she organized a reading program for children who live on a public dump site in Honduras. While Sarabeth enjoyed volunteering, she wanted to contribute financially to the family, and also wanted the validation that comes with a paycheck. Kyle wanted those things for her, too, and encouraged her to try to find work. But she realized that to earn "a living wage," she would need to teach in an international or State Department–sponsored school. Without a teaching credential, those jobs were out of reach. When she and Kyle originally signed on to the foreign service, she had no idea she wouldn't be able to earn the credential overseas. Sarabeth hadn't minded being home with her kids when they were young—in fact, she enjoyed being able to give her children the stable two-parent home life she'd missed out on as a kid. But when her youngest child started kindergarten, Sarabeth began looking for a full-time job and was deflated when the search didn't go well.

"I have a shitload of hands-on experience. My knowledge base is the same as a credentialed teacher, but I couldn't get a job that paid more than McDonald's." Sarabeth found herself wondering what else she could possibly do, now that she was ready to move back into the working world. She didn't think she was qualified to do anything but teach. One option she'd been contemplating was returning to graduate school to finish earning her teaching credentials the next time the family was stationed in DC. But Sarabeth worried that those master's programs were costly. "Right now, we're saving for our kids' college, not mine."

Sarabeth told us that her predicament is pretty common among foreign service spouses. "We don't work, we volunteer at our kids' schools and in community projects. The State Department is missing out on a very large pool of educated people that they could use." The State Department does use them, just not in the way that Sarabeth would prefer. As is the case for most foreign service spouses, Sarabeth serves a role that's integral to her husband's career but one that she finds disconcerting: hostess. One of the duties expected of a foreign service member's spouse—and in Sarabeth's experience, those spouses are nearly all women—is to entertain. These women organize coffees and dinners and social time outside the embassy for their husbands, and their husbands' professional associates and their wives. This kind of traditional societal role spurs palpable discomfort for Sarabeth, who has long considered herself an active feminist. "Whatever kind of social situation we are in, if we are at the ambassador's residence and I meet somebody on my own, I introduce myself, and eventually they ask, 'Who are you?' They are trying to place who I am, and eventually, I have to say, 'I'm Kyle's wife.' That's a little demoralizing. Your identity morphs into more traditional gender roles. 'I'm Kyle's wife, that's who I am.'"

While being a foreign service spouse made it difficult, if not impossible, for Sarabeth to find work, that impossibility also relieved her of any tension about staying home with her kids when they were young. "It was wonderful not to have that outside guilt" about leaving the workforce. "I was home, free and clear. I couldn't work even if I wanted to. That was actually a relief." But the flip side of that bargain was that Sarabeth was just "Kyle's wife," with many years of valuable higher education under her belt, and at a loss as to how to build a career of her own.

As her children grew older and more independent and she struggled to find work, Sarabeth found herself sometimes feeling envious of the fact that, not only does her husband work and have an identity unto himself, but he has a job he loves. For him, Sarabeth told us, it is "the best job in the world. Sometimes I think, 'I deserve to have the best job in the world too!' But not everybody gets to." Vacillating on this point even within the span of one sentence, Sarabeth assured us that she was going to find a way to pursue her dream of teaching again. "My time will come. Something is going to fall into place."

Sarabeth seemed to be ensnared in a catch-22 she couldn't find her way out of when we first spoke with her, so we were encouraged to hear how things had changed when we talked to her two years later. She and her family moved back to Washington, and Sarabeth enrolled in a university program, geared to spouses of foreign service members, to finally earn her teaching credential. "Tuition is high, but we thought, if I get a good job, I can make the money back within a year." She expects to earn her master's within five years and have her teaching license in two; when we spoke with her she was a year into the program and feeling buoyed by the vision of her life changes to come. She is also busy with homework, a teaching practicum, and the job of running a household with a tween and a teenager.

Her family has supported her transition back into teaching, Sarabeth says. Her children are happy for her, even if they have missed her being around for them all day, every day. "They've gotten on a good schedule, and it was time anyway. They were getting older and able to take on more."

Kyle, too, has been an advocate of Sarabeth's pursuit of her career after so many years. As she worried about the cost of graduate school tuition, he was the one who suggested she look at it as an investment—that after a year of her working again, they would be able to pay off the debt. Plus, Kyle is looking forward to not being the sole bearer of the financial burden of the family. "He is pretty excited I will be going back to work,"

Sarabeth says. Kyle acknowledges the value of Sarabeth's unpaid labor through childcare, domestic support, and volunteer work over the last two decades, but he is also more than ready for her to transition back into paid work, and perhaps to take a step back himself and have his own midlife career transition (he's been giddily signing up for retirement seminars, as he'll be eligible to retire from the foreign service in a few years).

But Sarabeth views the still materializing future for her and her family with open eyes. "I haven't worked full-time in a long time, and I had this forties crisis. I don't know what is in store for the future, but as long as we financially need it, I will continue [pursuing paid work]." If she had it to do over again, Sarabeth says, she would have finished her teaching credential before embarking on life and starting a family. After she earns her credential, she'll be open to jobs both in the States and abroad; living in this country as a family of four on a public servant's salary—or a school teacher's, for that matter—is a financial stretch for a family that is used to the perks of foreign service life, which sometimes includes live-in staff or country homes. But she's realistic about the breadth of her career options given her job history. "I didn't realize my opportunities would be so limited, but you have to prioritize what's important to you and how you want your life to look."

S arabeth's trajectory—returning to school and then work after a decade-plus out of the workforce raising children—was a traditional, and familiar, one. Many women we interviewed told us their own mothers, after staying home to raise them, went back to school to earn graduate degrees and then transitioned into careers later in life. In Sarabeth's case, she launched her entire career on a trajectory she knew was simply biding time until she could finally do what she wanted. But by delaying getting her teaching credential, she unwittingly committed herself to more than a decade of unpaid work. When we heard she'd worked out the economics and was back in school, we gave her a psychic high five, excited that even though it had taken a while, she'd finally be able to introduce herself as something other than "Kyle's wife."

Sarabeth was not the only friend we interviewed who followed the path laid out for her by others. Lucy, another friend who stayed home with her children for many years, felt that her path, too, had been heavily influenced by what her parents thought her life should look like. But unlike Sarabeth, whose mother had strong opinions about the type of career she should have, Lucy's parents had a heavy hand in guiding her toward the type of person they thought she should marry. That choice set forth a domino-like series of decisions that propelled Lucy down a path that, she discovered, left her deeply unsatisfied. So once Lucy hit her forties, she decided to take the domino set and throw it out the window.

Sometimes Your Original Plan Is the Polar Opposite of What You Really Want

Lucy arrived at Northwestern with pressed jeans, preppy bobbed hair, diamond studs, and monogrammed sheets. She'd grown up in a wealthy Chicago suburb where life had gone pretty smoothly for her. She'd been at the top of her class in high school, served as student body president her senior year, and arrived at college with a burst of energy—Northwestern was the next step in her well-planned life, and she was ready to move things along.

As with Sarabeth's mother, Lucy's parents made clear what was expected of her. She was to marry someone from a similarly wealthy Midwestern family, a man who earned a high wage and knew how to wear a tuxedo. She would stay home with her children, as her mother had done, and she would do volunteer work, sit on the boards of cultural institutions, and plan opulent charity balls. As a result, Lucy did what lots of college students do when they find themselves sprung free from their parents' watchful eyes: She rebelled. Lucy spent most of college dating people her parents considered wildly inappropriate: the much older TA from her psych class, a local bar owner, men from a range of socioeconomic backgrounds and ethnicities. (Needless to say, Lucy's parents never considered that she might bring home someone who wasn't white.) But when it came to figuring out her major and career path, Lucy wavered. She thought she might want to do something in the art world, and perhaps eventually go to graduate school, though she wasn't sure in what area, so she chose to major in art history.

After graduation Lucy found work at a Chicago auction house. "It was an environment of young, energetic people who came from affluent backgrounds. We all could work for no money, work long, crazy hours, and run this company at the age of twentysomething and just have a blast doing it, really enjoying each other and enjoying the work." She met her future husband at the auction house—he was another one of the young, affluent people at work who could afford to work long hours for minimal pay. He came from a suburb much like the one Lucy had grown up in, and the two quickly married at age twenty-three. Lucy's parents were pleased.

"I was going on some different paths with men, and my parents were ready to kill me. So ultimately I followed the path that I felt everyone expected of me. I was dating people who were ten, twenty years older than me and trying to find my great love. But at that age, I think you feel pressure to do what people expect of you."

After she married, Lucy struggled to find a solid direction for her career. She liked the auction house but didn't see it as viable long term—the hours were long and there was no way to move up. At her parents' urging, she enrolled in business school in Chicago, working her way through a degree over the course of three years while she did marketing for a high-profile photographer on the side. Her husband also returned to graduate school, earning a master's degree in journalism. Eventually he found work on a communications team for a pharmaceutical company. After business school, Lucy and her brother decided to start a toy company together, but never managed to get it off the ground. When she became pregnant with her first child and her career hadn't quite crystallized, it seemed like a no-brainer for Lucy to stay home and start leading the kind of life she'd always been expected to live.

"My career was in flux, I didn't really know what I wanted to do, and, as far as money was concerned, I didn't have to work. I didn't feel like I needed a paying job and I wanted to stay home with kids. Because that was the norm in my household growing up, and in my husband's household as well."

For years Lucy's life was filled with hands-on parenting, helping out at her kids' school planning talent shows and working on the art curriculum, and volunteer work, a parade of designer gowns worn to charity balls—the kind of life that might make some women envious. But as her kids grew older, she began to feel a hole in her life that she couldn't quite decipher. She kept poking at it, like a missing tooth. She had all the things in her life that she was supposed to want, and yet . . . something was amiss. The more she thought about it, the more she was certain the problem was her marriage. But she wasn't yet ready to call it quits, so instead she tried to fill the hole with work.

"Getting married that young and doing what I felt like everybody expected me to do, I didn't marry that great love of my life," Lucy told us. "We find ourselves struggling as our children get older—it's like, 'Now what?' Which is why I went back to work."

A part-time job had fallen into Lucy's lap, and it was a convenient foray back into the working world. She'd been a longtime customer of a service that allows women to buy designer clothing in their homes—a sort of personalized trunk show—and the company asked Lucy if she'd be interested in doing some selling and helping train other sellers. She took the job, but after a few years, instead of feeling that the hole had been filled, she now found herself dissatisfied with both her work and her marriage. She was at a point where she should have been loving life—her kids needed her less, her schedule was full of social commitments and volunteer work, and she had just demolished her house in order to rebuild it from scratch, which she described as "something on my bucket list." Instead, she found herself living with her parents while her house was under construction next door (literally—her parents literally lived next door—"I can see the house," she told us on one Skype call), contemplating separating from her husband. But in order to leave her husband, she knew she'd have to find more consistent work. She still had a wealthy family as a safety net, but for the first time in her life, she also wanted to be economically self-sufficient. She wanted to stop living the life that other people had told her to live. Unfortunately, she had no idea what a different kind of life might look like.

When we first interviewed Lucy, she had recently spent a seemingly hopeless afternoon talking to a career coach. "I walked in there and this woman looked at me and she's like, 'You need to figure out what you want to do before I can help you.' I said, 'Well, that's a little frustrating because I want you to help me figure out what to do.' So, that's where I am. I don't know what I want to do. This woman said, 'I can put you in front of any company right now and you could probably do whatever you want.' But I don't know what that is."

And living with her parents wasn't particularly constructive for a life restart, either. When she told her mother she was thinking about getting a divorce, her mother quickly reverted to old tropes.

"She said, 'If you're going to do it again, marry for money. Make it easier for yourself.' At forty-three years old, I just want to tell her to fuck off because I'm like, therein lies the problem. I've been doing everything to please everyone else for so long. The first time around I married for security. I didn't marry for love and fun and happiness. I'm not going to say that I've had this horrible life for the past twenty years, because I haven't. I've had a great life, but I feel like there's some big piece missing and it's not the money."

When we interviewed Lucy two years later, some things had changed in her life, and some hadn't. She and her husband had divorced. She and her kids were still living with her parents. She'd finished construction on her dream house and promptly sold it. And she'd started a new job, working as a part-time independent contractor for a company that helps plan large corporate meetings. It isn't anything close to what she'd planned on doing, but Lucy likes the client service aspect, the fact that she isn't chained to a desk, and the schedule flexibility. Plus, in addition to the income she needs the stimulation. "There's definitely a financial need. And, if I wasn't working, what would I do with my time?"

Lucy also has a new boyfriend, someone she's known since high school who, unlike her ex, doesn't have a high-paying job. For the first time in her life, she needs to think about money, and earning it for herself, but the trade-off is well worth it. "My lifestyle is going to be totally different," she told us. "It's the polar opposite of what I have been used to for the last twenty years of my life. But it's all good. That's not what's important. It takes a while to figure that out, and I'm okay with it." Plus, she assumes, sometime down the line, "I can go make money." If anyone can turn a seventeen-year employment gap into a lucrative career, it's Lucy, who has always been outgoing, with a take-charge personality. But she faces an uphill battle. While there are now several nonprofits and networking groups that help women who have taken caregiving breaks return to the workforce, statistics remain bleak on the prospects for middle-aged women finding those money jobs in today's workforce. Middle-aged women's résumés are overlooked based on age alone.[6] Since the 2008 recession, it has become even more difficult for older women to find long-term employment, with women over fifty accounting for half of the long-term unemployed.[7]

Even our friend Suzanne, who was roundly considered to be the highest-achieving, most-type-A, on-a-track-to-superstardom member of our class, struggled to return to work after a decade out of the workforce. After graduating with honors from Northwestern, earning an Ivy League law degree, interning at the Supreme Court, and becoming a Justice Department lawyer before opting out for fifteen years, she spent years working to find a government legal job at the same pay grade she had earned in 2001. Suzanne has now reentered the workforce as the legal adviser for a national religious organization. When we spoke with her most recently, she seemed to be enjoying her new role—but it was hard to imagine that she would ever regain the hard-hitting federal government career she once had. Or that Lucy would breezily be able to "go make money" at the very moment she wished to.

Lucy, like Sarabeth, adhered to her parents' dream for decades, and, in her mid-forties, is finally ready to pursue her own path. Having always felt she had to prioritize money—though not money she was responsible for earning—Lucy feels liberated, finally, that she is making relationship decisions not solely based on economics. She seems optimistic about the years to come. But we wonder what Lucy's life might have looked like if her parents, while encouraging her to prioritize wealth and lifestyle, had also encouraged her to create that wealth for herself rather than marry into it. The idea that Lucy might be the *provider* of a high-society lifestyle, rather than the beneficiary of one, never seemed to enter into either Lucy's or her parents' worldview. There was never any doubt that Lucy would pursue the life of a modern socialite, stay at home with her children, keep the house running smoothly for her high-earning husband, and raise money for charities in her downtime. She was groomed from an early age to inhabit the role she eventually slipped into in adulthood, despite the fact that her intelligence, skills, top-tier education, and charisma could have easily propelled her to a big career. So perhaps it isn't all that shocking that she was never able to find a career that called to her. Why bother, if no one else in your orbit expects you to have much of a career to begin with?

We interviewed other women who described themselves as parent-pleasers—choosing colleges, majors, careers, and even spouses because of their parents' hopes and dreams for them—but some of them came to the realization earlier in their trajectories that they didn't have to please their parents. Our friend Emily, the utilities executive whose passion is rescuing dogs from shelters, told us her dad "was a pretty big factor in what I studied at Northwestern because he was a professor and an engineer." She took a lot of finance, math, and engineering classes; even though she knew early on that she was interested in animals, she couldn't figure out how to turn that into a lucrative career. Her father tightly controlled which classes she took in college, reasoning, she said, that "'I'm paying for it, so this is what you're going to study.' Because he was a professor, I just followed along. I was a rule follower."

By senior year, once she had taken all her required classes, she was able to branch out a little more, but it wasn't until years later, after she met and married her husband, that she was able to "break free and start doing my own thing." She described her husband as "very much his own person. He will happily tell somebody to fuck off if they try to tell him to do something. I've learned a lot from [him], and that's made me much more of my own person. If I had it to do differently, I would have learned those lessons earlier, to find a way to explore more of my own passions. I don't know where I'd be now if I had done that." Some of our friends chose to assert their independence in ways that had nothing to do with career. Sarah, the Etsy artist and ACLU volunteer coordinator, told us she started getting tattoos at age forty-one because "I just decided that at this point, I could look my mother in the face and say, 'Fuck you,' so therefore, I can do what I want. Yay!" These women, along with Sarabeth, Lucy, and so many others in this group, are embracing being over forty as a time when they are finally able to claim the people they always wanted to be, but didn't have the self-confidence to become earlier in life.

For many of our friends, the very qualities that likely helped them get into Northwestern—being good at understanding what was being asked of them and delivering it, working hard to meet or exceed others' high expectations, achieving academically to please demanding parents—may also have been the qualities that prevented them from breaking free of others' demands when they were in their twenties, and, in some cases, their thirties. In this, they are not alone.

Aggressive girls are found to be less likeable than non-aggressive ones—a statistic surprising to no one—and well into adulthood, women suffer socially more than men do for expressing aggression. They are also more concerned that showing anger will damage their social relationships.[8] (Never mind their familial relationships, as in Sarabeth's and Lucy's cases.) Girls also care a lot more than boys whether everyone gets along, a trait that begins to emerge during adolescence.[9] Wanting to be liked, not wanting to rock the boat, are characteristics that carry well beyond childhood and adolescence for women. And that isn't doing us any favors professionally. The internalized need to be "nice, polite, modest, and selfless curtails our power and potential," argues Rachel Simmons in *The Curse of the Good Girl: Raising Authentic Girls with Courage and Confidence.*[10]

The demoralizing statistic that men apply for a job when they meet only 60 percent of the qualifications, while women abstain from applying unless they feel they have 100 percent of the skills requested,[11] has been cited in countless articles on the wage gap, by Sheryl Sandberg in *Lean In*, and as an explanation for why there aren't more women in [insert your favorite field here]. The statistic is likely not true, but it probably gets cited so frequently because it *feels* true.[12] Most working women (both of us, hands raised) can relate to the feeling that perhaps you are your own worst saboteur, as you check a list of job qualifications and reject yourself before anyone else has the chance to weigh in.

All of which, for our friends, sometimes meant decades lived in service of someone else's dream. While we wish some of our friends could have shrugged off the rules earlier in their lives, we understand how hard it is to defy the expectations of those closest to you, to disappoint those who love you, even in your own best interest. But we celebrated each time we interviewed someone who, in midlife, had gathered the courage to take charge of her own trajectory. There is a power conferred on women in their forties, a liberation upon realizing that, in ways both large and small, your life is your own to live, and that you can get divorced, get a job, or get a tattoo, and the world will not fall apart.

The Ambition Cap: Still a Thing in Your Forties

While some of our friends changed up their paths by asserting independence over their own trajectories, for others, reaching their mid-forties brought opportunities—sometimes by choice, sometimes via a swift kick in the pants—for them to radically redefine their life roles. For our friend Ariel, who spent her twenties flitting across careers and her thirties as the primary caregiver for her children, entering her forties meant a chance to pursue both a passion and a career, and the hope that the changes she made to her life would allow her husband to change his.

Switching Roles, Responsibilities, and Ambition Levels with a Spouse

Ariel started at Northwestern as a radio/television/film major. Her first quarter in, she attended a panel discussion with a director who told the audience he'd had to take a second mortgage on his mother's house to afford to make his films, warning the earnest new students that filmmaking is a grueling career that is also likely to bankrupt you. "He told us, 'If you didn't have the means to access that type of money, to take that type of risk, you were never going to be a filmmaker.'" The tough-love warning spooked Ariel—she didn't come from a wealthy family, and it sounded like that was the only way to work in film—so she hastily transferred into the School of Education and declared a math major. She was strong in math, liked kids, and thought maybe she'd teach in the inner city. The summer between her junior and senior years, her mother suggested she do something fun, so she took an acting class and discovered that she missed the arts. She graduated with the education degree, but then joined an acting conservatory in New York City for a couple of years. "There was a teacher there who told us, 'Take one small step every single day at your passion, whatever it is.' At that time, it was acting. Each day, I would go to an audition, schedule an audition, work on a monologue." Tiny steps, every day, was advice she would keep with her for many decades to come.

Ariel remained interested in acting and film, but also continued to want to teach, travel, and do all the things that an idealistic, artistic twenty-one-year-old wants to do. She also needed to earn a living, but in her early twenties, without commitments and with her loans generously paid off by her mother, she was content to try out the young-starving-artist life. She meandered through a mélange of creative jobs for little pay, spending time as a theater counselor at a camp, a teacher at an educational theater nonprofit, and an English teacher in South America. "My twenties were a lot of exploration. I spent time bouncing between teaching and the arts and writing, doing all kinds of crazy things. Kurt Vonnegut's advice to kids getting out of college was retire first and then decide what you want to do by the time you're forty. I kind of did that."

Five years post-graduation, when Ariel faced the reality that she "made no money," she began to revisit her math background. A friend worked at a financial brokerage as a trader, and thought Ariel's background would be a good fit. Ariel wasn't particularly interested in a career in finance, but it seemed as good an opportunity as any to increase her earnings, and she was looking to broaden her social life, too—at the nonprofit where she worked, there were just three people in the office. She took the trading job and enjoyed the greater income, but missed the creative life she had shelved. She ended up quitting that job after two years to return to teaching, but not before beginning to date a cute coworker who "at first was a little too edgy, too New York-y for me, but lo and behold, we ended up together."

Ariel stopped teaching during her first pregnancy, figuring she'd go back to work soon after giving birth. "I never wanted to stay home with my kids, ever," she told us, and soon after her daughter was born she went to a job interview for another position. Unexpectedly, "I cried the whole way home. She was six weeks old, and I didn't want to leave her. I decided I wasn't going to take the position. I was lucky that my husband made enough money that I could make that choice." Ariel emphasized to us how much she appreciated her husband taking on the financial burden for the family, particularly because he, too, was someone who had at one time dreamt of pursuing a career he felt passionate about. Like Ariel, he loved film. Also, children and sports. For a while he talked about quitting banking and becoming a physician or a sports coach, but he didn't end up pursuing either—medicine required too many years of education and "college coaches have to move everywhere, and he didn't want to do that to his family." Ariel's husband didn't love being a trader, but he was good at it, and he didn't feel he had the luxury to pursue a job he loved. He had a family to support, and trading was not only secure, it was lucrative.

Eventually, the couple had two more kids. Ariel spent her days caring for the children. Her husband stayed in his trading job; somebody had to pay the mortgage. "He didn't have something he was absolutely passionate about doing," Ariel reflected, so by default he pursued a traditional high-earning career, adhering to the role society ascribes to most men even now. "If I could make enough money off writing to support this family 24/7, he would be the best stay-at-home dad ever," Ariel told us in our first interview. But at that point, she couldn't make any money as a screenwriter (even working professional screenwriters sometimes struggle for a paycheck), and he didn't become a stay-at-home dad. Ariel's husband has been a faithful earner, committed to his job, but like many of our flex life–pursuing women friends, he felt ambivalent about how fast and furiously he wanted to climb the corporate finance ladder. A year after their first child was born, Ariel's husband's firm was bought out by a global investment bank, and he was offered a job at their headquarters, but the family would have had to move from Chicago to New York City. "Everyone said, 'You're going to New York,' like it's a given," Ariel remembered. "But he talked to his employer, realized what would be expected of him if he took the new position, and he was like, 'I'm not ready for that right now, with my daughter this young.' He gave up a very good position at a global investment bank because he wanted to spend time with his daughter." Ariel's husband, she says, has been a very present father to their kids, prioritizing being there physically as well as emotionally—and has also been very supportive of her part-time writing work, even though it yielded little income over those years.

Ariel was committed to writing, regardless of the income. Following the advice of her acting teacher back in New York City, during the years Ariel was home with her kids, she continued to work and create, taking small freelance jobs over the years in online teaching and writing, grabbing at filaments of time to work on writing projects. "I wrote all kinds of things, screenplays, plays, fiction, nonfiction. I wrote a novel. That was what kept me sane when my kids were little."

As a stay-at-home mother, finding time wasn't trivial. She often ended up dropping her kids off at the babysitting services at her gym, then sneaking off to write at a nearby café. She went away on solo writing weekends while her husband stayed home with the kids, even after long hours at the trading office. As her children have gotten older, Ariel has had more time to advance her writing. She went to graduate school for an MFA in film. She began submitting screenplays to film festivals in 2015 and started teaching an online screenwriting class at a community college.

When we first interviewed Ariel, she'd just won a prestigious award for undiscovered screenwriters and was hopeful it might take her somewhere. She talked about moving the family to LA, finding a job with a studio, spending less time with her kids and more time at work. She seemed to be at a transition point, turning over options and dreams and logistics in her mind, but it was unclear where any of it would lead.

When we interviewed her two years later, much had changed for Ariel and her family. After a couple of years at her online screenwriting gig, Ariel accepted a tenure-track position as a screenwriting professor at a private college in Chicago. The salary doesn't begin to approximate her husband's, but it's more money than she has made in many years. And the timing was good. A month after she took the professorship, Ariel's husband's division at the bank was eliminated and he lost his job. He could have pursued something else in the same vein, Ariel said, but "he's forty-eight now and doesn't want to keep trading." Ariel and her husband have found themselves at a crossroads.

Her husband is now taking some time off and serving as the primary caregiver to their kids—he and Ariel are seeing their fantasy of him as the stay-at-home dad bear out—while he considers what he wants to do next. "It's one of those things where you've been doing something for so long without ever thinking you had the possibility to do something else." Ariel's husband now has the opportunity to contemplate that something else—and she's in a position to give him the time and the space to do that, while in turn continuing to pursue her passion and earn some needed income for her family.

Ariel is slowly, finally, seeing some traction on all the work she has invested in her writing over the years. "A lot of good stuff has happened, but it's been a tremendous amount of work." One of her scripts is being financed by Amazon, she's looking for funding for another completed script, and she's shopping around a web series she wrote with a colleague. Ariel seems to have a dozen other little projects, too, as she has always had, some bringing in income, some not quite there yet. She credits staying in touch with all her professors, mentors, former employers, and students, plus a lot of hard work and some luck, with this later-in-life professional success. Her husband losing his job was a forced jump-start for Ariel to become the primary earner, but it's a role she's now embracing, even as it brings stresses at home.

"The kids still want me," Ariel says. "He's much stricter, so they're always like, 'When's Mom getting home?' It's been really tough to make that transition, from me being the primary caregiver and him getting the gravy." The kids have complained because, of course, Dad doesn't do things exactly the way Mom did. "He hates sitting down and going through their homework with them. But somebody has to. So he either is like, 'I'm not gonna do this,' or 'When you get home, you have to do this.' The balance isn't there, by any means. He doesn't want to go back to work at this full-time job again, but he's also like, 'This other stuff isn't all that fun, either!'" For Ariel, that means "there's major guilt. You're letting your spouse down, your kids down."

But the way we see it, Ariel isn't letting her husband down at all. She's helping to support him and the kids, as he supported her when she was off on weekend writing retreats, crafting her work in solitude. She's acknowledging that he is also a person with dreams and hopes, and showing him through her economic support that hers aren't the only viable goals. "He's always done a job for the sole reason of making money for his family. He never wanted to be a trader for the passion of it. He would much rather have been an ER doctor or a coach, but he never made those choices because of money."

As with Sarabeth and her husband Kyle's later-in-life work switch-up, this transition point might have been easier for Ariel and her husband if, earlier on, she had developed and maintained a career with greater economic potential, one that she could count on for a secure paycheck once she needed it. "There's a little bit of tension because I am doing something that makes a lot less money now than he made for our family, but takes the same number of hours," Ariel told us. But this was also the result of Ariel having stayed home and taken care of all the domestic duties during her husband's prime earning years, years when Ariel's unpaid labor supported her husband's ability to be financially and professionally successful. Unlike Sarabeth, Ariel has held other jobs outside of low-paying creative fields, but both women wanted to pursue careers that held more meaning for them, even if it meant economic compromise.

It's a point to which Ariel has given a lot of thought. She and her husband have ongoing discussions about the triangulation of their jobs, their passions, and their economic realities. "You have to decide what lifestyle you want. You have to decide it is more important to have a job you enjoy. But it has to be agreed upon across all parties. It's a conversation in constant transition." Ariel continues to urge her husband to "do something that he loves. I keep telling him, go coach now. It may make ten percent of the salary you once made," but she thinks he should do it anyway. We were rooting for him to do it anyway, too—understanding that their family may have to make some significant financial compromises in the next few years, but also hoping that as Ariel moves forward in her career, she'll find more financial success.

As we work toward a more gender-equal society, shouldn't men have as much opportunity to rethink and rework their life choices as women do? In a more equal world, shouldn't women consider it their duty to support the family as much as men do? In an ideal world, it was Ariel's turn to get the gravy, and her husband's turn to check the homework and then be afforded some solo weekends to hone his passions.

Change 233

At Forty, the Impossible Seems Worth a Shot

While for a number of our friends, reaching forty meant a chance for a life rethink, most of our High Achiever friends just kept on being High Achievers as they moved into middle age. Women who had been C-suite adjacent or senior executives when we began this project moved another rung up the corporate ladder. Our friend Amy, the insurance executive, moved from running a large group at a multinational insurance company to an even larger job overseeing the insurance division of a major management consultancy. Our friend Ellen the rabbi delivered the invocation to Congress this past winter.

Several friends, though, who had seemed content with their careers when we first interviewed them, decided a few years or even months later to totally shake things up. A few of these women told us unequivocally in those early interviews that they wanted to stay in flexible jobs that allowed them lots of hands-on parenting time. But then a short time later, they told us they'd decided to chase down a risky new opportunity even though they knew it would probably cause chaos for their families. These opportunities presented the chance to reposition their careers, or put them in another caliber of their field altogether, and yet they also created competing priorities: These women were still needed by their children at home, were still handling much of the second shift, and truly could not visualize how to reconcile the jobs they wanted with their parenting and household responsibilities without making themselves completely crazy. They did it anyway.

Investing in Chaos in Order to Level-Up a Career

Alison always knew she wanted to work in film or theater. In high school, she acted and sang in school productions, but once she arrived at Northwestern and met other students in the theater department, she changed directions. "I quickly realized that I'm a very nervous auditioner and also not that talented as an actor. There were people at Northwestern who grew up in New York and were in off-Broadway shows as kids. People were studying the Greeks and doing the Greek tragedies. It wasn't my thing." At the end of her second year at Northwestern, Alison enrolled in a competitive screenwriting program, which was much more her speed.

Her senior year, she auditioned for *The Mee-Ow Show*, a renowned comedy improv show at Northwestern boasting alumni like Julia Louis-Dreyfus, Ana Gasteyer, and Seth Meyers. "I loved being in that show. I love doing improv. Finally I had found a part of theater that I could excel at. You didn't have to be nervous because you weren't supposed to remember anything or do anything, it was just all based on you." Her confidence boosted, Alison began to think about writing comedy, and after graduation she went on to film school in LA.

On the first day of graduate school, Alison met Michael, a fellow student in her program. He was smart, confident, also a strong writer, and he shared Alison's comedic aesthetic. They hit it off right away and began collaborating on school projects. In their second year of school, they pooled their resources to produce a twenty-five-minute romantic comedy short. "We shot it on thirty-five millimeter. We put our credit cards in it and just did everything we could to make it happen." It was a big risk, racking up credit card debt for a graduate school thesis.

The short was set to be screened at a theater as part of a film school initiative for new filmmakers. "At that point, in the nineties, it was still a big deal because not everybody had a YouTube short." But the two assumed nothing much would come of the screening, so both had started jobs as production assistants, figuring they'd need to start at the bottom of the industry and slog their way up. To Alison and Michael's delight, after the short screened they began to get calls from producers. Propelled by the adrenaline of hope and confidence, Alison "decided I was going to quit my job and sell movies. So I did. We did. It was totally insane." Both assistants left their day jobs and, later that year, sold their pitch for a romantic comedy. "It was a total anomaly in my career, that we sold it [right away] and within a year had to write it, too. Within a year of selling it, it was going into production. Our entrance into the movie business was crazy." In 1999, Alison and Michael's first feature-length film was released, starring an A-list actor and grossing more than $80 million worldwide.

While in graduate school and working on their first script, Alison and Michael had also become a couple. After seven years and a brief engagement, they separated ("We're just not meant to be as a romantic couple," she said), but they've stayed together as a screenwriting team ever since, cowriting successful romantic comedies, as well as television pilots and a few other scripts along the way that didn't find financing. They both eventually married other partners and each have two children, but they work closely together, speak on the phone every day, vacation together, and spend many weekends together as families. "Our parents think it's kind of crazy that we were together for so long, and that our families vacation together. It's just all one big crazy family."

That crazy family has consistently produced some very funny, relatable, and commercially successful romantic comedies, about being insecure, falling in love, breaking up, and women's friendships, not necessarily in that order. Even so, Alison says that the benchmark for success in Hollywood is constantly moving—the "you're only as good as your last project" theory of life. When everyone in your industry is constantly chasing and reevaluating their success based on their most recent project, that leaves room for a lot of self-doubt. "When we sold our first script, I was like, Okay, I can go to a party and someone can say, 'What do you do?' And I can say, 'I sold a movie.' That was my benchmark at that point. I felt psyched. We were under an overall deal for three years at [a major studio]. We were twenty-six and we had an office and a golf cart and an assistant. We were getting paid a lot and it was like, 'Okay, now we've arrived.' But none of these things stay. It's all ephemeral." Even as that big-break success was unfolding for her, Alison questioned what would happen next. "I definitely felt that I had surpassed what I had hoped, but then that's over, and if your deal doesn't get re-upped and things change, then you're back to thinking, 'Oh, now what am I? A has-been?' Things continue to shift, and I would continue to feel like, 'Okay, now I have to prove myself again.'"

When we first interviewed her, Alison was in the process of putting herself back together after a pilot she and Michael had been working on for several years didn't get picked up. "It nearly broke me. I was the producer, so I had to call all the actors and tell them the show wasn't going to get picked up when we really felt like it was. I'm the boss, just crying into the phone and telling them how sorry and hurt I was, too. After that, I thought I would not recover. I stayed in bed and cried for a couple of days."

Industry highs and lows notwithstanding, one thing Alison loves about her job is the flexibility it gives her when it comes to being a hands-on parent. "Being a screenwriter is honestly the greatest job for being a parent, because I work a lot but I'm my boss. It's up to me. I can be sitting in the carpool lane and thinking about what I want to work on." Alison has a part-time nanny, but is intent on being home by six most days to make and eat dinner with her family, even if that means, when she's got a tight deadline, she might "put the kids to bed at nine and stay up until three in the morning banging out a script." In our first interview, when we asked Alison what else, after twenty years of screenwriting, she wanted to accomplish, she went back and forth on directing. She wanted to do it, but didn't see how she could take on such a time-consuming job while being a parent of young children. "Being a director is less of a perfect job for a mom. I would like to direct a movie because I'd like to see what it would be like to have creative control past when I hand off the script, but I really love writing. I love being the master of my own time-management destiny."

We had this first conversation with Alison in January. Not six months later, she and her writing partner signed on to direct a romantic comedy starring an A-list comedic actor. Alison, it seemed, had changed her mind.

The next time we talked to Alison, she was spending days in the edit room for her feature directorial debut, a big-budget romantic comedy helmed by one of the top stars of the decade. She'd been very satisfied as a comedy screenwriter, she said, but had long dreamt of directing one of her own scripts. "I got my master's in film production and I always wanted to direct. I've kept that in the back of my mind. There's frustration that builds up around not being able to see your script through. It gets away from you, you sell it, you don't then have any creative control. The more we wrote stuff that got produced, the more it became attractive to be able to continue to have a creative voice in what we came up with." Intent on realizing this dream on a who-knows-when time line, Alison and Michael took a few months off of paying work and cowrote a romantic comedy that they both really believed in. "We felt that if we were going to direct something, we wanted it to have something to say. This movie does, and I'm proud of that. It's a strong message about women, but not just for women."

The duo were hopeful but realistic about their prospects for getting the film made. "We weren't under some illusion that we'd be like, 'Okay, we want to direct,' and then Hollywood studios would be banging down our door, so we thought the best way was to write our way into it." They finished the script, and their message to producers and production companies was, "'It's a script we love and believe in, it's a very specific tone and we're the ones who can achieve it.' Anyone who was interested in it knew it was a package deal, with us as directors. We were comfortable doing it in a small-budget way or a big-budget way, we just wanted to have the experience of seeing our creative project through and to be involved in the casting and the tone and the music and all of that." Rather quickly and, Alison says, with no small amount of luck, they got the script to a producer who got it to a financier, who delivered it to the actor—who signed on. "We are still in awe. Stuff never happens like that, but it did."

But even though Alison had run headlong toward her dream of directing, all the worries around parenting and time came rushing back to her

the minute she learned her dream was going to come true. She hung up
the phone after hearing her film was going to be green-lit, and immediately began frantically sending out emails to try to find a nanny who could
help out while she was on set in New York. When Alison told this story to
a friend of hers, her friend pointed out how gendered Alison's reaction
was. "She's like, 'How many dudes do you think get something green-lit
and their first thought is, What's the nanny situation going to be?'"

While her husband stayed in LA, Alison moved her children to the
East Coast with her for the three months of filming. She found her East
Coast nanny, while retaining her Los Angeles nanny—and yes, having to
hire bicoastal nannies could possibly be one reason we don't see more
women directing big-budget films—and began a whirlwind summer of
logistics, camps, nannies, movie stars, and film production. Alison's
daughter is a competitive dancer and had to travel to Europe over the
summer to compete in an international tournament, which meant paying
one nanny to travel overseas while the other nanny stayed in New York,
while Alison herself was on set on the East Coast. Alison called herself
the "production manager of my family as well as the production manager
of the movie" during that summer. "It was insane. But I was fully like,
'This is going to be an adventure for all of us, this is a family project,' and
they were on board."

It was a stressful time, for sure, but Alison wouldn't have had it any
other way. She didn't want to be away from her children for three months,
and the production schedule fell over their summer break, so school
wasn't an issue. Her parents, she said, thought it was crazy to bring a six-
year-old and a nine-year-old along for her directorial debut, but Alison
found that having her kids with her helped ground her in reality. "I could
come home at night and normalize again, and remember, 'Oh right, I'm
still the same person. I am still the mom to these awesome kids. This is
my macro life, still beating.' My family was worried it would provide a
greater stress, but I think it did the opposite. Even if I had only an hour
when I got home and they were already in bed, and I could lie down with
them and tell stories, it was so awesome for me to not just continue about

whatever the crisis of the day was. I thought I was doing it for them, because I didn't think my son would do well with not seeing me all summer, but it ended up being the right decision for all of us."

In our last conversation with Alison, she was just off the high of production and into the rhythm of editing—and still very much in the throes of gratitude over bringing the biggest project of her career to fruition. She repeatedly told us that it was largely luck, and timing, that had made this possible. But she hopes the stars will align to make this kind of opportunity happen again. "If I could have another chance to direct something that I totally believed in, if I could do that for the rest of my career, write things and direct, it would be awesome." In the meantime, though, she is content to be in the moment of her first directing project, and also acutely aware of the larger implications of taking on a director role as a woman. "I had many women crew members who had never worked with a female director come up to me and tell me how gratifying it was to have a female director. It was a long time coming, and I felt empowered, and also like I want to get the ball farther down the field." Reflecting on her crazy summer, Alison said, "I get why women and moms don't make up as big a piece of the pie as I would like them to. The logistics of my family were cuckoo. It would be great if there were more of us, people I could talk to to guide me through that process."

A lison was right. Directing didn't fit her lifestyle. And yet she did it anyway. She invested in her career long-term by sowing chaos short-term, in the hopes that not only would she fulfill her directing dream, but that that fulfillment might alter the arc of her career. Ariel was also willing to endure her lifestyle being upended, over an indefinite time line, in exchange for the potential of great professional reward for her—and the hope for significant change for her husband, too. "I loved being with my kids for thirteen years, but I gave up a lot of myself because of that," Ariel concedes. Alison's and Ariel's midlife career changes illustrated for us how we come to think the structures of our lives are intractable—how our children won't possibly be able to survive without us being the ones to feed them their dinner every night, how our spouses may forget to check the homework folders or sign the permission slips or make the pediatrician appointments if we aren't 100 percent managing those details. But we also came to realize how flexible those structures can be, and are, if and when we choose to make them so. As many mothers can attest, we often put our own needs last, by necessity when our children are very young. It's hard to think about directing a movie for the first time when you're covered in spit-up or have a two-year-old clinging to your knees. When you've got a routine down of being there to meet the school bus, are used to working from home so you can run out for groceries in between conference calls, or have left work promptly at five every day for years to be there to help with homework, it seems impossible to live life any other way. But these stories remind us that sometimes, when women want something very badly, something that will dramatically boost their career or raise up their life's work, they deserve to pursue it, even as it disrupts their family life to do so. Ambition, even when shelved for twelve months, or twelve years, demands to be fed.

Scaling Back in Middle Age

Not all of our friends saw their forties as a chance to finally go full throttle on their careers. Some, in fact, were thinking of pumping the brakes a little. In particular, some of our friends who spent their twenties and thirties grinding away at big careers were ready for a break. Heather, the bank CMO, told us she was thinking about retiring early, having already earned and achieved what she needed, though she wasn't sure what she might want to do next. Three of our friends got engaged or married in their forties, and with the added income and a new partner in their life, two of them were now thinking about their next steps in new ways. Our friend Angela, who runs a life-coaching business and spent a few years taking care of her ailing parents, told us she wanted to downscale her life and spend more time fishing with her fiancé. Shortly after that conversation we began to see lots of pictures of her on social media with wide-mouthed freshly caught fish. And for our friend Meredith, her forties were a chance to make a home for herself and her new spouse, consider easing up on her career, and try living a different kind of life.

I May Take a Happy Derailment

Meredith, a Chicago-based friend who owns a public relations firm, is someone we enthusiastically classified as a High Achiever when we first spoke to her three years ago. A pull-herself-up-by-her-bootstraps kind of woman, she transferred to Northwestern our sophomore year (Northwestern was her dream school, but she hadn't gotten in for freshman year). Upon graduation, she interned at a sports radio station in Chicago and was eventually hired as the "tape librarian," the person who archives the interview tapes, for very low wages. Meredith also juggled three or four other small jobs, doing camera work and production for other radio and TV shows, pursuing her dream of being a television sports reporter. "I was doing everything I could to learn as much as I could, and make as much as I could, which never really amounted to more than $25,000." Five years after graduation, Meredith neared a crisis point. "I had been toiling for years, still not making anything, still living at home. I was broke. Broke, broke, broke. I was starting to rethink my dreams."

Through one of her radio jobs, Meredith met a woman who ran a public relations firm. The woman offered her a job starting a sports PR division within the firm. She said no the first time, then six months later, still broke broke broke, she accepted. "I left television behind, sort of tucked the dream away, but figured maybe there would be another opportunity" somewhere down the line. She changed jobs a couple more times, staying in sports PR and marketing, until an opportunity to do PR for a commercial real estate firm presented itself.

"This was a total crossroads in my life because I was interested in making more money—I was only making $40,000 and I was coming up on thirty at that point. When your friends are getting married and buying homes and you're still living at your parents' house chasing a dream, it was kind of like, whoa. I interviewed on a whim, thinking, 'I'll just see what they have to say.'" When the job came through, Meredith wavered. "They were offering to double my salary, and it was a chance for me to use my brains for once and get into corporate America." But she knew that if she took the job, she'd probably be leaving behind her dream of working in TV for good. The night before she was due to give an answer, she was certain she'd decline it. She woke up the next morning and called to accept. "I decided it was time to grow up, and I took the job. I've been in the commercial real estate business ever since."

She worked for a couple of different big firms over the years, surviving two corporate takeovers and a lot of uncertainty. Her personal life also brought uncertainty. She was in a four-year relationship that ended badly and abruptly, leaving her unexpectedly single at thirty-eight. Meredith had grown up in a close family with two brothers, with whom she remains very close. She had wanted to have a family of her own. "I woke up on my thirty-ninth birthday sobbing because I was thirty-nine. My prospect for having kids was probably gone because I was getting older. I had really been thrown for a big fat loop." Still stinging from the realization that she might not become a mother, Meredith got a call about a PR job at a New York–based commercial real estate firm. "In my industry, it was the biggest job I could get. I took it, thinking, 'Well, this is going to be a really good learning experience for me, and it's going to get me out of Chicago and put everything behind me.'" It did put some of the pain of her personal life behind her, and she thrived at the company. She also became close friends with a colleague, a man who was divorced with a young son.

After more than a decade of being all-in at her job, Meredith began to grow tired of the cutthroat work environment. "Commercial real estate is a mean, mean, mean business. Donald Trump has said it's one of the nastiest businesses on the planet." Finally, deciding that she "didn't want to work with assholes" any longer, Meredith quit her job, and within two weeks had her first client at her own firm. Her goal, she said, was simply to accept only clients who were "nice." After she left the big firm, she began dating the divorced dad.

When we first interviewed Meredith, her trajectory seemed pretty straightforward: possessed ambition, followed dream, shifted dream in order to make more money, had fruitful career, became happily partnered after forty. We asked her how she would categorize her ambition over the course of her career—to us, she seemed like a quintessential High Achiever who had identified what she wanted and had made it happen, even as that required some compromises over the years. But to our surprise, she told us that she was thinking about tearing it all down. "My level of ambition has not changed, but my goals have changed," Meredith reflected. "I reached the highest job I could reach in commercial real estate public relations. I grabbed the brass ring. I didn't like it. I'm over it."

Meredith ruminated on the state of her life at age forty-four: She was in a serious relationship with the former coworker, contemplating marriage. Her business was going well, but she could grow it even bigger, expanding it into other cities. "I would love for my company to be big and huge and successful, and I'd love to sell it to Rubenstein PR and call it a day. I don't want to sacrifice what I've created, because I've created something really freaking good. On the other hand, now that I think I've found the person that I can have a life with, I'm reevaluating my goals. I don't want to be married at fifty and be too old to enjoy that life."

Eighteen months later, we spoke with Meredith again. She was getting married in a few weeks—we would see about eight of our former sorority sisters on social media happily flanking our friend at the reception—and she would be moving to the East Coast to live full-time with her husband. A new home base will mean a new, much bigger potential client base. "Everything's changing in my world. I have a whole new market to conquer in New York. I've got clients out there, but I don't have a huge roster." She echoed the conundrum she raised with us during our first conversation. "My big question at this point is, do I blow this thing up as big as I think I could get it, have thirty-five people working for me and become huge, or do I just find a few more clients, make plenty of money to be happy, and have flexibility? Everything's coming to a head right now because I've got to make some of those decisions."

Having always been ambitious, Meredith is torn about what that ambition could, and should, look like in midlife. Acknowledging that she didn't take a break from her career to raise children, Meredith wonders if it might be time to slow down, temporarily, maybe. "At forty-six, I've been grinding for twenty-something years. I hadn't ever had the person in my life who I wanted to spend time with and love and do things with and create that life. I'm making plenty to support my retirement, and I'm happy. I don't need to be a bazillionaire. Do I enjoy a little bit of flexibility and focus on our life together and creating happiness at this point? People step away because they have babies, and they have this or that, and things derail. I just may take a happy sort of derailment." Meredith is, at forty-six, for the first time in her life contemplating her next shift in ambition—toward the flex life.

We talked to many women who had taken "happy derailments" earlier in their lives, mostly after having children, some after having big, exhausting careers that they felt done with. Meredith was one of several who is choosing that derailment later—she, like Angela the life coach, seemed to want to invest more time in pursuits like fly fishing and traveling, rather than being on call 24/7 for demanding clients. She still wants to work, but also wants to take the time to enjoy the fulfilling partnership she has always desired and finally found.

Meredith didn't expect to marry at forty-six, and we asked her why she felt the need to legally marry. She didn't need the financial support, she wasn't planning on having children, and, at forty-six, she certainly didn't need anyone else's approval (Meredith is the kind of woman who didn't need anyone's approval at nineteen, for that matter). She told us that she hadn't personally needed a wedding, but that her parents had always dreamt of it, so that was that. Also, she and her husband wanted to solidify their commitment to each other, both socially and legally.

"I don't need a man to baby me. I need a buddy to go through life with. I need a partner who makes my world brighter and better, but I don't rely on him for my happiness. He just makes everything in my world infinitely better." Meredith hasn't relied on anyone for her happiness, and, adhering to the way she has made her life decisions over twenty-five years, she is confident enough to continue to declare what she wants now. She can go "balls to the wall" with her career ambition, or chill out a little and build her new family and home life. She recognizes that both of those are good choices for her right now, and that she can pick either, free of the judgments that others or she herself might have inflicted on her earlier in life.

Meredith's story showed us, again, the degree to which ambition ebbs and flows over the course of our lives: There is no one set ambition level for any given person. You may want to follow your passion or follow the money, kill it in your career or ease up a bit to focus on creating a home. You can be the same person and want all of these things at different times in your life. Without guilt. No *I should be doing this* or *I should be wanting that*. What you want today is important and just as valid as the thing you'll want ten years from now, which, by the way, could easily be the exact opposite of the thing you're chasing now. The trick is to know what you want for yourself—not because your parents want it or your spouse wants it—and to carefully lay out the pieces that will give you the freedom to choose down the road. Our friends who knew what they wanted, who didn't let dreams fall by the wayside in favor of other people's wants and needs (because there will always be other people who want and need), and who invested in those dreams in even the smallest of ways (an hour of writing here, a volunteer teaching gig there) were ultimately able to gather up those pieces and snap them together like Lego bricks, discovering where pieces fit and what was missing, and building something they couldn't have pictured when the bricks were simply scattered across the rug.

There are infinite ways to shape your world at different stages in your life. Here's to building, rebuilding, and keeping the conversation in constant transition.

What We Know About Change in Midlife

▶ **The sooner you're able to brush off your parents' (or anyone else's) expectations of you, the sooner you can have the life you want.**

Our friends Sarabeth and Lucy subscribed to, and achieved, the life goals their parents had set for them. But because those goals conflicted with—or had nothing to do with—the things they themselves wanted to achieve, they landed in middle age with the nagging feeling that they hadn't done the things they'd wanted to. They then found themselves having to hit reset in their early forties. Emily, on the other hand, let her father be a primary driver in her life agenda through college and her early twenties, but chose to break free of his expectations when she reached her thirties. As a result, she abandoned her urban, not-fully-satisfying corporate life for a more flexible career and a life in the mountains. She still earns enough money that she envisions being able to retire early and launch her second career at an animal shelter. Many of our ambitious friends had parents with a strong hold over their lives; those who realized that breaking free, even in the smallest ways, was within their power seemed able to better direct their own lives.

▶ **If you are an ambitious person, don't beat yourself up if you witness your ambition waning.**

A good number of our friends took time off from their careers to raise their children, and others, like Meredith and our friend Sarah, who left her sales training job to pursue her art, took a "happy derail-ment" for other reasons. Ambition is not always a straight line be-tween two points, but can manifest as a curving, jagged one with a number of detours along the way. If you are ambitious, and you find your ambition slowing at some point in your life, don't throw your hands up in resignation, thinking your eye-of-the-tiger days are over and done with. It is likely that your ambition may wax again at a differ-ent point in your life. By making strategic decisions, you can position yourself to awaken your ambition even after a hibernation.

> **▶ Just because you haven't realized all your dreams by forty doesn't mean you won't.**

Your forties may be the time when you have the mental space, the skills, and the knowledge to go for things that previously seemed out of reach. A number of friends, like Alison, chose to upend their lives in middle age to take on new, daunting challenges that previously hadn't seemed feasible. Leilani moved with her partner and young son from Europe to Asia for a bigger job. Ariel has let some of the primary par-enting duties fall to her husband as she works her way toward building a career that can support her family down the road, allowing her hus-band to pursue his dreams.

The two of us have also let go of things we felt were sacrosanct in order to chase down career dreams. In her thirties, with young chil-dren at home, Hana felt she needed to be there at school pick-up to watch her children eat a granola bar while she heard about their days, or to shuttle them to gymnastics or the park or the dentist. She'd been unwilling to take a job that required her to be physically present in an office every day; those afternoon hours with her kids, though often tedious, felt necessary. Her career had idled accordingly, as she took on work that could be crammed in and around school hours. But by her early forties, with her kids in elementary and middle school, she was ready to pick up the pace on her career while also doing something that felt more meaningful and challenging. Through a friend she heard about an interesting tech job at the White House and applied on a whim (despite living a three-hour train ride from Washington, DC). When, to her surprise, she was offered the job, she did something that ran counter to everything she'd done around her career for the previous ten years: She took it. Like Alison, she saw an opportunity that might not come around again, and figured the details (like the fact that the job was in a different city) would work themselves out. Today, a year and thousands of miles of train track later, her career is in a much different place.

Liz still counts herself squarely in the Flex Lifer category, prioritizing yoga, homemade meals, and homework supervision. But with a couple of years of aggressive PTA volunteerism under her belt, she's cut back her unpaid work to pursue paying writing gigs, expanding her editing and writing portfolio to include advertising and content marketing.

And for both of us, of course, we have invested time in this project alongside other work, manipulating the giant Jenga blocks of our daily family logistics, always teetering between balance and collapse—yet we feel energized and intellectually challenged on a level that is new and thrilling. For this group, forty wasn't just sitting there like some dead end; it was more like a looking glass that, once we stepped through, offered up possibilities we couldn't have begun to imagine from the other side.

CONCLUSION,
OR GROUP THERAPY

feel like you guys are my therapists," one of our friends told us after our second eighty-minute Skype interview with her. We'd just covered some of the more dramatic moments in her relationship with her husband, how she'd felt out of place at Northwestern, and her dreams for her future life. "It took me a few hours to decompress after our last call."

She wasn't the only one who felt like our calls were therapy, or who needed time to process what we'd talked about. After every intense call, we had to decompress, too, often texting each other late into the night trying to wrap our minds around what we'd just heard, connect it with our own lives, our own decisions, the choices other friends made, the predictable and unexpected twists that everyone's trajectories had taken, and understand what it all meant.

One of the reasons for engaging in actual psychotherapy is the opportunity to be heard without judgment. At first unknowingly, we offered this kind of space to the friends we interviewed. By simply saying to our friends, "We want to hear about your life choices over the past two decades," by creating a common space for an hour or several, we gave them not only permission but encouragement to reflect on their life choices and share with us what they'd learned and lived. As middle-aged women with young children, we are not a group of people who are often asked how we are—how we really *are*. "How are the kids doing/how is school going/

what's for dinner/can you sign this permission slip/where is more toilet paper?" yes. But not, "No, really, how *are* you?"

And all of that not-being-asked perhaps led many of our friends to question whether they had anything worth saying. Time and again, our friends' initial replies to our requests for interviews were: Sure, happy to be interviewed, "but I might be too boring," or "I won't be very interesting compared to other people we graduated with." While none of us had become Beyoncé, Sheryl Sandberg, or Condoleezza Rice (surprise! No one turned out to be a platinum recording artist, the COO of Facebook, or secretary of state!) their stories were far from boring—and every one of them resonated with our own experiences.

The fact that many of these women's lives were somewhat ordinary, filled with routinized tasks that would make up weeks and years and a whole life, makes them all the more relatable. Here we were, all tackling the same mundane yet irritating challenges: How to figure out what your next career move should be. How to figure out what you really wanted out of life—passion, meaning, money, time alone in the woods, or all of the above. How to get everyone out the door in the morning, get ourselves to the office, excel as best we could at work, get home, get everyone fed and into bed, then start the whole thing over again the next morning. Oh, and not lose sight of your entire individual identity in the process.

Hearing other women share their struggles and triumphs, their moments monumental and tiny along the way, became as therapeutic for us as it was for some of our friends. This group of women, the majority of whom we had not had any contact with in more than twenty years, candidly opened up their lives to us as if no time at all had passed. They shared sometimes uncomfortable details about lost jobs, struggling marriages, infertility, cancer, children with health issues, sexual harassment and oblique sexism, wavering self-confidence, ambivalence about their ambition levels, and the things they felt were holding them back in their careers. At first, we patted ourselves on the back for being such good interviewers, for getting people to open up the moment their images appeared on our computer screens. It was only later that we realized our friends told us the innermost details of their lives because they needed to. That the interviews were as illuminating and surprising for some of them as they were for us.

As this project progressed over the years, we watched something totally unexpected happen: The women we interviewed began to reconnect with each other. At first it was just a spate of friending on social media. But then, they began to get together in person. Friends who asked, "What happened to Jenny?" were excited to find out she lived in a town only three hours away. Ten months later, we'd get an email about their get-together in a town halfway between them. When the two of us traveled to Washington, DC, one summer, we told a few of our sorority friends that we'd be in town—one or two were people we'd stayed in touch with and with whom we would have gotten together anyway, but others were friends we'd only reconnected with via interviews. One thing led to another, and we found ourselves seated at a gathering of twelve sorority sisters at a trendy Peruvian-Asian fusion restaurant, clinking Pisco cocktails, then stumbling out into the muggy air at one o'clock in the morning after shutting down the bar we'd decamped to post-dinner. Most of these women had not stayed awake past eleven p.m. in years. And some of the women weren't even part of our interview set, though they had been in our sorority. They'd heard about our project from other friends, a game of Telephone that, instead of leaving its players befuddled, pulled together women who were craving connection.

Our friends shared pictures of the Washington gathering on social media, and spurred by that get-together, where in each other's presence we all, for a moment, remembered what it was like to be a part of a sprawling community of women, friends in other parts of the country began meeting up and sharing their own pictures. Four of us had dinner in exurban Virginia with our families, the children running sock-footed through the house, fast friends though most had never met before. Five women posed near a rocky outcropping in the Southwest. One woman who had recently gotten married trumped everyone else when one of our friends shared a picture of eight sorority sisters clustered around the bride. "BOOM," she captioned the picture, a digital wink to what had somehow become a friendly, ridiculous competition to see who could get the most sorority sisters in the same place at the same time, twenty-five years post-college.

Once part of a somewhat randomly assembled collection of fierce young women, our friends relinked themselves to the same community, scattered and older, shaped by the wisdom of time passed, experiences gained, risks taken, things lost. By reconnecting with the two of us, sharing their stories, they were reconnecting with a nation they had forgotten they belonged to but, like a wrinkled $10 bill found in a freshly laundered pair of pants, were happy to rediscover. Collectively we've aged out of the scrabbling race to the top that dominated our college years. We no longer compete over grades or boyfriends or who has the best internship. Instead, now in our forties, we are able to genuinely bask in each other's accomplishments. A triumph for one of us is simply more evidence that we are all badass. We've loved watching these women reunite to celebrate each other and to offer a sisterhood that, at this time in our lives, we didn't even know we needed.

For the two of us, our friendship, like our ambition, has waxed and waned over twenty-seven years. When we first met, during New Student Week, we were cordial and had friends in common, but didn't feel a particularly special bond. By the time we reached our junior year, though, we'd begun to grow close. We found that we shared an interest in writing and feminism and digressive, impassioned speeches about the state of the world. In a college populated by students who had their favorite study carrel at the library, we bonded during road trips to rallies, a rave in an abandoned warehouse, and eventually time spent sitting cross-legged on a cheap rug in the living room of the apartment we shared with two other friends senior year.

There was a fierceness to our friendship then, an intensity that only young women with few demands on their time can harbor, but the moment passed. We were on to other friends and other lives. And yet, as close as we were then, coming back together to write this book has forged a friendship between the two of us that, while rooted in the rich earth of our college-age friendship, our history together, the fact that we *knew each other when*, is nothing like that first go-around. It would be an understatement to say we are in constant communication. We often have multiple Slack threads and text messages going at once, on topics that range from fiscal independence to whether one of us should go to yoga today. Two of our children ended up in the same elementary school class this year (previously they didn't even attend the same school), so we have sent library books back and forth via child–Pony Express, stashing heavy tomes on work-life balance and Marxist feminism in our children's backpacks with handwritten notes instructing, "Give this book to your mother." We are often the first people, outside of our families, we talk to in the morning, and the last at night.

As writing partners, we have also become each other's sounding boards, editors, loyal supporters, and work wives, and that communication has evolved into a language that is familiar and vital. In an age when most people of our generation and younger are loath to call anyone on a phone anymore, we schedule weekly phone check-ins—calls that sometimes feel obligatory and burdensome when we see them on our calendar but, once complete, serve as a psychic life preserver. It is a support system that, outside of our spouses and our parents, neither of us had ever experienced before—one which we now consider indispensable. We didn't come into this project looking to make a friend, or even knowing that we needed yet another person in our lives, but we have, for this moment in time, become intricately intertwined in each other's existence.

This project was initially our attempt to understand our own lives by setting them in context against the lives of our college friends. We wanted to answer the question: Is it just me? But what we ended up with was so much more. This project has changed our lives, and more than that, it has given us a deep friendship and a chorus of voices from other ambitious women all going through the same things. We feel less alone. We know we are doing the best we can.

More people—more women, specifically—need this type of community. Not everyone has access to a preestablished group of forty-three women they have known for decades, in close proximity, on social media, or at all. Perhaps this book will spur you to foster and grow your own groups of supportive friends, whatever that looks like for you: Book clubs! Pisco cocktails! Marches and rallies! Facebook groups with encouraging captions and fist-bump emojis! Dinners, manic text message threads with other passionate people, phone calls to say "I hear you, you are not alone," cheers to go for a big job or dial it back, and the continued reminder to allow your partner to take on their fair share of domestic work, and to be okay with how they choose to do it.

Or maybe all that sounds really overwhelming, which is in large part why we've shared these stories with you here. These stories, culminating in this book, gathered over several years and countless conversations, are our offering of community to you. The feeling of being part of something larger than yourself can also come from a group of women you don't know at all in real life, that you may never meet in person—we hope that experiencing these women's stories has provided a glimmer of that community, has helped you recognize the many different ways that women's lives can unfold, and given you an understanding of some of the difficult struggles therein. We hope it's made you feel less alone. Because you aren't alone. These are topics that women don't often talk openly about, but we should, because the more we talk about them, the more obvious it becomes that *it's not just you*. It's all of us. We are all facing the same challenges, wrestling late at night with the same questions, wondering if we are winning at life or fucking the whole thing up. We are all ruminating on the same topics, the ones we've covered in this book: *Do I move to a larger city for a "better" job? Do I chill in the perfectly decent job I have now? Do I have a second baby? Do I scale back work to be home with that baby more, but also make less income and maybe hinder my career path at the same time? Do I want a partner who is a stay-at-home parent? Do I want to go full throttle at work after forty, or do I want to pivot my career and have more time for fly fishing, or maybe something else altogether that I haven't even articulated yet?* We are all trying our best. We are all looking for a North Star to guide us to the place we know is right for us, if only we could make out exactly what that place looks like. It's like trying to find home without a map. Where, you might ask, is the damn map?

We, too, wanted a map. We wanted someone to tell us how to think about the big decisions in our lives. We wanted a mentor at work, a woman to model our lives after, a successful older sister, a cool aunt who had it all figured out, maybe a panel consisting of Amy Poehler, Oprah, Angela Merkel, Shonda Rhimes, Anna Kendrick, and Janelle Monáe installed permanently in our living room offering up suggestions. We wanted an understanding of the repercussions of the million decisions we make throughout our careers and at home, someone to tell us, "If you go this way, here's what's likely to happen . . . "

We started these interviews trying to answer difficult questions for ourselves, and rethinking decisions that we'd previously thought resolved: What career am I passionate about? How can I launch a career, and grow it? Will I earn enough money, and if not, what will I do about that? What does my work life look like with a spouse—and what does their work life look like? How can I have children and still grow that aforementioned career? What kind of parent do I want to be? If I have a spouse, which one of us is going to empty the dishwasher? The discussion these questions provoked, the resulting analysis, is this book—a tangible toolbox full of questions and answers, both existential and painstakingly practical. The quandaries and decision points our friends encountered during their biggest life transitions were the issues that led to the most chaos or crisis in their lives. Being able to anticipate these transitional watersheds can help manage that chaos, abate some of those crises, and lead to informed decisions rather than wild stabs in the dark.

As we wrote this book, we also lived it and put what we'd learned into practice. This led to statements like, "Do you know that in twelve years of having children I have been the only one who cuts their nails?" It's led to an understanding of why we both feel mildly unhinged when we aren't contributing to the household finances as much as we'd like to be. And it has led to a deep understanding of how we got where we are today, where we want to go next, and how to get there.

By sharing with you what we've learned, we've armed you with an arsenal of questions to draw from at different points in your life—questions for yourself, your friends, your partners, your mentors, your colleagues—and an understanding of the way your answers to those questions can play out over a lifetime. The conversations these questions will spur—both internal (totally cool if you want to talk to yourself in the mirror about the elements of motherhood you find nonnegotiable) and external—are the tools that will help you build the life you want. So you are no longer navigating in a pre–Google Maps world. This book is your map. And it is more than that. It is also a flashlight, a mirror, and a compass all rolled into one bound set of old-school printed pages. Use it to help guide the way. Revisit it often, as life transitions come up, as the things you're prioritizing shift and slide into different configurations. Head into those moments not only with questions, but with answers from women who've lived through them and possess the wisdom that only comes from being on the other side. Walk into the unknowns more empowered, more confident, and ready to let your ambition fly.

ACKNOWLEDGMENTS

To the forty-three old friends who indulged us in many hours of conversation about work, life, marriage, children, and dogs, and offered us invaluable candor, and more importantly, ongoing friendship and support, and without whom this book would not have been written. To our earliest interviewees, who let us fumble around with questions before we knew what we were doing, especially Stephanie Gerard Rowlands (aka Patient Zero) and other early interviewees who have championed this book, and us, over the years.

Libby McGuire, who over English breakfast tea assigned her belief to us and our ideas, along with her fierce protection, never wavering despite many mortifying F train fumblings, and whose vast world of connections and lobby pep talks led us like a trail of crumbs to long-awaited fruition. Laura Tisdel, for getting us at hello, for championing our friendship and our collaboration, for challenging our internal biases, nudging us always to *define* and push further, for indulging, encouraging even, twenty-five-minute digressive memories about the Indigo Girls, and for helping us distill a decent idea into a personal watershed. To Amy Sun, for digging deeper on everything from Harvard Business School graduates' "success" rates to Carrie Bradshaw's choice of Big over Aidan. And to the fabulous team at Viking, especially Carolyn Coleburn, Alison Klooster, and Lydia Hirt.

Rebecca Rosen, who listened patiently through a PowerPoint pitch, then green-lit and guided our *Atlantic* essays. Tiffany Dufu, who wisely advised us to keep looking, and to come to our first publicity meeting with our own spreadsheet. Meghan McNeer, whose enviable aesthetic and hungry eye for natural light drew out both of our best sides. Allison Lucas, for deep conversations on this topic over the years, thinking through all the worst-case scenarios, and the transcendental Melissa Etheridge concert. Noel Planet for bringing our friends' voices to life in spectacular animated form.

This book traveled the world with us. We wrote it on the beach in Hawaii, in a round house by a stream in Vermont, on the regional Amtrak between New York and Washington, in an airport in Costa Rica while waiting for power to be restored to the entire country, on the porch of a house in Stone Harbor, New Jersey, in backyards in Greenport, New York, and Del Mar, California, and on more than one stoop in Brooklyn. But perhaps the most memorable locale was the few days we spent together at the Highlights Foundation in Milanville, Pennsylvania. They provide an invaluable service to writers, and also taught us how not to get shot during bear season.

From Hana

Roger Schank, for obsessively reading me *Girls Can Be Anything* when I was a kid, and for believing it. Diane Schank, who derives such pleasure from spending time with my children that I felt comfortable taking a job in another city, which ultimately sparked the idea for this book. Margaret Rosenberg Schank, for showing me what an ambitious woman could do, and who I think would have been made proud by this book. Joshua Schank, who is always there for me in spirit, even when time zones make it impossible to have an actual conversation. Lindsey Schank reads and excitedly shares everything I write—thank you for being an ideal audience. The conversations I had with Katy Haynes and Deepa Kunapuli over coffees, lunches, martinis, and dinners helped shape many of the ideas in here. Thanks for hanging out with me even though I was usually the oldest person in the office, and for your enduring enthusiasm for this project. Naama Bloom told me the secret of selling a book proposal. It worked. Jessica Stone and Ellen Umansky for supporting this idea before we even really knew what it was. Milo Shaklan and Mira Shaklan for their curiosity around every stage of this project (Why are there a thousand Post-it notes on the wall? Why is your editor here with cheese? And what part are you writing now?), and for tolerating the years I talked about it at the dinner table. I still think *What Happened to Those Girls in My Sorority* is a great title suggestion. And to Steven Shaklan, my true partner. None of it would be possible without you.

From Elizabeth

To Van Nguyen Schramm, who defined ambition for me from a young age, who is a fighter, a survivor, and a champion, and who showed me that feminism has many different faces, and to Fred Schramm, her partner in the fruits of that high-achieving life. To Lynn Juel, who took me to Taylor's bookstore in suburban Texas every weekend of my childhood and urged me to buy books and to read them, who gave me my first fountain pen and urged me to start, and to keep, writing, and who showed me that there are indeed many different paths to fulfillment. To Jan Wallace, who explained why financial independence is important, introduced me to Kenny Rogers, and modeled for me that our quirks are our strengths. Tita Eberly, an admirable model of how ambition takes infinite forms. Shana Bass, you've believed in the awesome mess that I am since we met in eighth grade, seen me through many stages of friendship and hair, and never once wavered in your support or refusal to judge. Bradley Jacobs Sigesmund, you're a true believer and a real friend in a harsh city filled with doubt but also glitter—and your zeal for this project came early. Jessica Shaw, your empathy, humor, brilliance, ongoing dedication to finding the just-right pre-theater Sauvignon Blanc drive-by, and willingness to listen to, and read, my words for ten years now are tireless gifts. Nicole LaRosa, thank you for the present of being present, daily—your words as they flutter over iMessage, and your harmonies as they seamlessly channel Streisand and Ronstadt, are a source of invaluable comfort. To Clyde Eberly and Eli Eberly, for being the champions of That Thing You're Doing with Hana for the past several years, for showing me that through challenge emerges resilience and strength, for forcing me to slow down, and for reminding me to get to the point earlier. Ingrid Eberly, you have been here from the beginning, the middle, the end, all the do-overs in between, and the next stages, and any success I ever enjoy, I share equally with you.

BIBLIOGRAPHY

Bennets, Leslie. *The Feminine Mistake: Are We Giving Up Too Much?* New York: Voice, 2007.

Blau, Francine D., Marianne Ferber, and Anne E. Winkler. *The Economics of Women, Men and Work*, 5th ed. Upper Saddle River, New Jersey: Prentice Hall, 2005.

Burnett, Bill, and Dave Evans. *Designing Your Life: How to Build a Well-Lived, Joyful Life.* New York: Knopf, 2016.

Coontz, Stephanie. *Marriage, a History: How Love Conquered Marriage.* New York: Viking, 2005.

Duckworth, Angela. *Grit: The Power and Passion of Perseverance.* New York: Scribner, 2016.

Dufu, Tiffany. *Drop the Ball: Achieve More by Doing Less.* New York: Flatiron Books, 2017.

Dunn, Jancee. *How Not to Hate Your Husband After Kids.* New York: Little, Brown and Company, 2017.

Fels, Anna. *Necessary Dreams: Ambition in Women's Changing Lives.* New York: Pantheon, 2004.

Filipovic, Jill. *The H-Spot: The Feminist Pursuit of Happiness.* New York: Nation Books, 2017.

Gilman, Charlotte Perkins. *Women and Economics: A Study of the Economic Relation Between Men and Women as a Factor in Social Evolution.* New York: Harper & Row, 1966.

Gottleib, Lori. *Marry Him: The Case for Settling for Mr. Good Enough.* New York: Dutton, 2010.

Hamerstone, James, and Lindsay Musser Hough. *A Woman's Framework for a Successful Career and Life.* New York: Palgrave Macmillan, 2013.

Hirshman, Linda. *Get to Work: A Manifesto for Women of the World.* New York: Viking, 2006.

Hochschild, Arlie Russell, and Anne Machung. *The Second Shift: Working Families and the Revolution at Home.* New York: Penguin, 2012.

Huffington, Arianna. *Thrive: The Third Metric to Redefining Success and Creating a Life of Well-Being, Wisdom, and Wonder.* New York: Harmony, 2014.

Huston, Therese. *How Women Decide: What's True, What's Not, and What Strategies Spark the Best Choices.* New York: Houghton Mifflin Harcourt, 2016.

Newport, Cal. *So Good They Can't Ignore You: Why Skills Trump Passion in the Quest for Work You Love.* New York: Grand Central, 2012.

Sandberg, Sheryl. *Lean In: Women, Work, and the Will to Live.* New York: Knopf, 2015.

Schulte, Brigid. *Overwhelmed: How to Work, Love, and Play When No One Has the Time.* New York: Sarah Crichton Books, 2014.

Senior, Jennifer. *All Joy and No Fun: The Paradox of Modern Parenthood.* New York: Ecco, 2014.

Setiya, Kieran. *Midlife: A Philosophical Guide.* Princeton, New Jersey: Princeton University Press, 2017.

Shafir, Eldar, and Sendhil Mullainathan. *Scarcity: Why Having Too Little Means So Much.* New York: Times Books, 2013.

Sheehy, Gail. *Passages: Predictable Crises of Adult Life.* New York: Dutton, 1976.

Simmons, Rachel. *The Curse of the Good Girl: Raising Authentic Girls with Courage and Confidence.* New York: Penguin Press, 2009.

Slaughter, Anne-Marie. *Unfinished Business.* New York: Random House, 2015.

Thaler, Richard H., and Cass R. Sunstein. *Nudge: Improving Decisions about Health, Wealth, and Happiness.* New Haven, Connecticut: Yale University Press, 2008.

Tokumitsu, Miya. *Do What You Love: And Other Lies About Success and Happiness.* New York: Regan Arts, 2015.

Traister, Rebecca. *All the Single Ladies: Unmarried Women and the Rise of an Independent Nation.* New York: Simon & Schuster, 2016.

Valenti, Jessica. *Why Have Kids?* New York: New Harvest, 2012.

Waring, Marilyn. *If Women Counted: A New Feminist Economics.* New York: Harper & Row, 1988.

Warner, Judith. *Perfect Madness: Motherhood in the Age of Anxiety.* New York: Riverhead, 2005.

Zweigenhaft, Richard L., and William G. Domhoff. *The New CEOs: Women, African American, Latino, and Asian American Leaders of Fortune 500 Companies.* New York: Rowman & Littlefield Publishers, 2011.

NOTES

CHAPTER 1: Career

1. Sylvia Ann Hewlett and Carolyn Buck Luce, "Off-Ramps and On-Ramps: Keeping Talented Women on the Road to Success," *Harvard Business Review*, March 2005, https://hbr.org/2005/03/off-ramps-and-on-ramps -keeping-talented-women-on-the-road-to-success.
2. American Sociological Association, "Workplace Flexibility Benefits Employees, Study Says," Phys.org, January 13, 2016, https://phys.org/news /2016-01-workplace-flexibility-benefits-employees.html.
3. Brigid Schulte, "Flexible Work Alone Won't Create Gender Equality, but These Things Might," *Better Life Lab* (blog), *Slate*, October 27, 2017, http:// www.slate.com/blogs/better_life_lab/2017/10/27/will_more_flexible_work _close_the_gender_gap.html.

CHAPTER 2: Ambition

1. Robert Fiorentine, "Men, Women, and the Premed Persistence Gap: A Normative Alternatives Approach," *American Journal of Sociology* 92, no. 5 (March 1987): 1118, http://www.jstor.org/stable/2779998?seq=1#page_scan _tab_contents.
2. Edmond Costantini, "Political Women and Political Ambition: Closing the Gender Gap," *American Journal of Political Science* 34, no. 3 (August 1990): 741, http://www.jstor.org/stable/2111397?seq=1#page_scan_tab_contents.
3. Egon Zehnder, "Leaders & Daughters Global Survey 2017," 2017, https:// s3-eu-west-1.amazonaws.com/public-gbda/Leaders_Daughters_Final.pdf.
4. McKinsey & Company and LeanIn.Org, "Women in the Workplace 2017," accessed February 1, 2018, https://womenintheworkplace.com.
5. Katie Abouzahr et al., "Dispelling the Myths of the Gender 'Ambition Gap,'" The Boston Consulting Group, April 5, 2017, https://www.bcg.com

/publications/2017/people-organization-leadership-change-dispelling-the
-myths-of-the-gender-ambition-gap.aspx.

6. World Economic Forum, "Davos 2012—Women as the Way Forward," You-
Tube video, 57:51, published on January 29, 2012, https://www.youtube.com
/watch?v=6LO1rIoislk.

7. Jena McGregor, "The Number of Women CEOs in the Fortune 500 Is at an
All-Time High—of 32," *Washington Post*, June 7, 2017, https://www.wash
ingtonpost.com/news/on-leadership/wp/2017/06/07/the-number-of-women
-ceos-in-the-fortune-500-is-at-an-all-time-high-of-32/?utm_term=.737274
f34ba2.

8. Ashley Kirk, "Nobel Prize Winners: How Many Women Have Won Awards?"
The Telegraph, October 12, 2015, http://www.telegraph.co.uk/news/worldnews
/11922707/Nobel-Prize-winners-How-many-women-have-won-awards.html.

9. Lorena O'Neill, "Oscars: No Women Nominated for Best Director—Again,"
Hollywood Reporter, January 24, 2017, https://www.hollywoodreporter.com
/news/oscars-no-women-nominated-best-director-again-967284.

10. Hilarie M. Sheets, "Gender Gap Persists at Largest Museums," *New York
Times*, March 22, 2017, https://www.nytimes.com/2017/03/22/arts/design
/gender-gap-persists-at-largest-museums.html?_r=0.

11. Jerome Kagan and Howard A. Moss, *Birth to Maturity: A Study in Psychological Development* (Hoboken, NJ: John Wiley & Sons, 1962).

12. Anna Fels, "Do Women Lack Ambition?" *Harvard Business Review*, April
2004, https://hbr.org/2004/04/do-women-lack-ambition.

13. Bryan McIntosh et al., "Motherhood and Its Impact on Career Progression,"
Gender in Management: An International Journal 27, no. 5 (2012): 346–364,
http://www.emeraldinsight.com/doi/abs/10.1108/17542411211252651; Lorra
M. Brown, "The Relationship Between Motherhood and Professional Advancement: Perceptions Versus Reality," *Employee Relations* 32, no. 5
(2010): 470–494, http://www.emeraldinsight.com/doi/abs/10.1108/014254510
11061649; Elizabeth Aura McClintock, "Can Women Reduce the Career
Cost of Motherhood?," *Psychology Today*, October 8, 2014, https://www.psy
chologytoday.com/blog/it-s-man-s-and-woman-s-world/201410/can-women
-reduce-the-career-cost-motherhood.

14. Robin J. Ely, Pamela Stone, and Colleen Ammerman, "Rethink What You
'Know' About High-Achieving Women," *Harvard Business Review*, December
2014, https://hbr.org/2014/12/rethink-what-you-know-about-high-achieving
-women.

15. Peter V. Marsden, ed., *Social Trends in American Life: Findings from the General Social Survey Since 1972* (Princeton, NJ: Princeton University Press, 2012).
16. The *Social Trends* study cited above is full of fascinating findings, but our space is limited. Here are a few of our favorites: Over time people have grown increasingly comfortable with the idea that a man's career need not take precedence over a woman's career. However, at the same time, the percentage of people who agree with the statement that it is okay for married women to work for pay has leveled off since the mid-1980s, hovering around 80 percent. This means that 20 percent of people do not believe married women should have jobs. Another interesting tidbit: The percentage of people who think it's better if women stay home and men achieve in their careers dropped throughout the '70s and '80s, but has leveled off since the '90s, hovering between 30 and 40 percent. And finally, gender-based attitudes about how the division of labor should work in the home have not changed since 1989.
17. Herminia Ibarra, Nancy M. Carter, and Christine Silva, "Why Men Still Get More Promotions Than Women," *Harvard Business Review*, September 2010, https://hbr.org/2010/09/why-men-still-get-more-promotions-than-women.
18. McKinsey & Company and LeanIn.Org, "Women in the Workplace 2017," accessed February 1, 2018, https://womenintheworkplace.com.

CHAPTER 3: Marriage

1. Robert D. Mare, "Educational Homogamy in Two Gilded Ages: Evidence from Inter-generational Social Mobility Data," *ANNALS of the American Academy of Political and Social Science* 663, no. 1 (January 1, 2016): 117–139, http://journals.sagepub.com/doi/abs/10.1177/0002716215596967.
2. Lydia Saad, "The '40-Hour' Workweek Is Actually Longer—by Seven Hours," Gallup News, August 29, 2014, http://news.gallup.com/poll/175286/hour-workweek-actually-longer-seven-hours.aspx.
3. Lawrence Mishel, "Vast Majority of Wage Earners Are Working Harder, and for Not Much More," Economic Policy Institute, January 30, 2013, http://www.epi.org/publication/ib348-trends-us-work-hours-wages-1979-2007/.
4. Jennifer J. Deal, "Always On, Never Done? Don't Blame the Smartphone," Center for Creative Leadership, accessed February 1, 2018, http://www.ccl.org/wp-content/uploads/2015/04/AlwaysOn.pdf.

5. American Psychological Association, "Americans Stay Connected to Work on Weekends, Vacation and Even When Out Sick," September 4, 2013, http://www.apa.org/news/press/releases/2013/09/connected-work.aspx.

6. GfK Public Affairs & Corporate Communications, "Overwhelmed America: Why Don't We Use Our Earned Leave?," accessed February 4, 2018, https://www.projecttimeoff.com/sites/default/files/PTO_OverwhelmedAmerica_Report.pdf.

7. "Americans Stay Connected," http://www.apa.org/news/press/releases/2013/09/connected-work.aspx.

8. Linda K. Stroh and Jeanne M. Brett, "The Dual-Earner Dad Penalty in Salary Progression," *Human Resource Management* 35, no. 2 (June 1996): 181–201, http://onlinelibrary.wiley.com/doi/10.1002/(SICI)1099-050X(199622)35:2%3C181::AID-HRM3%3E3.0.CO;2-U/abstract.

9. Linda Hirshman, "Homeward Bound," *The American Prospect*, November 21, 2005, http://prospect.org/article/homeward-bound-0.

10. David Brooks, "The Year of Domesticity," *New York Times*, January 1, 2006, http://query.nytimes.com/gst/fullpage.html?res=9F07E6DB1030F932A35752C0A9609C8B63.

11. Carol Hymowitz, "Behind Every Great Woman," *Bloomberg Businessweek*, January 4, 2012, https://www.sbcf-famlaw.com/wp-content/uploads/2012/03/behind-every-great1.pdf.

12. James B. Stewart, "A C.E.O.'s Support System, aka Husband," *New York Times*, November 4, 2011, http://www.nytimes.com/2011/11/05/business/a-ceos-support-system-a-k-a-husband.html.

13. Ralph Gardner Jr., "Alpha Women, Beta Men," *New York Magazine*, November 17, 2003, accessed February 4, 2018, http://nymag.com/nymetro/news/features/n_9495.

14. Scott Stanley, "What Is the Divorce Rate, Anyway? Around 42 Percent, One Scholar Believes," Institute for Family Studies, January 22, 2015, https://ifstudies.org/blog/what-is-the-divorce-rate-anyway-around-42-percent-one-scholar-believes.

15. Brittany C. Solomon and Joshua J. Jackson, "The Long Reach of One's Spouse," *Psychological Science* 25, no. 12 (October 17, 2014): 2189–2198, http://journals.sagepub.com/doi/abs/10.1177/0956797614551370?rss=1&.

16. We came across this excerpt from *Heartburn* while reading Linda Hirshman's essay "Homeward Bound," and knew we to had to cite it. So thank you, Ms. Hirschman. Linda Hirschman, "Homeward Bound," *American Prospect*,

November 21, 2005, http://prospect.org/article/homeward-bound-0; Nora Ephron, *Heartburn* (New York: Vintage Books, 1983), 20.

17. Ellen Galinsky, Kerstin Aumann, and James T. Bond, "Times Are Changing: Gender and Generation at Work and at Home," 2008 National Study of the Changing Workforce, Families and Work Institute, revised August 2011, http://familiesandwork.org/downloads/TimesAreChanging.pdf.

18. Alexandra C. Achen and Frank P. Stafford, "Data Quality of Housework Hours in the Panel Study of Income Dynamics: Who Really Does the Dishes?," Panel Study of Income Dynamics, September 2005, https://psidon line.isr.umich.edu/publications/Papers/tsp/2005-04_Data_Qual_of_House hold_Hours-_Dishes.pdf.

19. Stephanie Coontz, *Marriage, a History: How Love Conqured Marriage* (New York: Penguin, 2005), 299.

CHAPTER 4: Parenting

1. Jessica Grose, "Parents Are Now Getting Arrested for Letting Their Kids Go to the Park Alone," *The XX Factor* (blog), *Slate*, July 15, 2014, http://www .slate.com/blogs/xx_factor/2014/07/15/debra_harrell_arrested_for_letting _her_9_year_old_daughter_go_to_the_park.html.

2. Andrea McCarren, "Parents in Trouble Again for Letting Kids Walk Alone," *USA Today*, April 13, 2015, https://www.usatoday.com/story/news/nation /2015/04/13/parents-investigated-letting-children-walk-alone/25700823/.

3. Lenore Skenazy, "I Let My 9-Year-Old Ride the Subway Alone. I Got Labeled the 'World's Worst Mom,'" *Washington Post*, January 16, 2015, https://www.wash- ingtonpost.com/posteverything/wp/2015/01/16/i-let-my-9-year-old-ride-the -subway-alone-i-got-labeled-the-worlds-worst-mom/?utm_term=.344f9da6d75f.

4. Sharon Hays, *The Cultural Contradictions of Motherhood* (New Haven, CT: Yale University Press, 1996).

5. Judith Warner, *Perfect Madness: Motherhood in the Age of Anxiety* (New York: Riverhead Books, 2005).

6. Philip Terzian, "The Great Day-Care Sexual-Abuse Panic," *The Weekly Standard*, July 7, 2017, http://www.weeklystandard.com/the-great-day-care -sexual-abuse-panic/article/2008742.

7. Warner, *Perfect Madness*, 138–139.

8. Jennifer Senior, *All Joy and No Fun: The Paradox of Modern Parenthood* (New York: HarperCollins, 2014), 122.

9. Arlie Russell Hochschild with Anne Machung, *The Second Shift: Working Parents and the Revolution at Home* (New York: Viking Penguin, 1989).

10. Judith Shulevitz, "Mom: The Designated Worrier," *New York Times*, May 8, 2015, https://www.nytimes.com/2015/05/10/opinion/sunday/judith-shulevitz-mom-the-designated-worrier.html.

11. Gemma Hartley, "Women Aren't Nags—We're Just Fed Up," *Harper's Bazaar*, September 27, 2017, http://www.harpersbazaar.com/culture/features/a12063822/emotional-labor-gender-equality; Rose Hackman, "'Women Are Just Better at This Stuff': Is Emotional Labor Feminism's Next Frontier?," *The Guardian*, November 8, 2015, https://www.theguardian.com/world/2015/nov/08/women-gender-roles-sexism-emotional-labor-feminism; Dana McMahan, "I Said 'No' to Unpaid Emotional Labor by Saying Goodbye to This Word," *Better* (blog), *NBC News*, October 26, 2017, https://www.nbcnews.com/better/health/i-said-no-emotional-labor-saying-goodbye-word-ncna814356; Soraya Chemaly, "At Work as at Home, Men Reap the Benefits of Women's 'Invisible Labor,'" *Quartz*, January 22, 2016, https://qz.com/599999/at-work-as-at-home-men-reap-the-benefits-of-womens-invisible-labor; Christine Hutchinson, "Why Women Are Tired: The Price of Unpaid Emotional Labor," *Huffington Post*, updated on December 6, 2017, https://www.huffingtonpost.com/psyched-in-san-francisco/why-women-are-tired-the-p_b_9619732.html.

12. Robin J. Ely, Pamela Stone, and Colleen Ammerman, "Rethink What You 'Know' About High-Achieving Women," *Harvard Business Review*, December 2014, https://hbr.org/2014/12/rethink-what-you-know-about-high-achieving-women.

13. Charles Opondo et al., "Father Involvement in Early Child-Rearing and Behavioural Outcomes in Their Pre-Adolescent Children: Evidence from the Alspac UK Birth Cohort," *BMJ Open*, November 22, 2016, http://bmjopen.bmj.com/content/6/11/e012034.

14. Maria del Carmen Huerta et al., "Fathers' Leave, Fathers' Involvement and Child Development: Are They Related? Evidence from Four OECD Countries," *OECD Social, Employment and Migration Working Papers*, no. 140 (January 14, 2013), https://econpapers.repec.org/paper/oecelsaab/140-en.htm.

15. Senior, *All Joy and No Fun*, 123.

CHAPTER 5: Economics

1. Fidelity Viewpoints, "Women & Money: How to Take Charge," Fidelity Investments, March 23, 2016, https://www.fidelity.com/viewpoints/personal-finance/women-manage-money. Fidelity Investments 2015 Money FIT Women Study

found that eight out of ten women refrain from having financial conversations, and only 47 percent are confident discussing money and investing with a professional, as opposed to 77 percent who are comfortable discussing medical issues with their physician.

2. The same Fidelity Viewpoints study cited above found a range of negative attitudes around the idea of discussing money and finances openly. Twenty-seven percent of respondents said they were raised not to discuss finances, 32 percent reported feeling uncomfortable discussing money, and 16 percent called the topic taboo. More than half of the women in the study thought money was "too personal" a topic to discuss with friends or family.

3. Greg Rosenberg, "UBS Invest Watch Report Reveals Couples Say They Share Financial Decisions, But Not Investing Decisions," *UBS Investor Watch*, April 29, 2014, https://www.ubs.com/us/en/wealth/news/wealth-management -americas-news.html/en/2014/04/29/ubs-investor-watch-2014-2Q.html.

4. Linda Babcock and Sara Laschever, *Women Don't Ask: Negotiation and the Gender Divide* (New York: Bantam Books, 2007), 2.

5. The Agenda, "Why Is It So Hard for Us to Talk About Money?," *Elle*, May 29, 2015, http://www.elle.com/culture/career-politics/news/a28298/the -last-taboo-money/.

6. W. Bradford Wilcox, "The Evolution of Divorce," *National Affairs* 34 (Winter 2018), https://www.nationalaffairs.com/publications/detail/the-evolution -of-divorce: "From 1960 to 1980, the divorce rate more than doubled—from 9.2 divorces per 1,000 married women to 22.6 divorces per 1,000 married women. [. . .] And approximately half of the children born to married parents in the 1970s saw their parents part."

7. "Labor Force Statistics from the Current Population Survey," Bureau of Labor Statistics, accessed April 19, 2018, https://data.bls.gov/timeseries/LNS14000000.

8. Christine Romans, "Remembering the Worst Day in Wall Street History," *Romans' Numeral* (blog), *CNN Money*, October 19, 2017, http://money.cnn .com/2017/10/19/investing/romans-numeral-black-monday/index.html.

9. Charlotte Perkins Gilman, *Women and Economics: A Study of the Economic Relation Between Men and Women as a Factor in Social Evolution* (New York: Harper & Row, 1966).

10. Dan A. Black, Hoda R. Makar, Seth G. Sanders, and Lowell J. Taylor, "The Earnings Effects of Sexual Orientation," *ILR Review* 56, no. 3 (April 2003): 449–469, https://www.jstor.org/stable/3590918?seq=1#page_scan_tab_contents.

11. S.K., "Why Lesbians Tend to Earn More than Heterosexual Women," *The Economist Explains* (blog), *The Economist,* February 15, 2016, https://www .economist.com/blogs/economist-explains/2016/02/economist-explains-8.

12. Heather Antecol, Anneke Jong, and Michael Steinberg, *IZA DP, Number 2945*, July 2017, https://pdfs.semanticscholar.org/7b58/ef1680bfc5aee1a1871a 183e0c5bebb31f88.pdf.
13. Miya Tokumitsu, *Do What You Love: And Other Lies About Success and Happiness* (New York: Regan Arts, 2015), 5.
14. Miya Tokumitsu, "In the Name of Love," *Jacobin Magazine*, January 2014, https://www.jacobinmag.com/2014/01/in-the-name-of-love.
15. Tokumitsu, "In the Name of Love."
16. Cal Newport, *So Good They Can't Ignore You: Why Skills Trump Passion in the Quest for Work You Love* (New York: Grand Central, 2012), 4.
17. Newport, *So Good They Can't Ignore You*, 21.
18. Newport, *So Good They Can't Ignore You*, 6.
19. Catherine Rampell, "Women May Earn Less, but They Find Their Work More Meaningful," *Economix* (blog), *New York Times*, February 16, 2012, https://economix.blogs.nytimes.com/2012/02/16/women-may-earn-less-but -they-find-their-work-more-meaningful/?_r=1.
20. Lina Nilsson, "How to Attract Female Engineers," *New York Times*, April 27, 2015, https://www.nytimes.com/2015/04/27/opinion/how-to-attract-female -engineers.html.
21. Newport, *So Good They Can't Ignore You*, 16–17.
22. "U.S. College Majors: Median Yearly Earnings vs. Gender Ratio," Randal S. Olson (blog), August 16, 2015, http://www.randalolson.com/2015/08/16/u-s-college -majors-median-yearly-earnings-vs-gender-ratio.
23. Andrew Chamberlain, Ph.D., and Jyotsna Jayaraman, "The Pipeline Problem: How College Majors Contribute to the Gender Pay Gap," Glassdoor, April 2017, https://www.glassdoor.com/research/app/uploads/sites/2/2017/04 /FULL-STUDY-PDF-Gender-Pay-Gap2FCollege-Major.pdf.

CHAPTER 6: Change

1. Megan Garber, "When *Newsweek* 'Struck Terror in the Hearts of Single Women,'" *The Atlantic*, June 2, 2016, https://www.theatlantic.com/entertain ment/archive/2016/06/more-likely-to-be-killed-by-a-terrorist-than-to-get -married/485171/.
2. "5 Reasons to Hire Women Over 40 at Your Tech Startup," *theBoardlist* (blog), *Medium*, February 17, 2017, https://medium.com/@theBoardlist /5-reasons-to-hire-women-over-40-at-your-tech-startup-2294a038f02c.

3. Perri Konecky, "Zara's Stunning New Campaign Features Only Models Over 40," *PopSugar*, September 2, 2017, https://www.popsugar.com/fashion/Zara-Timeless-Woman-Campaign-Fall-2017-43961371.
4. "MILF," Urban Dictionary, last modified April 12, 2012, https://www.urbandictionary.com/define.php?term=Stifler%27s%20Mom.
5. Emine Saner, "Women on the Verge of a Midlife Crisis," *The Guardian*, January 27, 2017, https://www.theguardian.com/lifeandstyle/2017/jan/27/women-on-the-verge-of-a-midlife-crisis.
6. Saner, "Women on the Verge of a Midlife Crisis."
7. Federal Bank of St. Louis, "Long-Term Unemployment Affected Older Women Most Following Recession," *On the Economy* (blog), November 17, 2015, https://www.stlouisfed.org/on-the-economy/2015/november/older-women-recession-long-term-unemployment.
8. Agneta H. Fischer, ed., *Gender and Emotion: Social and Psychological Perspectives* (New York: Cambridge University Press, 2000), 25.
9. Florence R. Rosenberg and Roberta G. Simmons, "Sex Differences in the Self-concept in Adolescence," *Sex Roles* 1, no. 2 (June 1975), https://link.springer.com/article/10.1007%2FBF00288008?LI=true.
10. Rachel Simmons, *The Curse of the Good Girl: Raising Authentic Girls with Courage and Confidence* (New York: Penguin Press, 2009).
11. Tara Sophia Mohr, "Why Women Don't Apply for Jobs Unless They're 100% Qualified," *Harvard Business Review*, August 25, 2014, https://hbr.org/2014/08/why-women-dont-apply-for-jobs-unless-theyre-100-qualified.
12. Curt Rice, "Anecdata, or How McKinsey's Story Became Sheryl Sandberg's Fact," Science in the Balance, April 22, 2014, http://curt-rice.com/2014/04/22/what-happens-when-under-qualified-women-apply-for-jobs-and-why-sheryl-sandberg-and-mckinsey-wrongly-think-we-dont-know.